speeches
that changed the world

the stories and transcripts of the moments that made history

with an introduction by
Simon Sebag Montefiore

Quercus

Quercus Publishing Plc
21 Bloomsbury Square
London
WC1A 2NS

First published 2005
This edition published 2007

A catalogue record for this book is available from the British Library.

ISBN 10: 1 84724 087 9
ISBN 13: 978 1 84724 087 3

Printed in China

The editors and publisher are grateful to those historians, writers and commentators who have recorded, transcribed or translated the great speeches of history.

The publishers would like to thank the following for source material and permission to reproduce copyright material:

For the speeches of: Adolf Hitler: The Speeches of Adolf Hitler 1922-1939, Oxford University Press 1942; Winston Churchill: reproduced by kind permission of the Crown Copyright; J. Robert Oppenheimer: University of Chicago; Nelson Mandela: archive of the African National Congress; Martin Luther King Jr: The Estate of Dr Martin Luther King Jr; Malcolm X: Speeches and Statements, Grove Press, New York; Shirley Chisholm: Documents from the Woman's Liberation Movement; Pierre Trudeau: www.collectionscanada.ca; Ronald Reagan: The Reagan Foundation; F.W. de Klerk: reproduced by kind permission of Hansard; Chaim Herzog: reproduced by kind permission of Minister Isaac Herzog

For the audio recordings of: Neville Chamberlain, Mother Teresa, F.W. de Klerk: BBC Worldwide Limited; Winston Churchill: 'This was their finest hour'; 'Blood, toil, tears, and sweat': EMI Gold Label release, 'Churchill Speeches', Catalogue number 474 5642; 'Never in the field of human conflict...': Licensed from Decca Music Group Limited, a division of Universal Music Group (LXT6200); Jawaharlal Nehru: Harappa; Nelson Mandela: The National Archives and Records Service of South Africa; SABC; Chaim Herzog: The Arthur and Luce Klein Audio Collection, World of Words, Inc., The Yale Collection of Historical Sound Recordings, Yale University Music Library

For pictures: Moses, ©Corbis; Jesus, ©Bettmann/Corbis; Mohammed, ©Bettmann/Corbis; St Francis of Assisi, ©Archivo Iconografico, S.A./Corbis; Elizabeth I, ©Bettmann/Corbis; Charles I, ©Classic Image/Alamy; Oliver Cromwell, ©Bettmann/Corbis; George Washington, ©Corbis; Thomas Jefferson, ©Bettmann/Corbis; Napoleon Bonaparte, ©Archivo Iconografico, S.A./Corbis; Abraham Lincoln, ©Bettmann/Corbis; Emmeline Pankhurst, ©Hulton-Deutsch Collection/Corbis; Marie Curie, ©Hulton-Deutsch Collection/Corbis; Mahatma Gandhi, ©Bettmann/Corbis; V I Lenin, ©Popperfoto/Alamy; Woodrow Wilson, ©Corbis; Clarence Darrow, ©Bettmann/Corbis; Neville Chamberlain, ©Hulton-Deutsch Collection/Corbis; Adolf Hitler, ©Hulton-Deutsch Collection/Corbis; Joseph Stalin, ©Popperfoto/Alamy; Winston Churchill, ©Hulton-Deutsch Collection/Corbis; Vyacheslav Molotov, ©Bettmann/Corbis; Franklin D. Roosevelt, ©Bettmann/Corbis; Charles de Gaulle, ©Bettmann/Corbis; General George S Patton, ©Bettmann/Corbis; Emperor Hirohito, ©Bettmann/Corbis; Jawaharlal Nehru, ©Bettmann/Corbis; Robert Oppenheimer, ©Bettmann/Corbis; General Douglas MacArthur, ©Bettman/Corbis; Nelson Mandela, ©Alexander Caminada/Alamy; Eamon de Valera, ©Hulton-Deutsch Collection/Corbis; John F. Kennedy, ©Bettmann/Corbis; Martin Luther King Jr, ©Flip Schulke/Corbis; Malcolm X, ©Bettmann/Corbis; Shirley Chisholm, ©Corbis; Pierre Trudeau, ©Corbis; Golda Meir, ©David Rubinger/Corbis; Richard Nixon, ©Bettmann/Corbis; Indira Gandhi, ©Sipa Press/Rex Features; Chaim Herzog, ©Bettmann/Corbis; Mother Teresa, ©Bettmann/Corbis; Pope John Paul II, ©Bettmann/Corbis; Ronald Reagan, ©Bettmann/Corbis; Mikhail Gorbachev, ©Jacques Langevin/Corbis Sygma; F W de Klerk, ©Richard Olivier/Corbis; Vaclav Havel, ©J A Giordano/Corbis Saba; Elie Wiesel, ©Robert Maass/Corbis; George W. Bush, ©Reuters/Corbis

Cover picture: Nelson Mandela © Reuters/CORBIS

Every effort has been made to contact copyright holders. However, the publishers will be glad to rectify in future editions any inadvertent omissions brought to their attention.

Researched, compiled and edited by Cambridge Editorial Partnership, Michael Young Centre, Purbeck Road, Cambridge CB2 2PF, with thanks to Martin Hall, Carol Schaessens and Martin Walters.

Designed by Zoe Naylor on behalf of Hart McLeod.

Introduction

Simon Sebag Montefiore

A great speech does not just capture the truth of its era; it can also capture the big lie. This wonderful collection of speeches contains uplifting hymns to democratic freedom that encapsulate the principles of decency and liberty that we cherish, good words that enlightened the world. But we can also read some of the most despicable speeches that darkened the horizons of the free world. It is the speeches by the monsters of history that are the real lessons.

Many of these speeches contain eternal truths, particularly a classic such as the Gettysburg Address, or less known orations by those such as Vaclav Havel, dissident and future Czech President, or Chaim Herzog, Israeli President. As a rule, simplicity of language marks superb speechmaking, as with Mohammed, Jesus or Martin Luther King, and it helps when the orator has written the words himself. But many reek of evil and folly; their lesson is that fine, philanthropic words can mask and distort as much as they reveal and enlighten. Some speeches are distinctly Orwellian. Some are simply untrue, some wicked and some we can simply judge better now with the tool of historical hindsight.

Emperor Napoleon's 'adieu to the Old Guard' is tear-jerking hokum, because he had never put his country before himself and his ambitions had layered the fields of Europe with the bodies of the young and innocent. Two speeches show bad men as superb political animals. In Lenin's 'all power to the Soviets' speech in September 1917, it is hard to count the lies for he had no intention of giving power to the Soviets, the peasants or the workers; power was for himself and his Party oligarchs. The disdain and cynicism are overwhelming. Adolf Hitler's speeches reveal his virtuosity as a political agitator, national actor and speechwriter, but are riddled with cynical, brutal lies and camp, ludicrous posturing. Conversely, though Stalin's views are despicably ruthless, the self-consciously 'modest' cobbler's son delivers them with surprising plainness.

Then, of course, there are the poseurs, the deluded and the well-intentioned. Richard Nixon promised to prevent the very whitewash he was determined to accomplish. General Douglas MacArthur's farewell is magnificent but reeks of vain delusion. When President Mikhail Gorbachev praised 'freedom of choice', he certainly did not mean his own people to receive so much of it that they threw him out – along with his beloved Communism. Neville Chamberlain is even more the butt of the sad joke of hindsight in his 'peace in our time' speech; it is hard to imagine a greater error of judgement and a more pathetic delusion of achievement, expressed in simple words.

Many of these speeches thus reveal the character flaws and virtues of their orators, but each is also a window onto a great occasion in history. In the age of radio or television, most people would recall where they were when they heard George W. Bush's speech on 9/11, Franklin Roosevelt's after Pearl Harbour or Vyacheslav Molotov's stammered reading of what were actually Stalin's words after the Nazi invasion of the Soviet Union. Speeches delivered spontaneously are even more powerful: Charles I's address must have been unforgettable but reveals the stubborn arrogance and proud pathos of the doomed monarch. Lord Protector Cromwell's dismissal of Parliament reveals both his furious will and sanctimonious conviction of divine providence. Yet, for me, the best speech is one that marks no great event but merely pinpoints with splendid language, moral rigour and righteous fury, the essence of all decent civilization, a theme that runs through so many of these speeches: Elie Wiesel's millennium address on the 'perils of indifference'. We should know ALL these speeches. But if the reader remembers just Wiesel's thoughts on history and the private individual, this book will truly have succeeded.

Simon Sebag Montefiore

Contents

‘Thou shalt have no other gods before me.’

Moses

The Ten Commandments, Exodus 20. 1–17

The Ten Commandments, or Decalogue, are acknowledged in Judaism, Christianity and Islam as a summary of the central rules of behaviour that God expects of humankind. The book of Exodus, in the Old Testament, tells that they were given by God to Moses, the great prophet and leader of the Hebrews, after he led them to freedom from slavery in Egypt. These rules have been at the heart of Jewish and Christian morality for over 3,000 years. In Judaism, the first five commandments identify duties towards God; the second five, duties towards other people. Jesus reiterated the commandments in his Sermon on the Mount, which is regarded as the manifesto of Christian law. Within Islam, the Koran appears to refer to the Decalogue and to urge that it should be followed.

Moses

Born c. 1527 BCE in Egypt.

Moses was born a Hebrew in Egypt and raised at the court of Pharaoh. He was commanded by God to lead the Hebrew slaves to freedom (the Exodus, c. 1447 BCE). At Mount Sinai in Palestine God delivered **the Ten Commandments** to Moses (date speculative).

Died c. 1407 BCE.

Moses was born in Egypt, during a time when Pharaoh ordered the male children of Hebrew slaves to be killed. When his mother could no longer keep her baby concealed she put him in a basket made of bulrushes and floated it down the Nile. Pharaoh's daughter found the basket and adopted the baby, giving him the Egyptian name Moses, which means 'saved' or 'taken from water'.

Little is written about Moses' early life. After he killed an Egyptian he found mistreating a Hebrew slave, he was forced to flee Egypt and escaped to Midian. It was here that he was commanded by God to return to Egypt and demand freedom for the Hebrew slaves, who were to be allowed to go to the Promised Land of Israel. Moses was reluctant at first: 'I [am] slow of speech, and of a slow tongue'. He was allowed to take his brother Aaron as his spokesman.

Their first encounter with Pharaoh ended in failure. Egypt relied on slave labour and Pharaoh was unwilling to release so many vital workers. The slaves were made to work even harder. He relented only after God had sent the Egyptians ten plagues, culminating in the death of every Egyptian first born. The Hebrews (Israelites) left Egypt under Moses' leadership but Pharaoh changed his mind and sent his army to bring them back. When they reached the Sea of Reeds God divided the water, allowing the Israelites to pass through to freedom, while the Egyptian army drowned.

Moses led his people to Mount Sinai in Palestine, where God gave him two stone tablets inscribed with the Ten Commandments. He died never having reached the Promised Land.

1 And God spake all these words, saying,

2 I am the LORD thy God, which have brought thee out of the land of Egypt, out of the house of bondage.

3 Thou shalt have no other gods before me.

4 Thou shalt not make unto thee any graven image, or any likeness of any thing that is in heaven above, or that is in the earth beneath, or that is in the water under the earth:

5 Thou shalt not bow down thyself to them, nor serve them: for I the LORD thy God am a jealous God, visiting the iniquity of the fathers upon the children unto the third and fourth generation of them that hate me;

6 And showing mercy unto thousands of them that love me, and keep my commandments.

7 Thou shalt not take the name of the LORD thy God in vain; for the LORD will not hold him guiltless that taketh his name in vain.

8 Remember the sabbath day, to keep it holy.

9 Six days shalt thou labour, and do all thy work:

10 But the seventh day is the sabbath of the LORD thy God: in it thou shalt not do any work, thou, nor thy son, nor thy daughter, thy manservant, nor thy maidservant, nor thy cattle, nor thy stranger that is within thy gates:

11 For in six days the LORD made heaven and earth, the sea, and all that in them is, and rested the seventh day: wherefore the LORD blessed the sabbath day, and hallowed it.

12 Honour thy father and thy mother: that thy days may be long upon the land which the LORD thy God giveth thee.

13 Thou shalt not kill.

14 Thou shalt not commit adultery.

15 Thou shalt not steal.

16 Thou shalt not bear false witness against thy neighbour.

17 Thou shalt not covet thy neighbour's house, thou shalt not covet thy neighbour's wife, nor his manservant, nor his maidservant, nor his ox, nor his ass, nor any thing that is thy neighbour's.

‘Blessed are the poor in spirit: for theirs is the kingdom of heaven.’

Jesus of Nazareth

The Sermon on the Mount, Matthew 5–7

For many people the sayings of Jesus, gathered together in the Sermon on the Mount, represent the essence of Christianity – what Jesus teaches. Jesus of Nazareth was a first-century Jewish teacher crucified by the Romans. Christians believe him to have risen from the dead and to be the Son of God, through whom God revealed himself to the world and whose death reconciles the world to God. Christianity is one of the world's major religions and is based on the teachings of Jesus and his followers recorded in the New Testament of the Bible.

In historical terms Jesus has been viewed variously as a moral reformer, political revolutionary, Palestinian peasant, and charismatic rabbi. In the Gospels Jesus is characterized as someone with immense personal authority and miraculous powers, as a prophet whose unique relationship to God was shown through divine signs at his baptism and a later transfiguring experience. At the same time he is portrayed as living a life without material security or family support, often mixing with the poor and society's outcasts, and constantly teaching that he would be rejected by the authorities, persecuted, suffer and die in order to fulfil God's purpose.

Born c. 4 BCE in Palestine.
Jesus preached a radical version of Jewish scripture. His teaching, healing and the performance of miracles drew large numbers of followers and the attention of religious and political leaders, who saw him as a threat to stability in Roman-occupied Palestine. Some Christian thinkers view **The Sermon on the Mount** as a collection of discrete sayings gathered together by early Christian writers, rather than a speech delivered on a particular historic occasion.
Died c. 26 in Palestine.

Jesus was born in Roman-ruled Palestine during the reign of Emperor Augustus, growing up in Nazareth and becoming an itinerant preacher in North Palestine for three years, during which he gathered many followers attracted by his interpretation of Jewish law and the miracles he performed. His criticism of Jewish religious leaders and warnings of the imminence of God's rule replacing human rule provoked opposition from the Jewish and Roman establishment. While Pontius Pilate was governor of Judea he was executed by crucifixion, a form of execution used by the Romans on non-Roman citizens who threatened Roman authority. Jesus' followers claimed that God then raised him from the dead. The Christian movement quickly spread throughout the Mediterranean and was savagely suppressed in the first century by the Roman Emperors Claudius and Nero. By the end of the century Jewish authorities in Palestine had adopted policies aimed at sharply differentiating Christians from Jews.

Matthew 5

1 And seeing the multitudes, he went up into a mountain: and when he was set, his disciples came unto him:

2 And he opened his mouth, and taught them, saying,

3 Blessed are the poor in spirit: for theirs is the kingdom of heaven.

4 Blessed are they that mourn: for they shall be comforted.

5 Blessed are the meek: for they shall inherit the earth.

6 Blessed are they which do hunger and thirst after righteousness: for they shall be filled.

7 Blessed are the merciful: for they shall obtain mercy.

8 Blessed are the pure in heart: for they shall see God.

9 Blessed are the peacemakers: for they shall be called the children of God.

10 Blessed are they which are persecuted for righteousness' sake: for theirs is the kingdom of heaven.

11 Blessed are ye, when men shall revile you, and persecute you, and shall say all manner of evil against you falsely, for my sake.

12 Rejoice, and be exceeding glad: for great is your reward in heaven: for so persecuted they the prophets which were before you.

13 Ye are the salt of the earth: but if the salt have lost his savour, wherewith shall it be salted? it is thenceforth good for nothing, but to be cast out, and to be trodden under foot of men.

14 Ye are the light of the world. A city that is set on an hill cannot be hid.

15 Neither do men light a candle, and put it under a bushel, but on a candlestick; and it giveth light unto all that are in the house.

16 Let your light so shine before men, that they may see your good works, and glorify your Father which is in heaven.

17 Think not that I am come to destroy the law, or the prophets: I am not come to destroy, but to fulfil.

18 For verily I say unto you, Till heaven and earth pass, one jot or one tittle shall in no wise pass from the law, till all be fulfilled.

19 Whosoever therefore shall break one of these least commandments, and shall teach men so, he shall be called the least in the kingdom of heaven: but whosoever shall do and teach them, the same shall be called great in the kingdom of heaven.

20 For I say unto you, That except your righteousness shall exceed the righteousness of the scribes and Pharisees, ye shall in no case enter into the kingdom of heaven.

21 Ye have heard that it was said of them of old time, Thou shalt not kill; and whosoever shall kill shall be in danger of the judgement:

22 But I say unto you, That whosoever is angry with his brother without a cause shall be in danger of the judgement: and whosoever shall say to his brother, Raca, shall be in danger of the council: but whosoever shall say, Thou fool, shall be in danger of hell fire.

23 Therefore if thou bring thy gift to the altar, and there rememberest that thy brother hath ought against thee;

'Love your enemies.'

24 Leave there thy gift before the altar, and go thy way; first be reconciled to thy brother, and then come and offer thy gift.

25 Agree with thine adversary quickly, whiles thou art in the way with him; lest at any time the adversary deliver thee to the judge, and the judge deliver thee to the officer, and thou be cast into prison.

26 Verily I say unto thee, Thou shalt by no means come out thence, till thou hast paid the uttermost farthing.

27 Ye have heard that it was said by them of old time, Thou shalt not commit adultery:

28 But I say unto you, That whosoever looketh on a woman to lust after her hath committed adultery with her already in his heart.

29 And if thy right eye offend thee, pluck it out, and cast it from thee: for it is profitable for thee that one of thy members should perish, and not that thy whole body should be cast into hell.

30 And if thy right hand offend thee, cut it off, and cast it from thee: for it is profitable for thee that one of thy members should perish, and not that thy whole body should be cast into hell.

31 It hath been said, Whosoever shall put away his wife, let him give her a writing of divorcement:

32 But I say unto you, That whosoever shall put away his wife, saving for the cause of fornication, causeth her to commit adultery: and whosoever shall marry her that is divorced committeth adultery.

33 Again, ye have heard that it hath been said by them of old time, Thou shalt not forswear thyself, but shalt perform unto the Lord thine oaths:

34 But I say unto you, Swear not at all; neither by heaven; for it is God's throne:

35 Nor by the earth; for it is his footstool: neither by Jerusalem; for it is the city of the great King.

36 Neither shalt thou swear by thy head, because thou canst not make one hair white or black.

37 But let your communication be, Yea, yea; Nay, nay: for whatsoever is more than these cometh of evil.

38 Ye have heard that it hath been said, An eye for an eye, and a tooth for a tooth:

39 But I say unto you, That ye resist not evil: but whosoever shall smite thee on thy right cheek, turn to him the other also.

40 And if any man will sue thee at the law, and take away thy coat, let him have thy cloak also.

41 And whosoever shall compel thee to go a mile, go with him twain.

42 Give to him that asketh thee, and from him that would borrow of thee turn not thou away.

43 Ye have heard that it hath been said, Thou shalt love thy neighbour, and hate thine enemy.

44 But I say unto you, Love your enemies, bless them that curse you, do good to them that hate you, and pray for them which despitefully use you, and persecute you;

45 That ye may be the children of your Father which is in heaven: for he maketh his sun to rise on the evil and on the good, and sendeth rain on the just and on the unjust.

46 For if ye love them which love you, what reward have ye? do not even the publicans the same?

47 And if ye salute your brethren only, what do ye more than others? do not even the publicans so?

48 Be ye therefore perfect, even as your Father which is in heaven is perfect.

Matthew 6

1 Take heed that ye do not your alms before men, to be seen of them: otherwise ye have no reward of your Father which is in heaven.

2 Therefore when thou doest thine alms, do not sound a trumpet before thee, as the hypocrites do in the synagogues and in the streets, that they may have glory of men. Verily I say unto you, They have their reward.

3 But when thou doest alms, let not thy left hand know what thy right hand doeth:

4 That thine alms may be in secret: and thy Father which seeth in secret himself shall reward thee openly.

5 And when thou prayest, thou shalt not be as the hypocrites are: for they love to pray standing in the synagogues and in the corners of the streets, that they may be seen of men. Verily I say unto you, They have their reward.

6 But thou, when thou prayest, enter into thy closet, and when thou hast shut thy door, pray to thy Father which is in secret; and thy Father which seeth in secret shall reward thee openly.

7 But when ye pray, use not vain repetitions, as the heathen do: for they think that they shall be heard for their much speaking.

8 Be not ye therefore like unto them: for your Father knoweth what things ye have need of, before ye ask him.

9 After this manner therefore pray ye: Our Father which art in heaven, Hallowed be thy name.

10 Thy kingdom come, Thy will be done in earth, as it is in heaven.

11 Give us this day our daily bread.

12 And forgive us our debts, as we forgive our debtors.

13 And lead us not into temptation, but deliver us from evil: For thine is the kingdom, and the power, and the glory, for ever. Amen.

14 For if ye forgive men their trespasses, your heavenly Father will also forgive you:

15 But if ye forgive not men their trespasses, neither will your Father forgive your trespasses.

16 Moreover when ye fast, be not, as the hypocrites, of a sad countenance: for they disfigure their faces, that they may appear unto men to fast. Verily I say unto you, They have their reward.

‘Give us this day our daily bread.’

17 But thou, when thou fastest, anoint thine head, and wash thy face;

18 That thou appear not unto men to fast, but unto thy Father which is in secret: and thy Father, which seeth in secret, shall reward thee openly.

19 Lay not up for yourselves treasures upon earth, where moth and rust doth corrupt, and where thieves break through and steal:

20 But lay up for yourselves treasures in heaven, where neither moth nor rust doth corrupt, and where thieves do not break through nor steal:

21 For where your treasure is, there will your heart be also.

22 The light of the body is the eye: if therefore thine eye be single, thy whole body shall be full of light.

23 But if thine eye be evil, thy whole body shall be full of darkness. If therefore the light that is in thee be darkness, how great is that darkness!

24 No man can serve two masters: for either he will hate the one, and love the other; or else he will hold to the one, and despise the other. Ye cannot serve God and mammon.

25 Therefore I say unto you, Take no thought for your life, what ye shall eat, or what ye shall drink; nor yet for your body, what ye shall put on. Is not the life more than meat, and the body than raiment?

26 Behold the fowls of the air: for they sow not, neither do they reap, nor gather

into barns; yet your heavenly Father feedeth them. Are ye not much better than they?

27 Which of you by taking thought can add one cubit unto his stature?

28 And why take ye thought for raiment? Consider the lilies of the field, how they grow; they toil not, neither do they spin:

29 And yet I say unto you, That even Solomon in all his glory was not arrayed like one of these.

30 Wherefore, if God so clothe the grass of the field, which to day is, and to morrow is cast into the oven, shall he not much more clothe you, O ye of little faith?

31 Therefore take no thought, saying, What shall we eat? or, What shall we drink? or, Wherewithal shall we be clothed?

32 (For after all these things do the Gentiles seek:) for your heavenly Father knoweth that ye have need of all these things.

33 But seek ye first the kingdom of God, and his righteousness; and all these things shall be added unto you.

34 Take therefore no thought for the morrow: for the morrow shall take thought for the things of itself. Sufficient unto the day is the evil thereof.

Matthew 7

1 Judge not, that ye be not judged.

2 For with what judgement ye judge, ye shall be judged: and with what measure ye mete, it shall be measured to you again.

3 And why beholdest thou the mote that is in thy brother's eye, but considerest not the beam that is in thine own eye?

4 Or how wilt thou say to thy brother, Let me pull out the mote out of thine eye; and, behold, a beam is in thine own eye?

5 Thou hypocrite, first cast out the beam out of thine own eye; and then shalt thou see clearly to cast out the mote out of thy brother's eye.

6 Give not that which is holy unto the dogs, neither cast ye your pearls before swine, lest they trample them under their feet, and turn again and rend you.

7 Ask, and it shall be given you; seek, and ye shall find; knock, and it shall be opened unto you:

8 For every one that asketh receiveth; and he that seeketh findeth; and to him that knocketh it shall be opened.

9 Or what man is there of you, whom if his son ask bread, will he give him a stone?

10 Or if he ask a fish, will he give him a serpent?

11 If ye then, being evil, know how to give good gifts unto your children, how much more shall your Father which is in heaven give good things to them that ask him?

12 Therefore all things whatsoever ye would that men should do to you, do ye even so to them: for this is the law and the prophets.

13 Enter ye in at the strait gate: for wide is the gate, and broad is the way, that leadeth to destruction, and many there be which go in thereat:

14 Because strait is the gate, and narrow is the way, which leadeth unto life, and few there be that find it.

15 Beware of false prophets, which come to you in sheep's clothing, but inwardly they are ravening wolves.

16 Ye shall know them by their fruits. Do men gather grapes of thorns, or figs of thistles?

17 Even so every good tree bringeth forth good fruit; but a corrupt tree bringeth forth evil fruit.

18 A good tree cannot bring forth evil fruit, neither can a corrupt tree bring forth good fruit.

19 Every tree that bringeth not forth good fruit is hewn down, and cast into the fire.

20 Wherefore by their fruits ye shall know them.

21 Not every one that saith unto me, Lord, Lord, shall enter into the kingdom of heaven; but he that doeth the will of my Father which is in heaven.

'Strait is the gate, and narrow is the way, which leadeth unto life, and few there be that find it.'

22 Many will say to me in that day, Lord, Lord, have we not prophesied in thy name? and in thy name have cast out devils? and in thy name done many wonderful works?

23 And then will I profess unto them, I never knew you: depart from me, ye that work iniquity.

24 Therefore whosoever heareth these sayings of mine, and doeth them, I will liken him unto a wise man, which built his house upon a rock:

25 And the rain descended, and the floods came, and the winds blew, and beat upon that house; and it fell not: for it was founded upon a rock.

26 And every one that heareth these sayings of mine, and doeth them not, shall be likened unto a foolish man, which built his house upon the sand:

27 And the rain descended, and the floods came, and the winds blew, and beat upon that house; and it fell: and great was the fall of it.

28 And it came to pass, when Jesus had ended these sayings, the people were astonished at his doctrine:

29 For he taught them as one having authority, and not as the scribes.

‘Turn your face towards the Sacred Mosque.’

Mohammed

Koran 2, 144–45, 147–50

These words were delivered by Mohammed, the Prophet and founder of Islam, and concerned the direction in which prayers should be offered to God.

In 610 Mohammed, a merchant in the important trading centre of Mecca, had received a vision from the Angel Gabriel in which he was called on to preach the message entrusted to him by God. In 622, after a hostile response in his home city to his new religion and the persecution of his followers, Mohammed fled further north to Medina. Here he established a strong community of believers. This move was known as the *hegira*, or *hijra*, and the year in which it happened marked the first year of the Muslim calendar.

Born in 570 in Mecca.
In 610 Mohammed received a vision of the Angel Gabriel and began to preach a new religion. Persecuted, he fled to Medina in 622. About this time, he received instructions from God to pray towards the Ka'ba in Mecca ('**Turn your face towards the Sacred Mosque**'). In 630 Mohammed's forces captured Mecca and in his final pilgrimage there in 632 Mohammed declared the brotherhood of all Muslims, repudiating distinctions of class, colour and race.
Died in 632 in Medina.

The other religious groups active in Medina were Jews, Nazarenes and Christians who all offered their prayers towards Jerusalem, believing many of their prophets had preached from there. There were also unbelievers in Medina who would turn towards the Ka'ba, an ancient religious shrine and site of pilgrimage in Mecca that had become desecrated by superstition, idol worship and myth. In Medina Mohammed had at first offered his prayers towards Jerusalem rather than towards the Ka'ba but was uncertain about doing this. He felt drawn towards offering his prayers towards Ka'ba, the house that his ancestors and the prophets Abraham and Ishmael had rebuilt many centuries before. He was troubled by this until God (Allah) directed him to do so. From then onwards Mohammed and his followers faced the Ka'ba in Mecca when praying.

Born in 570 and orphaned at a young age, Mohammed was brought up by his grandfather and uncle. At 25 he married a wealthy widow and became a merchant in her business. In 610, while he was in a cave on Mount Hira outside Mecca, Mohammed received the vision that led him to preach a new religion that, although connected to both Judaism and Christianity, was a revision of both faiths and had a greater appeal to the Arab people. Mohammed attacked the superstition and idolatry he believed was corrupting the other major religions. He taught that people should live a moral life respecting an all-powerful, just and merciful God, whose mercy was obtained by regular prayer, fasting and alms-giving. Mohammed was a means for transmitting the word of

God to the people: there is no word of Mohammed's in the Koran. He called himself 'the seal of the prophets', meaning that he was the last in a long line of predecessors. Prophets from other religions were important to Mohammed and he regarded Abraham as the supreme example because he had submitted to the will of God in preparing to sacrifice his son to Him. The word 'Islam' means 'submission to the will of God'.

From Medina, Mohammed waged a victorious war on Mecca. In 630 the city was forced to accept Islam, and Mohammed's final pilgrimage there confirmed Mecca as the focal point of the religion. By the time of his death in 632, Islam had spread across the whole of central and southern Arabia.

We have seen you turning your face towards the heaven. We shall surely turn you to a direction that shall satisfy you. So turn your face towards the Sacred Mosque (built by Abraham); wherever you are, turn your faces to it. Those to whom the Book was given know this to be the truth from their Lord. Allah is not inattentive of what they do. But even if you brought those to whom the Book had been given every proof, they would not accept your direction, nor would you accept theirs; nor would any of them accept the direction of the other. If after all the knowledge you have been given you yield to their desires, then you will surely be among the harmdoers...

'Allah is never inattentive of what you do.'

The truth comes from your Lord, so do not be among the doubters. And for everyone is a direction for which he turns... And wherever you are, Allah will bring you all together. He has power over all things. From wherever you emerge, turn your face towards the Sacred Mosque. This is surely the truth from your Lord. Allah is never inattentive of what you do. From wherever you emerge, turn your face towards the Sacred Mosque, and wherever you are, face towards it, so that the people will have no argument against you, except the harm doers among them. Do not fear of them, fear Me, so that I will perfect My Favour to you and that you will be guided.

'My little sisters, the birds, much bounden are ye unto God.'

St Francis of Assisi

Sermon to the birds, c.1220

The preaching of St Francis of Assisi to the sparrows at Alviano is one of the many legends about this popular saint described in the anthology *Little Flowers of St Francis*. Francis believed that nature was the mirror of God and referred to all creatures as brothers and sisters. His fondness for birds is memorably captured in the famous fresco by the Florentine painter Giotto, which shows him feeding them.

Born in 1182, Francis was the son of a wealthy cloth merchant in Assisi, Italy. He had little formal education and lived a fun-loving life. In 1202 Assisi went to war with nearby Perugia and Francis volunteered for the cavalry. Captured after the first battle, he was imprisoned for several months. After this he fell ill and his outlook on life gradually underwent a transformation.

Francis began to seek solitude and prayer to know the will of God. After a vision of Christ in a grotto in Assisi, he left home and devoted himself to the care of lepers and the rebuilding of neglected churches in and around Assisi.

In 1209 he received a calling to live in total poverty and to preach the word of God. He soon attracted followers and in 1210 they sought the permission of the Pope to found a new religious order. The Franciscans preached the need for a simple lifestyle based on the ideals of the gospels. Followers were not to handle money and if not paid for work in food and clothing had to beg for what they needed. At that time the church had lost touch with large sections of lay people and a heretical group, the Cathars, were preaching that the material world was evil and the hierarchy of the Roman Church a false one. In contrast, Francis was loyal to the church hierarchy, and emphasised that God's world was fundamentally good.

Born in 1182 in Assisi, Italy.
In 1206, Francis publicly renounced his father's wealth and left home to live in poverty. He founded the Franciscan order in 1210 and the Poor Clares, an order for women, in 1212. The Third Order, a lay order, was founded in 1221. In 1224, Francis received the stigmata (wounds of Christ).
Francis died in 1226 and was canonized in 1228. In 1476 the first known edition of the *Little Flowers of St Francis*, containing the **Sermon to the birds**, was published in Italy.

Francis had a special devotion to the human figure of Jesus and it was he who made the Christmas crib popular.

The Franciscan movement spread quickly throughout Europe, with separate orders for women and lay people established in 1212 and 1221. Francis retired to contemplation. In 1224 he began a 40-day fast during which he received a vision and the stigmata of Christ's wounds appeared on his body. Living a hard life of penance and fasting, Francis spent the last two years of his life in constant pain and almost blind. After his death he was declared a saint by Pope Gregory (1228) and in the same year a church was built to house his relics.

Francis was an unprepossessing figure, small and very thin. There were many movements in the Middle Ages based on poverty but his own was popular because of his personal charisma and dedication. He lived austerely but with gentleness and with infectious enthusiasm. He gave simple, sincere sermons that touched people's hearts. Once when preaching before a cardinal and unable to express in words his joy in Christ, he conveyed it instead by dancing. The Franciscan order has continued to thrive and today still cares for the poor, educates young people and carries out other good works.

'Because ye know not how to spin or sow, God clotheth you, you and your children.'

My little sisters, the birds, much bounden are ye unto God, your Creator, and always in every place ought ye to praise Him, for that He hath given you liberty to fly about everywhere, and hath also given you double and triple raiment; moreover He preserved your seed in the ark of Noah, that your race might not perish out of the world; still more are ye beholden to Him for the element of the air which He hath appointed for you; beyond all this, ye sow not, neither do you reap; and God feedeth you, and giveth you the streams and fountains for your drink; the mountains and valleys for your refuge and the high trees whereon to make your nests; and because ye know not how to spin or sow, God clotheth you, you and your children; wherefore your Creator loveth you much, seeing that He hath bestowed on you so many benefits; and therefore, my little sisters, beware of the sin of ingratitude, and study always to give praises unto God.

'I have the heart and stomach of a king.'

Queen Elizabeth I

Speech to the English troops at Tilbury, 1588

Queen Elizabeth I gave this speech rallying her assembled troops at Tilbury near London, gathered to fight an expected Spanish invasion.

After the execution of Mary Queen of Scots in 1587, growing Catholic opposition to England was encouraged by the Pope and King Philip II of Spain, widower of Elizabeth's sister Mary, who wanted to depose Elizabeth and reinstate a Catholic monarch in England. In the late summer of 1588 the Spanish Armada approached England. One of the most famous naval battles in history followed, in which the Spanish Armada was unexpectedly defeated by the superior seamanship of the British.

Elizabeth was the daughter of Henry VIII and Ann Boleyn, whom Henry had married after divorcing his first wife, Catherine of Aragon, thus breaking with the Papacy. With one daughter (Mary Tudor) from his first marriage, Henry desperately needed an heir. Unable to produce one, Ann Boleyn was executed in 1536 and Henry married Jane Seymour who had a son, Edward, in 1537. Mary Tudor became Queen after their brother's early death and England reverted to Catholicism.

Following Mary's death in 1558 Elizabeth became Queen, warmly welcomed by all Protestants. She broke ties between the English church and Rome but was otherwise moderate in religious reforms, despite Parliament's desire for stronger measures. Later in her reign tougher measures were passed, following Catholic plots to assassinate Elizabeth after Mary Queen of Scots' arrival in England in 1568. After much prevarication by Elizabeth, Mary was eventually executed in 1587, leading to the train of events surrounding the Tilbury speech.

Born 7 September 1533 in Greenwich, England.
Elizabeth Tudor ascended the throne in 1558. Key events during her reign included the enforcement of the Protestant religion in England in 1559 and the defeat of the Spanish Armada, which followed her **speech at Tilbury**, in 1588.
Died 24 March 1603 at Richmond Palace, England.

Queen Elizabeth I ruled England for over half a century, during which the country flourished politically, economically and in the arts, especially literature. Though she resisted marriage, she had several 'favourites' including Robert Dudley, Earl of Leicester and, at the end of her life, the Earl of Essex (eventually executed for treason). Elizabeth was variously known as Good Queen Bess, the Virgin Queen and 'Gloriana', reflecting her immense popularity with her subjects, her refusal to marry, and her overseeing of a glorious period of creativity in England.

My loving people,

We have been persuaded by some that are careful of our safety, to take heed how we commit ourselves to armed multitudes, for fear of treachery; but I assure you I do not desire to live to distrust my faithful and loving people.

'I know I have the body but of a weak and feeble woman; but I have the heart and stomach of a king, and of a king of England too.'

Let tyrants fear, I have always so behaved myself that, under God, I have placed my chiefest strength and safeguard in the loyal hearts and good-will of my subjects; and therefore I am come amongst you, as you see, at this time, not for my recreation and disport, but being resolved, in the midst and heat of the battle, to live and die amongst you all; to lay down for my God, and for my kingdom, and my people, my honour and my blood, even in the dust.

I know I have the body but of a weak and feeble woman; but I have the heart and stomach of a king, and of a king of England too, and think foul scorn that Parma or Spain, or any prince of Europe, should dare to invade the borders of my realm; to which rather than any dishonour shall grow by me, I myself will take up arms, I myself will be your general, judge, and rewarder of every one of your virtues in the field. I know already, for your forwardness you have deserved rewards and crowns; and We do assure you in the word of a prince, they shall be duly paid you. In the mean time, my lieutenant general shall be in my stead, that whom never prince commanded a more noble or worthy subject; not doubting but by your obedience to my general, by your concord in the camp, and your valour in the field, we shall shortly have a famous victory over those enemies of my God, of my kingdom, and of my people.

‘I go from a corruptible to an incorruptible crown.’

King Charles I

Speech on the scaffold, 30 January 1649

These are the last words spoken by King Charles I just before his execution by beheading in January 1649. This act of regicide concluded a reign characterized by conflicts between the King and Parliament that had led to civil war in England and, ultimately, to a period during which the English monarchy was abolished.

Charles I, the son of James VI of Scotland, was 25 when he acceded to the throne and in the same year he married the French Roman Catholic Princess Henrietta Maria. Charles' reign was beset with problems from the start. His marriage did not please his Protestant country and he was soon at odds with Parliament over money. Royal revenues having been eroded during the previous century, English monarchs were dependent for grants from Parliament. When Parliament attempted to use its power to coerce Charles into granting it greater powers, he resisted and in 1629 dissolved Parliament and ruled without it for 11 years, raising money by other means.

Although Charles was brave, sincere, a loyal husband and father and a great patron of the arts, he was also reserved, shy, inflexible, politically deceitful, over-confident and a poor strategist. He was deeply religious and also influenced by his wife, who believed strongly in absolute monarchy. This did not help his cause as King in a country where Parliament wanted to move towards constitutional monarchy.

Born 19 November 1600 in Fife, Scotland. In 1625, Charles acceded to the throne and married Princess Henrietta Maria of France. He suspended Parliament in 1629, ruling alone for 11 years. In 1642, the English Civil Wars began. Charles was accused of treason by the republican Parliamentarians and sentenced to death. He faced his death bravely, as his **speech from the scaffold** records. Executed 30 January 1649, in London.

In 1637 Charles came into conflict with the Scots while trying to impose an Anglican form of worship on the mainly Presbyterian population. This led to the 'Bishops' Wars', which forced Charles to recall Parliament to access funds to squash the Scottish uprising. This 'Short Parliament' was dissolved after a month when it refused to give Charles the money. Continuing unrest in the north and in Ireland meant Charles then had to recall Parliament and the struggle between them for authority eventually led to outright conflict and the outbreak of civil war in 1642.

The Royalist forces fought the Parliamentarians (the Roundheads) over a period of six years, during which the fortunes of each side fluctuated but finally the Royalists were crushed. The Parliamentarian army, headed by Oliver Cromwell, accused Charles of being 'the grand author of our troubles', holding him responsible for the bloodshed of the Civil Wars. He was charged with treason but would not accept the legal validity of the court, or case, against him, and refused to speak in his own defence. Cromwell pushed through the death warrant and Charles I went bravely to his death.

I shall be very little heard of anybody here ... Indeed, I could hold my peace very well, if I did not think that holding my peace would make some men think that I did submit to the guilt, as well as to the punishment: but I think it is my duty to God first, and to my country, for to clear myself both as an honest man, and a good King and a good Christian.

I shall begin first with my innocency. In troth I think it not very needful for me to insist upon this, for all the world knows that I never did begin a war with the two Houses of Parliament, and I call God to witness, to whom I must shortly make an account, that I never did intend for to incroach upon their privileges, they began upon me, it is the militia they began upon, they confess that the militia was mine, but they thought it fit for to have it from me.

God forbid that I should be so ill a Christian, as not to say that God's judgements are just upon me: many times he does pay justice by an unjust sentence, that is ordinary: I will only say this, that an unjust sentence that I suffered to take effect, is punished now by an unjust sentence upon me, that is, so far I have said, to show you that I am an innocent man.

Now for to show you that I am a good Christian: I hope there is a good man that will bear me witness, that I have forgiven all the world, and even those in particular that have been the chief causers of my death: who they are, God

'I could hold my peace very well, if I did not think that holding my peace would make some men think that I did submit to the guilt, as well as to the punishment.'

knows, I do not desire to know, I pray God forgive them.

But this is not all, my charity must go farther, I wish that they may repent, for indeed they have committed a great sin in that particular: I pray God with St

Stephen, that this be not laid to their charge, nay, not only so, but that they may take the right way to the peace of the kingdom, for my charity commands me not only to forgive particular men, but my charity commands me to endeavour to the last gasp the peace of the kingdom ...

... For the people: and truly I desire their liberty and freedom as much as any body whomsoever, but I must tell you, that their liberty and their freedom consists in having of Government; those laws, by which their life and their goods may be most their own.

It is not for having share in government (Sir) that is nothing pertaining to them; a subject and a sovereign are clean different things, and therefore until they do that, I mean, that you do put the people in that liberty as I say, certainly they will never enjoy themselves. Sirs, it was for this that now I am come here: if I would have given way to an arbitrary way, for to have all laws changed according

'A subject and a sovereign are clean different things.'

to the power of the sword, I needed not to have come here, and therefore I tell you (and I pray God it be not laid to your charge) that I am the martyr of the people.

In troth Sirs, I shall not hold you much longer, for I will only say thus to you, that in truth I could have desired some little time longer, because I would have put then that I have said in a little more order, and a little better digested than I have done, and therefore I hope you will excuse me.

I have delivered my conscience, I pray God that you do take those courses that are best for the good of the kingdom, and your own salvations.

... In troth Sirs, my conscience in religion I think is very well known to all the world, and therefore I declare before you all, that I die a Christian, according to the profession of the Church of England, as I found it left me by my father, and this honest man I think will witness it.

... I have a good cause, and a gracious God on my side ... I go from a corruptible to an incorruptible crown; where no disturbance can be, no disturbance in the world.

'In the name of God, go!'

Oliver Cromwell

Dismisses the Rump Parliament, 20 April 1653

English soldier, and later statesman, Oliver Cromwell delivered this speech when forcibly dissolving the so-called Rump Parliament in 1653, prior to replacing it with his own assembly of 140 men – the Barebones Parliament – to whom he resigned all his power.

Born in Huntingdon, Cromwell was educated at Cambridge University and as a result of a strong conversion experience was a lifelong Puritan. In 1628 he was elected to Parliament for Huntingdon and in 1640 represented Cambridge in the Long Parliament. Here he made strong attacks on the Church of England bishops and urged the purification of the Church. As conflicts grew between Charles I and Parliament and sides began to be drawn up, Cromwell first raised a troop and then a cavalry regiment in Huntingdon.

During the first English Civil War Cromwell helped to win most of East Anglia for the Parliamentarian cause and was appointed Lieutenant General. He helped defeat the Royalists at the Battle of Marsden Moor and then took a major role in the Battle of Naseby as second in command to Sir Thomas Fairfax.

After the King's alliance with the Scots in the second Civil War failed, Cromwell argued that Charles I was personally responsible for renewing civil war and brought pressure for him to be tried for treason. Many people believe Cromwell was responsible for the execution of the King, although 59 others also signed the King's death warrant. Cromwell described the King's death as a 'cruel necessity'.

This speech demonstrates Cromwell's characteristic beliefs: that God had been behind his victories in the Civil Wars and that he had been chosen to enact God's will on earth. To establish a godly society in England he believed he needed to get rid of the current Parliament. This had been called 'the Rump' because it was what remained after the Long Parliament had been forcibly purged by Cromwell's army in 1648. Cromwell felt it was dragging its feet in producing political and religious reforms and so took decisive action to replace it. However, the Barebones Parliament was just as divided and by the end of the year it was dissolved. Cromwell was made Lord Protector of the Commonwealth of England, Scotland and Ireland, a position he held for five years enjoying many of the powers King Charles had once had.

Born 25 April 1599 in Huntingdon, England.
Cromwell became a Member of Parliament in 1628 and took the republican (Roundheads) side in the Civil Wars. His New Model Army destroyed King Charles I's forces at the Battle of Naseby in 1645. Cromwell was one of the signatories to the King's death warrant in 1649. He established the Commonwealth and in 1653 began a five-year rule as Lord Protector.
The 'shining bauble' **in this speech** refers to the House of Commons' ceremonial mace, made in 1649 and still in use today.
Died 3 September 1658 in London.

On Cromwell's death in 1658 the foundations of constitutional government had been laid and England was wealthy. He did not, however, produce a constitution for the country and his system of government did not last. He is widely remembered for the bloody and brutal methods he used to achieve and maintain his rule, rather than his godly intentions.

It is high time for me to put an end to your sitting in this place, which you have dishonoured by your contempt of all virtue, and defiled by your practice of every vice; ye are a factious crew, and enemies to all good government; ye are a pack of mercenary wretches, and would like Esau sell your country for a mess of potage,

'Is there a man amongst you that has the least care for the good of the Commonwealth?'

and like Judas betray your God for a few pieces of money; is there a single virtue now remaining amongst you? Is there one vice you do not possess? Ye have no more religion than my horse; gold is your God; which of you have not barter'd your conscience for bribes? Is there a man amongst you that has the least care for the good of the Commonwealth? Ye sordid prostitutes have you not defil'd this sacred place, and turn'd the Lord's temple into a den of thieves, by your immoral principles and wicked practices? Ye are grown intolerably odious to the whole nation; you were deputed here by the people to get grievances redress'd, are yourselves become the greatest grievance. Your county therefore calls upon me to cleanse this Augean stable, by putting a final period to your iniquitous

'Make haste! Ye venal slaves be gone!'

proceedings in this House; and which by God's help, and the strength he has given me, I am now come to do; I command ye therefore, upon the peril of your lives, to depart immediately out of this place; go, get you out! Make haste! Ye venal slaves be gone! Go! Take away that shining bauble there, and lock up the doors. In the name of God, go!

‘A passionate attachment of one nation for another produces a variety of evils.’

As the first President of the United States of America, George Washington holds a special place in history. Born on 22 February 1732, the son of a Virginia planter, he became a soldier and saw early action in the French and Indian War (1754–1763), the bloodiest American war of the eighteenth century.

The years 1759–75 were more peaceful for Washington, who concentrated on managing his land around Mount Vernon and served in the Virginia House of Burgesses. During this period, he and other landowners felt increasingly exploited and restricted by British regulations, and Washington became vocal in his objections.

By the autumn of 1760, the British controlled all the North American frontier, and in 1763 France surrendered all her American possessions to Britain and Spain. Conflict between the British and the Native Americans gradually led to worsening relations between England and her colonies and to the Revolutionary War itself, in which Washington was to play a central role.

Born 22 February 1732 in Virginia.
Combining a distinguished military career with politics, Washington led American troops to victory against the British in the War of Independence. He chaired the convention that drafted the American Constitution and was elected first President of the United States, serving for two terms. His **farewell address** emphasizes the importance of the Union.
Died 14 December 1799 in Virginia.
Washington's birthday is a public holiday in the US, celebrated on the third Monday in February.

In 1774 and 1775, Washington took part in two Continental Congresses held by the American colonies against British rule, and in 1775 he became Commander of the Continental Army, raised by the colonists. In July that year he began his involvement in the War of Independence, which was to last six years. It was under his leadership that America eventually triumphed, notably through the decisive battle at Yorktown in 1781.

In 1787, Washington chaired the Philadelphia convention that drafted the American Constitution, and at the end of April 1789 he was elected President, by unanimous vote of the Electoral College, taking his oath of office on the balcony of Federal Hall in New York's Wall Street. He was President for two terms.

As President, Washington concerned himself especially with foreign policy. When hostilities between the French and British flared, he insisted on following a policy of neutrality, rather than siding with either, and his powerful Farewell Address includes a warning against America forming long-term alliances.

In retirement he returned to Mount Vernon and when he died in December 1799 he was mourned by the nation for months.

Friends and fellow-citizens: the period for a new election of a citizen, to administer the executive government of the United States, being not far distant, and the time actually arrived when your thoughts must be employed in designating the person who is to be clothed with that important trust, it appears to me proper, especially as it may conduce to a more distinct expression of the public voice, that I should now apprise you of the resolution I have formed, to decline being considered among the number of those out of whom a choice is to be made ...

... I have the consolation to believe that, while choice and prudence invite me to quit the political scene, patriotism does not forbid it.

... A solicitude for your welfare which cannot end but with my life, and the apprehension of danger, natural to that solicitude, urge me, on an occasion like the present, to offer to your solemn contemplation, and to recommend to your frequent review, some sentiments which are the result of much reflection, of no inconsiderable observation, and which appear to me all-important to the permanency of your felicity as a people. These will be offered to you with the more freedom, as you can only see in them the disinterested warnings of a parting friend, who can possibly have no personal motive to bias his counsel. Nor can I forget, as an encouragement to it, your indulgent reception of my sentiments on a former and not dissimilar occasion.

‘Your Union ought to be considered as a main prop of your liberty, and that the love of the one ought to endear to you the preservation of the other.’

Interwoven as is the love of liberty with every ligament of your hearts, no recommendation of mine is necessary to fortify or confirm the attachment.

The unity of government, which constitutes you one people, is also now dear to you. It is justly so; for it is a main pillar in the edifice of your real independence, the support of your tranquillity at home, your peace abroad; of your safety; of your prosperity; of that very Liberty, which you so highly prize. ... Citizens, by birth or choice, of a common country, that country has a right to concentrate your affections. The name of American, which belongs to you, in your national capacity, must always exalt the just pride of patriotism, more than any appellation derived from local discriminations. With slight shades of difference, you have the same religion, manners, habits and political principles. You have in a common cause fought and triumphed together; the Independence and Liberty you possess are the work of joint counsels, and joint efforts, of common dangers, sufferings and successes.

But these considerations, however powerfully they address themselves to your sensibility, are greatly outweighed by those, which apply more immediately to your interest. Here every portion of our country finds the most commanding motives for carefully guarding and preserving the Union of the whole. ... [Y]our Union ought to be considered as a main prop of your liberty, and that the love of the one ought to endear to you the preservation of the other.

... Observe good faith and justice towards all nations; cultivate peace and harmony with all. Religion and morality enjoin this conduct; and can it be, that good policy does not equally enjoin it? It will be worthy of a free, enlightened, and, at no distant period, a great nation, to give to mankind the magnanimous and too novel example of a people always guided by an exalted justice and benevolence. Who can doubt, that, in the course of time and things, the fruits of such a plan would richly repay any temporary advantages, which might be lost by a steady adherence to it? Can it be, that Providence has not connected the permanent felicity of a nation with its virtue? The experiment, at least, is recommended by every sentiment which ennobles human nature. Alas! Is it rendered impossible by its vices?

... A passionate attachment of one nation for another produces a variety of evils. Sympathy for the favourite nation, facilitating the illusion of an imaginary common interest, in cases where no real common interest exists, and infusing into one the enmities of the other, betrays the former into a participation in the quarrels and wars of the latter, without adequate inducement or justification. It leads also to concessions to the favourite nation of privileges denied to others, which is apt doubly to injure the Nation making the concessions; by unnecessarily parting with what ought to have been retained; and by exciting jealousy, ill-will, and a disposition to retaliate, in the parties from whom equal privileges are withheld. And it gives to ambitious, corrupted or deluded citizens (who devote themselves to the favourite nation) facility to betray or sacrifice the interests of their own country, without odium, sometimes even with popularity; gilding, with the appearances of a virtuous sense of obligation, a commendable deference for public opinion, or a laudable zeal for public good, the base or foolish compliances of ambition, corruption, or infatuation ...

... Against the insidious wiles of foreign influence (I conjure you to believe me, fellow-citizens,) the jealousy of a free people ought to be constantly awake; since history and experience prove, that foreign influence is one of the most baneful foes of republican government. But that jealousy, to be useful, must be impartial; else it becomes the instrument of the very influence to be avoided, instead of a defence against it. Excessive partiality for one foreign nation, and excessive dislike of another, cause those whom they actuate to see danger only on one side, and serve to veil and even second the arts of influence on the other. Real patriots, who may resist the intrigues of the favourite, are liable to become suspected and odious; while its tools and dupes usurp the applause and confidence of the people, to surrender their interests ...

The great rule of conduct for us, in regard to foreign nations, is, in extending our commercial relations, to have with them as little political connection as possible. So far as we have already formed engagements, let them be fulfilled with perfect good faith. Here let us stop.

‘Observe good faith and justice towards all Nations; cultivate peace and harmony with all.’

Europe has a set of primary interests, which to us have none, or a very remote relation. Hence she must be engaged in frequent controversies, the causes of which are essentially foreign to our concerns. Hence, therefore, it must be unwise in us to implicate ourselves, by artificial ties, in the ordinary vicissitudes of her politics, or the ordinary combinations and collisions of her friendships or enmities.

Our detached and distant situation invites and enables us to pursue a different course. If we remain one people, under an efficient government, the period is not far off, when we may defy material injury from external annoyance; when we may take such an attitude as will cause the neutrality, we may at any time resolve upon, to be scrupulously respected; when belligerent nations, under the impossibility of making acquisitions upon us, will not lightly hazard the giving us provocation; when we may choose peace or war, as our interest, guided by justice, shall counsel.

Why forego the advantages of so peculiar a situation? Why quit our own to stand upon foreign ground? Why, by interweaving our destiny with that of any part of Europe, entangle our peace and prosperity in the toils of European ambition, rivalship, interest, humour or caprice?

It is our true policy to steer clear of permanent alliances with any portion of the foreign world; so far, I mean, as we are now at liberty to do it; for let me not be understood as capable of patronizing infidelity to existing engagements. I hold the maxim no less applicable to public than to private affairs, that honesty is always the best policy. I repeat it, therefore, let those engagements be observed in their genuine sense. But, in my opinion, it is unnecessary and would be unwise to extend them.

'Europe has a set of primary interests, which to us have none, or a very remote relation.'

Taking care always to keep ourselves, by suitable establishments, on a respectable defensive posture, we may safely trust to temporary alliances for extraordinary emergencies.

... Though, in reviewing the incidents of my administration, I am unconscious of intentional error, I am nevertheless too sensible of my defects not to think it probable that I may have committed many errors. Whatever they may be, I fervently beseech the Almighty to avert or mitigate the evils to which they may tend. I shall also carry with me the hope, that my country will never cease to view them with indulgence; and that, after forty-five years of my life dedicated to its service with an upright zeal, the faults of incompetent abilities will be consigned to oblivion, as myself must soon be to the mansions of rest.

Relying on its kindness in this as in other things, and actuated by that fervent love towards it, which is so natural to a man, who views it in the native soil of himself and his progenitors for several generations; I anticipate with pleasing expectation that retreat, in which I promise myself to realize, without alloy, the sweet enjoyment of partaking, in the midst of my fellow-citizens, the benign influence of good laws under a free government, the ever favourite object of my heart, and the happy reward, as I trust, of our mutual cares, labours and dangers.

‘We are all Republicans, we are all Federalists.’

Thomas Jefferson was born on 13 April 1743, in Virginia. His father was a landowning planter and surveyor and his mother belonged to a famous colonial family, the Randolphs.

At the College of William and Mary in Williamsburg, Jefferson studied mathematics, natural sciences, French, Latin, Greek, Spanish, Italian and Anglo-Saxon. He also played the violin and sang, and was a keen sportsman and rider.

He was admitted to the Bar in 1767, though his legal career was hampered by his weakness as a public speaker. Aware of abuses in the law, he became increasingly interested in politics. Although not excelling in oratory, he crafted his speeches with immense care and intelligence, best exemplified by the famous Declaration of Independence, which he drafted in 1776 at the age of 33. The bill he wrote establishing religious freedom was enacted in 1786.

Jefferson spent the years 1784 to 1789 in Paris, as Minister to France, and became deeply interested in the events leading up to the French Revolution, an experience that influenced his views of equality and democracy. However, his sympathies with the French Revolution led him into conflict with the US government and he resigned from the Cabinet in 1793. Two parties then emerged: the Federalists and the Democratic-Republicans. Jefferson became leader of the latter, cleverly positioning himself as able to unite the two factions.

In 1796 he became Vice-President under John Adams and President in 1801. Re-elected for a second term in 1804, with a large majority, his time in office was praised for its simplicity and vision. He maintained that all people are equally worthy of respect, abolished expensive state balls and ceremonies, reduced the army and navy and cut government expenses.

He retired from office in March 1809, refusing to be a candidate for re-election, although many urged him to stand again. In his twilight years he devoted himself to establishing the University of Virginia at Charlottesville, planning the buildings, and overseeing the organization. He died on 4 July 1826, the fiftieth anniversary of the Declaration of Independence.

Born 13 April 1743 in Virginia.
The Declaration of Independence, which Jefferson wrote, was adopted by Congress on 4 July 1776. Jefferson served as President for two terms. His **inaugural address** is famed for its forthright statement of his republican ideals. A lifelong scholar, Jefferson retired from politics in 1809 to concentrate on the establishment of the University of Virginia.
Died 4 July 1826.
Jefferson wrote his own epitaph for his gravestone: 'Here was buried Thomas Jefferson, author of the Declaration of American Independence, of the statute of Virginia for religious freedom, and father of the University of Virginia.'

Friends and fellow-citizens: Called upon to undertake the duties of the first executive office of our country, I avail myself of the presence of that portion of my fellow-citizens which is here assembled to express my grateful thanks for the favour with which they have been pleased to look toward me, to declare a sincere consciousness that the task is above my talents, and that I approach it with those anxious and awful presentiments which the greatness of the charge and the weakness of my powers so justly inspire. A rising nation, spread over a wide and fruitful land, traversing all the seas with the rich productions of their industry, engaged in commerce with nations who feel power and forget right, advancing rapidly to destinies beyond the reach of mortal eye – when I contemplate these transcendent objects, and see the honour, the happiness and the hopes of this beloved country committed to the issue, and the auspices of this day, I shrink from the contemplation, and humble myself before the magnitude of the undertaking. Utterly, indeed, should I despair did not the presence of many whom I here see remind me that in the other high authorities provided by our Constitution I shall find resources of wisdom, of virtue and of zeal on which to rely under all difficulties. To you, then, gentlemen, who are charged with the sovereign functions of legislation, and to those associated with you, I look with encouragement for that guidance and support which may enable us to steer with safety the vessel in which we are all embarked amidst the conflicting elements of a troubled world.

‘I believe this … the strongest Government on earth.’

During the contest of opinion through which we have passed the animation of discussions and of exertions has sometimes worn an aspect which might impose on strangers unused to think freely and to speak and to write what they think; but this being now decided by the voice of the nation, announced according to the rules of the Constitution, all will, of course, arrange themselves under the will of the law, and unite in common efforts for the common good. All, too, will bear in mind this sacred principle, that though the will of the majority is in all cases to prevail, that will to be rightful must be reasonable; that the minority possess their equal rights, which equal law must protect, and to violate would be oppression. Let us, then, fellow-citizens, unite with one heart and one mind. Let us restore to social intercourse that harmony and affection without which liberty and even life itself are but dreary things. And let us reflect that, having banished from our land that religious intolerance under which mankind so long bled and suffered, we have yet gained little if we countenance a political intolerance as despotic, as wicked, and capable of as bitter and bloody persecutions. During the throes and convulsions of the ancient world, during the agonizing spasms of infuriated man, seeking through blood and slaughter his long-lost liberty, it was not wonderful that the agitation of the billows should reach even this distant and peaceful shore; that this should be more felt and feared by some and less by others, and should divide opinions as to measures of safety. But every difference of opinion is not a difference of principle. We have called by different names

> '... freedom of religion; freedom of the press, and freedom of person under the protection of the habeas corpus, and trial by juries impartially selected.'

brethren of the same principle. We are all Republicans, we are all Federalists. If there be any among us who would wish to dissolve this Union or to change its republican form, let them stand undisturbed as monuments of the safety with which error of opinion may be tolerated where reason is left free to combat it. I know, indeed, that some honest men fear that a republican government cannot be strong, that this Government is not strong enough; but would the honest patriot, in the full tide of successful experiment, abandon a government which has so far kept us free and firm on the theoretic and visionary fear that this Government, the world's best hope, may by possibility want energy to preserve itself? I trust not. I believe this, on the contrary, the strongest Government on earth. I believe it the only one where every man, at the call of the law, would fly to the standard of the law, and would meet invasions of the public order as his own personal concern. Sometimes it is said that man can not be trusted with the government of himself. Can he, then, be trusted with the government of others? Or have we found angels in the forms of kings to govern him? Let history answer this question.

Let us, then, with courage and confidence pursue our own Federal and Republican principles, our attachment to union and representative government. Kindly separated by nature and a wide ocean from the exterminating havoc of one quarter of the globe; too high-minded to endure the degradations of the others;

possessing a chosen country, with room enough for our descendants to the thousandth and thousandth generation; entertaining a due sense of our equal right to the use of our own faculties, to the acquisitions of our own industry, to honour and confidence from our fellow-citizens, resulting not from birth, but from our actions and their sense of them; enlightened by a benign religion, professed, indeed, and practised in various forms, yet all of them inculcating honesty, truth, temperance, gratitude and the love of man; acknowledging and adoring an overruling Providence, which by all its dispensations proves that it delights in the happiness of man here and his greater happiness hereafter – with all these blessings, what more is necessary to make us a happy and a prosperous people? Still one thing more, fellow-citizens – a wise and frugal Government, which shall restrain men from injuring one another, shall leave them otherwise free to regulate their own pursuits of industry and improvement, and shall not take from the mouth of labour the bread it has earned. This is the sum of good government, and this is necessary to close the circle of our felicities.

About to enter, fellow-citizens, on the exercise of duties which comprehend everything dear and valuable to you, it is proper you should understand what I deem the essential principles of our Government, and consequently those which ought to shape its Administration. I will compress them within the narrowest compass they will bear, stating the general principle, but not all its limitations. Equal and exact justice to all men, of whatever state or persuasion, religious or political; peace, commerce, and honest friendship with all nations, entangling alliances with none; the support of the State governments in all their rights, as the most competent administrations for our domestic concerns and the surest bulwarks against anti-republican tendencies; the preservation of the General Government in its whole constitutional vigour, as the sheet anchor of our peace at home and safety abroad; a jealous care of the right of election by the people – a mild and safe corrective of abuses which are lopped by the sword of revolution where peaceable remedies are unprovided; absolute acquiescence in the decisions of the majority, the vital principle of republics, from which is no appeal but to force, the vital principle and immediate parent of despotism; a well-disciplined militia, our best reliance in peace and for the first moments of war, till regulars may relieve them; the supremacy of the civil over the military authority; economy in the public expense, that labour may be lightly burthened; the honest payment of our debts and sacred preservation of the public faith; encouragement of agriculture, and of commerce as its handmaid; the diffusion of information and arraignment of all abuses at the bar of the public reason; freedom of religion;

freedom of the press and freedom of person under the protection of the habeas corpus, and trial by juries impartially selected. These principles form the bright constellation which has gone before us and guided our steps through an age of revolution and reformation. The wisdom of our sages and blood of our heroes have been devoted to their attainment. They should be the creed of our political faith, the text of civic instruction, the touchstone by which to try the services of those we trust; and should we wander from them in moments of error or of alarm, let us hasten to retrace our steps and to regain the road which alone leads to peace, liberty and safety.

'I shall often go wrong through defect of judgement.'

I repair, then, fellow-citizens, to the post you have assigned me. With experience enough in subordinate offices to have seen the difficulties of this the greatest of all, I have learnt to expect that it will rarely fall to the lot of imperfect man to retire from this station with the reputation and the favour which bring him into it. Without pretensions to that high confidence you reposed in our first and greatest revolutionary character, whose pre-eminent services had entitled him to the first place in his country's love and destined for him the fairest page in the volume of faithful history, I ask so much confidence only as may give firmness and effect to the legal administration of your affairs. I shall often go wrong through defect of judgement. When right, I shall often be thought wrong by those whose positions will not command a view of the whole ground. I ask your indulgence for my own errors, which will never be intentional, and your support against the errors of others, who may condemn what they would not if seen in all its parts. The approbation implied by your suffrage is a great consolation to me for the past, and my future solicitude will be to retain the good opinion of those who have bestowed it in advance, to conciliate that of others by doing them all the good in my power, and to be instrumental to the happiness and freedom of all.

Relying, then, on the patronage of your good will, I advance with obedience to the work, ready to retire from it whenever you become sensible how much better choice it is in your power to make. And may that Infinite Power which rules the destinies of the universe lead our councils to what is best, and give them a favourable issue for your peace and prosperity.

'Soldiers of my Old Guard: I bid you farewell.'

Napoleon Bonaparte

Farewell to the Old Guard, 20 April 1814

This speech bidding farewell to his army was delivered by Napoleon Bonaparte after his failed invasion of Russia and defeat by the Allies, leading to his forced abdication as Emperor of France.

The man who led France to military glory, and became possibly the most famous military leader in history, was actually born in Corsica. In 1779 he began military school in France, where he earned the nickname 'the Little Corporal' because of his short stature. In 1785 Bonaparte was commissioned as a 2nd Lieutenant in artillery and in 1793 gained national recognition and promotion to Brigadier after a successful defeat of the British at Toulon. Bonaparte was not active in French politics in the early years of the French Revolution but in 1795, when the royalists attempted to overthrow the Directory, he was involved in the defence of Paris.

After heading campaigns through which France gained control of Italy and an unsuccessful campaign in Egypt, Napoleon returned to Paris where in 1799 he seized political power in a *coup d'état*, overthrowing the Directory. Bonaparte was named First Consul and given supreme power as head of a military dictatorship. He instituted many reforms in government and education and in 1804 had himself crowned as Emperor of France, with his wife, Josephine, his Empress.

Born 15 August 1769 in Corsica, of Italian descent.
Napoleon became an army officer in 1785 and had a brilliant military career. In 1796 he married Josephine de Beauharnais, later divorcing her to marry Marie Louise, daughter of the Austrian Emperor. He became First Consul in 1799 and Emperor of the French five years later. Under his rule, France became a European superpower. He abdicated twice, first in 1814 when Paris fell to his enemies (**Farewell to the Old Guard**) and again in 1815.
Died in exile under British arrest 5 May 1821.

The following year saw his greatest victory, the Battle of Austerlitz, in which he defeated the combined forces of Austria and Russia. By 1808 he was master of continental Europe. Determined to defeat the British, he attempted to ruin their economy through a blockade. However, when the Russians refused to cooperate Napoleon began his 1812 campaign against them. Although he defeated the Russian army at Borodino and occupied Moscow, the end result was the destruction of the French Grand Army as 500,000 troops withdrew through the terrible Russian winter. The Napoleonic system, under which three of the Emperor's brothers had sat on European thrones, also broke up.

In 1813 Napoleon suffered defeat at the Battle of the Nations and in 1814 Paris fell to forces allied against France. Napoleon said goodbye to his Old Guard and went into exile on the island of Elba, which was given to him as a Principality. He was allowed to retain the title of Emperor. Napoleon was later to make one last bid for power. Alarmed for the safety of his wife and son in France, after the monarchy was reinstated, he escaped from exile and returned to the mainland on 1 March 1815. Soldiers sent to capture him joined him instead and he regained his empire once more. His rule lasted only 100 days and ended with his final defeat in the Battle of Waterloo. After his second abdication Napoleon was jailed on St Helena in the Atlantic off the coast of Africa. He died five years later aged 52.

By repeated victories over a variety of European coalitions, Napoleon extended French rule over most of Europe and revolutionized military organization and training. However, the cost of this was thousands of French lives and, in any case, French dominance of Europe was not sustained. He is nevertheless regarded as a French hero, with a national tomb in Les Invalides in Paris. Napoleon's lasting legacy is the system of civil law (*Code Napoléon*) and the many institutions bearing his name that still exist in France today.

Soldiers of my Old Guard: I bid you farewell. For twenty years I have constantly accompanied you on the road to honour and glory. In these latter times, as in the days of our prosperity, you have invariably been models of courage and fidelity.

> 'I go, but you, my friends, will continue to serve France. Her happiness was my only thought.'

With men such as you our cause could not be lost; but the war would have been interminable; it would have been civil war, and that would have entailed deeper misfortunes on France.

I have sacrificed all of my interests to those of the country.

I go, but you, my friends, will continue to serve France. Her happiness was my only thought. It will still be the object of my wishes. Do not regret my fate; if I have consented to survive, it is to serve your glory. I intend to write the history of the great achievements we have performed together. Adieu, my friends. Would I could press you all to my heart.

‘Four score and seven years ago our fathers brought forth on this continent a new nation...’

Abraham Lincoln

The Gettysburg Address, 19 November 1863

Born in Hardin County, Kentucky, on 12 February 1809, Abraham Lincoln had a rural upbringing. His family moved to Indiana when he was eight and his mother died when he was ten. He summarized this stage of his life vividly: '... It was a wild region, with many bears and other wild animals still in the woods. There I grew up ... Of course when I came of age I did not know much. Still, somehow, I could read, write, and cipher ... but that was all.' The young Lincoln studied avidly by himself, urged on by his stepmother. As a boy he read widely, including the Bible, *Robinson Crusoe, The Pilgrim's Progress*, Aesop's fables, the poetry of Robert Burns, Shakespeare and books about the history of the United States.

At the age of 21 he teamed up with Denton Offutt, an itinerant trader and storekeeper, who helped him build a flatboat and took this down the Sangamon, Illinois and Mississippi rivers to New Orleans. In 1831 Offutt employed him in his country store in New Salem. This was not a busy store and Lincoln had ample time to study and improve his knowledge. Contemporary reports say he was devoted to self-education and read avidly.

Born 12 February 1809 in Kentucky. Self-educated, Lincoln served as a senator for many years before gaining the presidency, which he held for two terms. On New Year's Day 1863, Lincoln declared the emancipation of all slaves on US territory. **The Gettysburg Address** was given in commemoration of the three-day Battle of Gettysburg, a turning point in the Civil War, which left over 51,000 casualties. Assassinated 14 April 1865 in Washington.

He began to study law, which particularly appealed to him, and also became more and more interested in politics. In 1832 he was a candidate for the Illinois House of Representatives but the election was interrupted by the Black Hawk Indian War. Lincoln duly volunteered and joined one of the Sangamon County companies, where he was appointed Captain. However, he saw little action and his short military career seems to have been rather undistinguished.

He then went into business with his friend William Berry, buying a small country store. This was not a success and when the store was sold to pay its creditors in the spring of 1833 Lincoln was left with debts that took him 15 years to settle. In May 1833 he became postmaster of New Salem, a relatively poorly-paid job, and the same year he was appointed deputy to the surveyor of Sangamon County.

Lincoln was elected a member of the Illinois House of Representatives in 1834, re-elected in 1836, 1838 and 1840, and served in the post until 1842. In 1858 he ran for Senator, and although he lost, he gained popularity through his debates and won the Republican nomination in the 1860 presidential campaign, which he won. However, only the northern States supported Lincoln. Most of the southern States left the Union after

Lincoln's election and formed a rebel government. The resulting civil war overshadowed Lincoln's first presidency.

On 1 January 1863 he issued the famous Emancipation Proclamation, declaring the slaves of the Confederacy for ever free. He is most famous for the short but moving speech he made when dedicating the military cemetery at Gettysburg, the words of which are familiar to millions of Americans today.

Lincoln was re-elected for a second term in 1864 and in the following year a series of triumphs signalled the end of the bloody Civil War. Lincoln was notably generous in victory and focused on restructuring the governments of the conquered states.

His life ended tragically, however. On Good Friday, 14 April 1865, he was shot by John Wilkes Booth at Ford's Theatre in Washington. He died early the following day.

Four score and seven years ago our fathers brought forth on this continent a new nation, conceived in liberty and dedicated to the proposition that all men are created equal. Now we are engaged in a great civil war, testing whether that nation or any nation so conceived and so dedicated can long endure. We are met

'The world will little note nor long remember what we say here, but it can never forget what they did here.'

on a great battlefield of that war. We have come to dedicate a portion of that field as a final resting-place for those who here gave their lives that that nation might live. It is altogether fitting and proper that we should do this. But in a larger sense, we cannot dedicate, we cannot consecrate, we cannot hallow this ground. The brave men, living and dead who struggled here have consecrated it far above our poor power to add or detract. The world will little note nor long remember what we say here, but it can never forget what they did here. It is for us the living rather to be dedicated here to the unfinished work which they who fought here have thus far so nobly advanced. It is rather for us to be here dedicated to the great task remaining before us–that from these honoured dead we take increased devotion to that cause for which they gave the last full measure of devotion–that we here highly resolve that these dead shall not have died in vain, that this nation under God shall have a new birth of freedom, and that government of the people, by the people, for the people shall not perish from the earth.

‘I am here as a soldier who has temporarily left the field of battle.’

Emmeline Pankhurst

Speech on women’s suffrage, 13 November 1913

Emmeline Pankhurst, born Emmeline Goulden in 1858, was a British suffragist. She campaigned for British women's right to vote at a time when only men could elect the government. Born in Manchester, in 1879 she married Richard Marsden Pankhurst, a radical Manchester barrister who believed women should have the same rights as men. In the year of his death (1889), Emmeline founded the Women's Franchise League and in 1903, with her daughter Christabel (1880–1958), the Women's Social and Political Union (WSPU). She fought for women to have the same political status as men. The motto of the suffragettes was 'deeds, not words'.

Born 14 July 1858 in Manchester, England.
Married to a man who shared her conviction about women's rights, Emmeline founded the Women's Franchise League in 1889 and later the Women's Social and Political Union (WSPU), which campaigned aggressively for female suffrage (votes for women) in Britain. Her speech '**I am here as a soldier**' was given in the US, after a year punctuated by a dozen spells in prison.
Died 14 June 1928 in London.

The first actions of the movement were non-violent and consisted of disrupting political meetings, something unheard of at the time, especially by a group of middle-class women. In 1910, refused entry into the House of Commons to protest against the dropping of a bill that would have given women the right to vote, 100 women were arrested and brutally treated. The day was dubbed Black Friday.

From 1912 Emmeline and her followers fought for the vote by more violent means. Emmeline was arrested on several occasions and went on hunger strike while in prison. By the time of this speech, in 1913, the WSPU had become notorious for more violent attacks on the property of people opposed to female suffrage and the movement had still not succeeded in achieving its goal.

Emmeline Pankhurst was a striking woman and an inspiring speaker. An earlier Pankhurst speech from 1908 – she made hundreds during her life – includes the following stirring words: 'I for one, friends, looking round on the muddles that men had made, looking round on the sweated and decrepit members of my sex, I say men have had the control of these things long enough. … We are tired of it. We want to be of use; we want to have this power [to vote] in order that we may try to make the world a much better place for men and women than it is today. … Perhaps it is difficult to rouse women; they are long-suffering and patient, but now that we are roused, we will never be quiet again.'

With the outbreak of World War I, and the release of all suffragettes from prison, Emmeline turned her leadership skills towards urging women to work for their country. After some years living in Canada, she returned to Britain in 1926 and died while standing for Parliament as a Conservative candidate in 1928.

In June 1918 British women over 30 won the right to vote. On 2 July 1928, just three weeks after Emmeline Pankhurst's death, a law was passed allowing all women over the age of 21 to vote.

I do not come here as an advocate, because whatever position the suffrage movement may occupy in the United States of America, in England it has passed beyond the realm of advocacy and it has entered into the sphere of practical politics. It has become the subject of revolution and civil war, and so tonight I am not here to advocate woman suffrage. American suffragists can do that very well for themselves. I am here as a soldier who has temporarily left the field of battle in order to explain – it seems strange it should have to be explained – what civil war is like when civil war is waged by women. I am not only here as a soldier temporarily absent from the field of battle; I am here – and that, I think, is the strangest part of my coming – I am here as a person who, according to the law courts of my country, it has been decided, is of no value to the community at all; and I am adjudged because of my life to be a dangerous person, under sentence of penal servitude in a convict prison. So you see there is some special interest in hearing so unusual a person address you. I dare say, in the minds of many of you – you will perhaps forgive me this personal touch – that I do not look either very like a soldier or very like a convict, and yet I am both. ...

'I do not look either very like a soldier or very like a convict, and yet I am both...'

Now, I want to say to you who think women cannot succeed, we have brought the government of England to this position, that it has to face this alternative; either women are to be killed or women are to have the vote. I ask American men in this meeting, what would you say if in your State you were faced with that alternative, that you must either kill them or give them their citizenship, – women, many of whom you respect, women whom you know have lived useful lives, women whom you know, even if you do not know them personally, are animated with the highest motives, women who are in pursuit of liberty and the power to do useful public service? Well, there is only one answer to that alternative; there is only one way out of it, unless you are prepared to put back civilization two or three generations; you must give those women the vote. Now that is the outcome of our civil war.

'The scientific history of radium is beautiful.'

Marie Curie

On the discovery of radium, Vassar College, New York 14 May 1921

Marie Curie was born Maria Sklodowska on 7 November 1867 in Warsaw, Poland. She became famous for her research into radioactivity and was the first woman to win a Nobel Prize.

Her family valued education but women could not attend university in Russian-dominated Poland. In 1891 she went to Paris to study mathematics, chemistry and physics at the Sorbonne, adopting the name Marie, and was the first woman to teach there. She met Pierre Curie, professor of physics. Marie and Pierre married in 1895 and for many years this remarkable partnership worked on radioactive substances.

Born 7 November 1867 in Poland.
Marie Curie went to Paris to study science in 1891, as Polish universities were not open to women. She married her colleague Pierre Curie in 1895 and they worked together on research into radiation, jointly winning a Nobel Prize in 1903. Marie Curie won a second Nobel Prize in 1911. **'On the discovery of radium'** is a rare spoken account of her work. The Radium Institute (later Curie Institute) in Paris was founded in her honour in 1914.
Died 4 July 1934 in Paris.

Searching for the source of radioactivity, a word coined by Marie, the Curies discovered two highly radioactive elements, radium and polonium (the latter named after Marie's Polish origins). They won the 1903 Nobel Prize for physics for their discovery, sharing the award with another French physicist, Antoine Henri Becquerel (1852–1908), who had discovered natural radioactivity. In 1906 Pierre was run over by a horse-drawn wagon and died. Marie, alone with two small daughters to bring up, took his place as professor of physics, the first woman in the post.

Marie Curie continued her work on radioactive elements and in 1911 won her second Nobel Prize, for isolating radium and studying its chemical properties. In 1914 she helped found the Radium Institute in Paris and was its first director. When World War I broke out, Marie Curie, who promoted the therapeutic properties of radium and its usefulness in destroying cancerous cells, realised that X-rays would help to locate bullets and facilitate surgery. She invented X-ray vans to send out to wounded soldiers.

Marie Curie was quiet, dignified and unassuming, and admired by scientists everywhere. Her work is recorded in numerous papers in scientific journals, and reflected in many awards. In addition to the two Nobel Prizes she also received, jointly with her husband, the Davy Medal of the Royal Society in 1903. In 1921 President Harding, on behalf of the women of America, presented her with one precious gram of radium for her Institute, 'more than a hundred thousand times dearer than gold'.

Although used to the publication of learned papers, Marie rarely gave speeches. This one, delivered in 1921, describes the history and significance of her scientific discoveries, characteristically paying tribute both to Pierre and to the work of other scientists who preceded them.

In 1934, at the age of 67, Marie Curie died of leukaemia, probably caused by exposure to the high levels of radiation involved in her research. After her death the Radium Institute was renamed the Curie Institute in her honour. Her daughter Irène Joliot-Curie became one of the twentieth century's foremost chemists.

I could tell you many things about radium and radioactivity and it would take a long time. But as we cannot do that, I shall only give you a short account of my early work about radium. Radium is no more a baby, it is more than twenty years old, but the conditions of the discovery were somewhat peculiar, and so it is always of interest to remember them and to explain them.

We must go back to the year 1897. Professor Curie and I worked at that time in the laboratory of the school of Physics and Chemistry where Professor Curie held his lectures. I was engaged in some work on uranium rays which had been discovered two years before by Professor Becquerel.

I spent some time in studying the way of making good measurements of the uranium rays, and then I wanted to know if there were other elements, giving out rays of the same kind. So I took up a work about all known elements, and their compounds, and found that uranium compounds are active and also all thorium compounds, but other elements were not found active, nor were their compounds.

'What is considered particularly important is the treatment of cancer.'

Then I took up measurements of minerals and I found that several of those which contain uranium or thorium or both were active. But then the activity was not what I could expect, it was greater than for uranium or thorium compounds like the oxides which are almost entirely composed of these elements.

Then I thought that there should be in the minerals some unknown element having a much greater radioactivity than uranium or thorium. And I wanted to find and to separate that element, and I settled to that work with Professor Curie. We thought it would be done in several weeks or months, but it was not so. It took many years of hard work to finish that task. There was not one new element, there were several of them. But the most important is radium, which could be separated in a pure state.

Now, the special interest of radium is in the intensity of its rays which are several million times greater than the uranium rays. And the effects of the rays make the radium so important. If we take a practical point of view, then the most important property of the rays is the production of physiological effects on the cells of the human organism. These effects may be used for the cure of several diseases. Good results have been obtained in many cases. What is considered particularly important is the treatment of cancer. The medical utilization of radium makes it necessary to get that element in sufficient quantities. And so a factory of radium was started to begin with in France, and later in America where a big quantity of ore named carnotite is available. America does produce many grams of radium every year, but the price is still very high because the quantity of radium contained in the ore is so small. The radium is more than a hundred thousand times dearer than gold.

But we must not forget that when radium was discovered no one knew that it would prove useful in hospitals. The work was one of pure science. And this is a proof that scientific work must not be considered from the point of view of the direct usefulness of it. It must be done for itself, for the beauty of science, and then there is always the chance that a scientific discovery may become like the radium a benefit for humanity.

The scientific history of radium is beautiful. The properties of the rays have been studied very closely. We know that particles are expelled from radium with a very great velocity near to that of the light. We know that the atoms of radium are destroyed by expulsion of these particles, some of which are atoms of helium. And in that way it has been proved that the radioactive elements are constantly disintegrating and that they produce at the end ordinary elements, principally helium and lead. That is, as you see, a theory of transformation of atoms which are not stable, as was believed before, but may undergo spontaneous changes.

... There is always a vast field left to experimentation and I hope that we may have some beautiful progress in the following years. It is my earnest desire that some of you should carry on this scientific work and keep for your ambition the determination to make a permanent contribution to science.

‘There is no salvation for India.’

Mohandas Gandhi

The speech from which these extracts are taken was given on 4 February 1916 at Benares Hindu University. It illustrates Gandhi's early thoughts on India's need to gain independence from British rule. His beliefs led to his repeated imprisonment before independence was finally achieved in 1947. This, together with his self-sacrificing lifestyle, work for religious unity and championing of the rights of the poor, earned him the title *Mahatma* ('great soul').

Born 2 October 1869 in Porbandar, India. Gandhi studied law in England and once qualified worked in India and South Africa, where he remained for 20 years. Returning to India during World War I, he entered politics. **'There is no salvation for India'** is a plea for India to retrieve its own language, culture and independence after years of British rule. Gandhi's campaign for passive resistance was to lead to imprisonment. He was involved in negotiations leading to independence (1947). Assassinated 30 January 1948 in Delhi, India.

Born in India in 1869, Mohandas Gandhi cited his mother, a keen follower of Jainist beliefs in the importance of non-violence and vegetarianism, as the biggest influence on him. He described her life as 'an endless chain of fasts and vows'. Married by arrangement at the age of 13, Gandhi went to London to study law and was admitted to the Bar in 1891. In 1893 he joined an Indian firm in South Africa, where he stayed until 1914. During his time there he organized fellow Indians passively to resist discriminatory laws against them.

Through reading Thoreau, Tolstoy, the New Testament and the Hindu scriptures, Gandhi developed a creed of non-violent resistance known as *satyagraha* ('steadfastness in truth'). He believed that truth was vindicated not by inflicting suffering on one's opponent but on oneself and that the opponent must be weaned from error by patience and sympathy. This was more than passive resistance because it depended upon a positive and continuous interaction between the two parties with the aim of reconciliation. Gandhi was very concerned about how to bring about change and always put as much stress on the means as on the end.

Gandhi returned to India in 1914 and rapidly became known as a champion for people's rights. Initially he believed the British were a force for good. However, as vague promises for self-government given during World War I were not kept, and Indian people were oppressed by emergency war restrictions on liberties, he began to start training people in civil disobedience tactics.

He organized resistance against unpopular British measures such as the Salt Tax in 1930 and led a boycott of British goods. He was repeatedly imprisoned by the British but continued to protest, demanding the total withdrawal of the British in the Quit India

Movement during World War II. He also worked hard to improve the status of the *harijans* (untouchables) and tried to create closer bonds between Muslims and Hindus. When independence was finally achieved in 1947, following negotiations in which he took a major part, Gandhi was downcast by the outbreak of violence between Hindus and Muslims and prepared to fast until death in protest. His action worked and fighting stopped. However, at a prayer meeting in January 1948 Gandhi was assassinated by a Hindu extremist.

Gandhi spent 2,338 days in jail and fasted on many occasions. He left a legacy of non-violent teachings that influenced political activists around the world, including Martin Luther King Jr.

'... It is a matter of deep humiliation and shame for us that I am compelled this evening under the shadow of this great college, in this sacred city, to address my countrymen in a language that is foreign to me.

... I was present at the sessions of the great Congress in the month of December. There was a much vaster audience, and will you believe me when I tell you that the only speeches that touched the huge audience in Bombay were the speeches that were delivered in Hindustani? In Bombay, mind you, not in Benaras where everybody speaks Hindi. But between the vernaculars of the Bombay Presidency on the one hand and Hindi on the other, no such great dividing line exists as there does between English and the sister language of India; and the Congress audience was better able to follow the speakers in Hindi. I am hoping that this University will see to it that the youths who come to it will receive their instruction through the medium of their vernaculars. Our languages [are] the reflection of ourselves, and if you tell me that our languages are too poor to express the best thought, then say that the sooner we are wiped out of existence the better for us. Is there a man who dreams that English can ever become the national language of India? Why this handicap on the nation? Just consider for one moment what an equal race our lads have to run with every English lad.

'Our languages [are] the reflection of ourselves.'

... The charge against us is that we have no initiative. How can we have any, if we are to devote the precious years of our life to the mastery of a foreign tongue? ... The only education we receive is English education. Surely we must show something for it. But suppose that we had been receiving during the past fifty years education through our vernaculars, what should we have today? We should have today a free India, we should have our educated men, not as if they were foreigners in their own land but speaking to the heart of the nation; they would be working amongst the poorest of the poor, and whatever they would have gained during these fifty years would be a heritage for the nation. Today even our wives are not the sharers in our best thought ...

‘I am laying my heart bare.’

... I have turned the searchlight all over, and as you have given me the privilege of speaking to you, I am laying my heart bare. Surely we must set these things right in our progress towards self-government. I now introduce you to another scene. His Highness the Maharaja who presided yesterday over our deliberations spoke about the poverty of India. Other speakers laid great stress upon it. But what did we witness in the great pandal in which the foundation ceremony was performed by the Viceroy? Certainly a most gorgeous show, an exhibition of jewellery, which made a splendid feast for the eyes of the greatest jeweller who chose to come from Paris. I compare with the richly bedecked noble men the millions of the poor. And I feel like saying to these noble men, ‘There is no salvation for India unless you strip yourselves of this jewellery and hold it in trust for your countrymen in India’. I am sure it is not the desire of the King-Emperor or Lord Hardinge that in order to show the truest loyalty to our King-Emperor, it is necessary for us to ransack our jewellery boxes and to appear bedecked from top to toe. I would undertake, at the peril of my life, to bring to you a message from King George himself that he expects nothing of the kind.

Sir, whenever I hear of a great palace rising in any great city of India, be it in British India or be it in India which is ruled by our great chiefs, I become jealous at once, and say, ‘Oh, it is the money that has come from the agriculturists’. Over seventy-five per cent of the population are agriculturists and Mr Higginbotham told us last night in his own felicitous language, that they are the men who grow two blades of grass in the place of one. But there cannot be much spirit of self-government about us, if we take away or allow others to take away from them almost the whole of the results of their labour. Our salvation can only come through the farmer. Neither the lawyers, nor the doctors, nor the rich landlords are going to secure it.

'Power to the Soviets.'

Vladimir Ilyich Lenin

Moscow, September 1917

Vladimir Ilyich Lenin, Marxist revolutionary and leader of the Bolshevik Party in Russia, published this speech in September 1917 just weeks before the Bolsheviks seized power in the October Revolution. In it Lenin attacks the Provisional Government, a coalition of political groups that had overthrown the Tsarist regime in March that year. Lenin believed the March Revolution was just a first stage that must be followed by a second revolution. In this, power would be taken into the hands of the working people (the proletariat) and the peasants, rather than being held by the bourgeoisie (the middle classes) who only wanted moderate changes.

Since its establishment the Provisional Government had faced competition from workers' councils or 'Soviets'. The Soviets controlled the transport system and national industrial resources. The Provisional Government lacked any real power and could not resolve Russia's serious economic crisis and food shortages. Its commitment to the war against Germany was also unpopular.

By the end of 1917, Petrograd was in turmoil. Workers were taking over factories and Lenin's slogan, 'Power to the Soviets', was becoming reality. Together with Leon Trotsky, head of the Petrograd Soviet, Lenin and other top Bolsheviks hurriedly planned for an armed uprising. On the night of 6 November 1917 Lenin ordered his Red Guards to take over key institutions in Petrograd, including the Provisional Government's headquarters in the Winter Palace. With very little bloodshed, the Bolsheviks seized power in the second 1917 Russian Revolution.

Lenin was born in 1870 into a middle-class family. His real name was Vladimir Ilyich Ulyanov. Both his parents were teachers deeply committed to improving the lot of ordinary Russians. Lenin's older brother, Alexander, introduced Vladimir to revolutionary ideas and when Alexander was executed in 1887 for his role in plotting against the Tsar, Lenin was deeply affected. He immersed himself in radical writings, particularly those of Communist thinker Karl Marx. Lenin attended university in Kazan but was expelled and exiled for his radical views.

Born 10 April 1870 in Ulianovsk, Russia.
In 1891 Lenin gained a degree in law from St Petersburg University (first in his class). Arrested for subversive activities in 1895, he was exiled to Siberia for three years. At the 2nd Congress of the Russian Social Democratic Party in 1903 Lenin provoked a split between the Bolsheviks and Mensheviks. He was in exile in Switzerland until 1917. On 15 March 1917 the Tsarist regime was overthrown and Nicholas II abdicated. The following month Lenin returned to Petrograd. **'Power to the Soviets'** was given a few days before the 1917 October (November) Bolshevik Revolution. Lenin was the First Soviet head of state (1917–1924).
Died 21 January 1924 in Moscow.
October Revolution Day was the main public holiday in Soviet times, celebrated on 7 November. The Russian Parliament abolished the holiday in 2004.

After gaining a law degree as an external student of St Petersburg University in 1891, Lenin briefly practised law. His main interest, however, was planning for revolutionary change in Russia through adapting Marx's ideas. The Russian working class had failed to fulfil Marx's predictions that they would spontaneously rise up and gain power. Lenin believed that radical awareness had to be created in them through agitation by a well-organized revolutionary party that would act as a vanguard in the revolution.

After being imprisoned and sent to Siberia during 1897 and 1900, Lenin went abroad where he organized a secret newspaper *Iskra* (The Spark). During this time he became the leader of the Bolshevik faction of the Russian Socialist Democratic Labour Party. On arrival in Russia from Switzerland on 16 April 1917, Lenin received a triumphant welcome from his followers.

After the October Revolution, as head of the first Soviet government, Lenin guided the Soviet state successfully through its early years, including a civil war between 1918 and 1921. In 1922 he had the first of a series of strokes that led to his death in 1924. His body was embalmed and displayed in a glass coffin that became a great Communist shrine for those who revere Lenin as the founder of Russian Communism and the formulator of Marxism-Leninism. It is still visited today. Although famed for his political thinking, Lenin's main historical significance is as a revolutionary leader who managed to seize and retain power through his skills in political strategy and his organizing abilities.

The key question of every revolution is undoubtedly the question of state power. Which class holds power decides everything. When *Dyelo Naroda*, the paper of the chief governing party in Russia, recently complained that, owing to the controversies over power, both the question of the Constituent Assembly and that of bread are being forgotten, the Socialist-Revolutionaries should have been answered, 'Blame yourselves. For it is the wavering and indecision of *your* party that are mostly to blame for "ministerial leapfrog", the interminable postponements of the Constituent Assembly, and the undermining by the capitalists of the planned and agreed measures of a grain monopoly and of providing the country with bread.'

The question of power cannot be evaded or brushed aside, because it is the key question determining *everything* in a revolution's development, and in its foreign and domestic policies. It is an undisputed fact that our revolution has 'wasted' six months in wavering over the system of power; it is a fact resulting from the wavering policy of the Socialist-Revolutionaries and Mensheviks. In the long run, these parties' wavering policy was determined by the class position of the petty bourgeoisie, by their economic instability in the struggle between capital and labour.

'Which class holds power decides everything.'

The whole issue at present is whether the petty-bourgeois democrats have learned anything during these great, exceptionally eventful six months. If not, then the revolution is lost, and only a victorious uprising of the proletariat can save it. If they have learned something, the establishment of a stable, unwavering power must be begun immediately. Only if power is based, obviously and unconditionally, on a majority of the population can it be stable during a popular revolution, i.e., a revolution which rouses the people, the majority of the workers and peasants, to action. Up to now state power in Russia has virtually remained in the hands of the *bourgeoisie*, who are compelled to make only particular concessions (only to begin withdrawing them the following day), to hand out promises (only to fail to carry them out), to search for all sorts of excuses to cover their domination (only to fool the people by a show of 'honest coalition'), etc., etc. In words it claims to be a popular, democratic, revolutionary government, but in deeds it is an anti-popular, undemocratic, counter-revolutionary, bourgeois government. This is the contradiction which has existed so far and which has been a source of the complete instability and inconsistency of power, of that 'ministerial leapfrog' in which the SRs and Mensheviks have been engaged with such unfortunate (for the people) enthusiasm.

In early June 1917 I told the All-Russia Congress of Soviets that either the Soviets would be dispersed and die an inglorious death, or all power must be transferred to them. ...The slogan, 'Power to the Soviets', however, is very often, if not in most cases, taken quite incorrectly to mean a cabinet of the parties of the Soviet majority. We would like to go into more detail on this very false notion. ...

'Power to the Soviets' means radically reshaping the entire old state apparatus, that bureaucratic apparatus which hampers everything democratic. It means removing this apparatus and substituting for it a new, popular one, i.e., a truly democratic apparatus of Soviets, i.e., the organized and armed majority of the people – the workers, soldiers and peasants. It means allowing the majority of the people initiative and independence not only in the election of deputies, but also in state administration, in effecting reforms and various other changes.

To make this difference clearer and more comprehensible, it is worth recalling a valuable admission made some time ago by the paper of the governing party of the SRs, *Dyelo Naroda*. It wrote that even in those ministries which were in the hands of socialist Ministers (this was written during the notorious coalition with the Cadets, when some Mensheviks and SRs were ministers), the entire administrative apparatus had remained unchanged, and hampered work.

'Only the dictatorship of the proletariat and the poor peasants is capable of smashing the resistance of the capitalists.'

Let those who say: 'We have no apparatus to replace the old one, which inevitably gravitates towards the defence of the bourgeoisie', be ashamed of themselves. For this apparatus exists. It is the Soviets. Don't be afraid of the people's initiative and independence. Put your faith in their revolutionary organizations, and you will see in all realms of state affairs the same strength, majesty and invincibility of the workers and peasants as were displayed in their unity and their fury against Kornilov.

There is no middle course. This has been shown by experience. Either all power goes to the Soviets both centrally and locally, and all land is given to the peasants immediately, pending the Constituent Assembly's decision, or the landowners and capitalists obstruct every step, restore the landowners' power, drive the peasants into a rage and carry things to an exceedingly violent peasant revolt.

Only the dictatorship of the proletariat and the poor peasants is capable of smashing the resistance of the capitalists, of displaying truly supreme courage and determination in the exercise of power, and of securing the enthusiastic, selfless and truly heroic support of the masses both in the army and among the peasants.

Power to the Soviets – this is the only way to make further progress gradual, peaceful and smooth, keeping perfect pace with the political awareness and resolve of the majority of the people and with their own experience. Power to the Soviets means the complete transfer of the country's administration and economic control into the hands of the workers and peasants, to whom nobody would dare offer resistance and who, through practice, through their own experience, would soon learn how to distribute the land, products and grain properly.

'The world must be made safe for democracy.'

Woodrow Wilson

Speech to Congress, 2 April 1917

This speech was made by Woodrow Wilson, the 28th President of the United States, in 1917 and marked the entry of America into World War I. Up to this point the country had been neutral – although Wilson had actively mediated for peace, both overtly and secretly, since 1914. In 1917 Germany renewed its all-out submarine warfare and, as a result of public opinion and the pressure of world events, Wilson asked Congress to declare war on Germany, a decision passed by a majority.

The son of a Presbyterian minister, Wilson grew up in an academic household and lived his later life by a strict personal code of conduct. After studying law and being admitted to the Bar in 1881, he turned to academia. He taught at Princeton University (where he was elected President) for 12 years. He then moved into Democratic politics, working his way up until he became President of the United States in 1913. Wilson strongly believed in the rights of all men and set out to establish equality of opportunity within the country. During his presidency he tried to maintain peaceful relations with foreign countries by avoiding the use of threat or force.

Once America was involved in the war, Wilson worked to influence the peace settlement. In 1918 he presented a 14-point peace plan that brought the Allies and Germans to the bargaining table in late 1918. Wilson headed the US delegation to the Versailles Peace Conference, where he was greeted as a hero. He was successful in gaining acceptance that a League of Nations should be part of the treaty. He was, however, dismayed by the nationalistic aspirations of the different countries attending and was forced to make concessions to national, territorial and economic demands. It was only his shrewd bargaining that prevented harsher terms being imposed on Germany.

However, Wilson faced opposition to the League in the US. His dream of America being part of the League of Nations was never realized, due in part to his own refusal to allow the treaty to be modified. He launched himself on a gruelling national tour defending the League and arguing that US membership was essential to lasting world peace. The strain provoked a stroke in 1919. He continued to oppose restrictions to the League from his bed and viewed the 1920 presidential election as a referendum on the League. The Republican Warren Hardy, an opponent of the League, won by a landslide.

Born 28 December 1856 in Virginia.
Woodrow Wilson was a lawyer and academic before entering politics as a Democrat. He became President in 1913 and served two terms in office. His speech to Congress in 1917, which took the US into World War I, expresses the kernel of his belief in an international organization committed to establishing and maintaining world peace.
Died 3 January 1924 in Washington DC.

In 1919 Woodrow Wilson was awarded the Nobel Peace Prize, in recognition of his vision of an international organization that would work for world peace.

Gentlemen of the Congress: ...The present German submarine warfare against commerce is a warfare against mankind. It is war against all nations ... The challenge is to all mankind.

Each nation must decide for itself how it will meet it. The choice we make for ourselves must be made with a moderation of counsel and temperateness of judgement befitting our character and our motives as a nation. We must put excited feeling away. Our motive will not be revenge or the victorious assertion of the physical might of the nation, but only the vindication of right, of human right, of which we are only a single champion.

‘It is a fearful thing to lead this great peaceful people into war.’

... Armed neutrality is ineffectual enough at best; in such circumstances and in the face of such pretensions it is worse than ineffectual; it is likely only to produce what it was meant to prevent; it is practically certain to draw us into the war without either the rights or the effectiveness of belligerents. There is one choice we cannot make, we are incapable of making: we will not choose the path of submission and suffer the most sacred rights of our nation and our people to be ignored or violated. The wrongs against which we now array ourselves are no common wrongs: they cut to the very roots of human life.

With a profound sense of the solemn and even tragical character of the step I am taking ... I advise that the Congress declare the recent course of the Imperial German Government to be in fact nothing less than war against the government and people of the United States; that it formally accept the status of belligerent which has thus been thrust upon it; and that it take immediate steps not only to put the country in a more thorough state of defence but also to exert all its power and employ all its resources to bring the Government of the German Empire to terms and end the war.

... [W]e should keep constantly in mind the wisdoms of interfering as little as possible in our own preparation and in the equipment of our own military forces with the duty – for it will be a very practical duty – of supplying the nations already at war with Germany with the materials which they can obtain only from us or by our assistance. They are in the field and we should help them in every way to be effective there.

... While we do these things, these deeply momentous things, let us be very clear, and make very clear to all the world what our motives and our objects are ... Our object ... is to vindicate the principles of peace and justice in the life of the world as against selfish and autocratic power and to set up amongst the really free and self-governed peoples of the world such a concert of purpose and of action as will henceforth ensure the observance of those principles.

... A steadfast concert for peace can never be maintained except by a partnership of democratic nations. No autocratic government could be trusted to keep faith within it or observe its covenants. It must be a league of honour, a partnership of opinion.

... The world must be made safe for democracy. Its peace must be planted upon the tested foundations of political liberty. We have no selfish ends to serve.

We desire no conquest, no dominion. We seek no indemnities for ourselves, no material compensation for the sacrifices we shall cheerfully make. We are but one of the champions of the rights of mankind. We shall be satisfied when those rights have been made as secure as the faith and the freedom of nations can make them.

... It is a distressing and oppressive duty, Gentlemen of the Congress, which I have performed in thus addressing you. There are, it may be, many months of fiery trial and sacrifice ahead of us. It is a fearful thing to lead this great peaceful people into war, into the most terrible and disastrous of all wars, civilization itself seeming to be in the balance.

But the right is more precious than peace, and we shall fight for the things which we have always carried nearest our hearts, for democracy, for the right of those who submit to authority to have a voice in their own governments, for the rights and liberties of small nations, for a universal dominion of right by such a concert of free peoples as shall bring peace and safety to all nations and make the world at last free.

To such a task we can dedicate our lives and our fortunes, everything that we are and everything that we have, with the pride of those who know that the day has come when America is privileged to spend her blood and her might for the principles that gave her birth and happiness and the peace which she has treasured. God helping her, she can do no other.

‘I believe in the law of love.’

Clarence Darrow

Closing speech in defence of Henry Sweet, April 1926

This extract is from Clarence Darrow's seven-hour closing defence argument in Henry Sweet's trial for murder in April 1926. Sweet was a member of a black family who reacted with force against a white mob trying to evict them from their home in a white neighbourhood in Detroit.

Born 18 April 1857 in Ohio.
Clarence Darrow made his reputation as a defence lawyer, acting in some of the most notorious and high-profile cases in the US, including the Leopold–Loeb and Scopes 'Monkey' trials. His courtroom oratory, as demonstrated by his **summing-up in the Henry Sweet trial,** has inspired generations of lawyers – and many courtroom dramas.
Died 13 March 1938 in Chicago.

The growing car industry brought an influx of black workers to Detroit in the early 1920s and racial hatred was stirred up by Ku Klux Klan rallies, with white mobs driving out black professionals living in largely white housing areas and threatening others planning to move in. The night the Sweets moved into their home an organized riot broke out, and rocks were thrown at the house. The Sweets reacted by firing from an upper floor and Leon Breiner, a white man, was killed. The Sweets were tried for murder as a family and defended by Darrow. The jury failed to reach a verdict and the defendants were released on bail. Darrow then defended Henry Sweet, who admitted to firing a gun, in the first of individual trials of each family member. Darrow believed that if he could secure an acquittal for Sweet, the case for the other trials would disappear.

In his long summing-up Darrow demonstrated his superb qualities as a lawyer – immense courtroom skill, strong dramatic instincts and powerful persuasive abilities. Darrow argued that the case was about racism not murder: 'I insist that there is nothing but prejudice in this case; that if it was reversed and eleven white men had shot and killed a black while protecting their home and their lives against a mob of blacks, nobody would have dreamed of having them indicted ... Now, that is the case, gentlemen, and that is all there is to this case. Take the hatred away, and you have nothing left.' The jury took four hours to reach a 'not guilty' verdict and in July 1926 the other defendants' charges were dropped. Although the case ended in triumph for Darrow, the Sweets' story is less happy. They returned to their home but several family members, including Henry Sweet, died of tuberculosis within years of the trial and his co-accused brother Ossian later took his own life.

Born in 1857 in rural Ohio, Darrow grew up in an atmosphere of radical agnosticism. He read law in Ohio, was admitted to the Bar in 1878 and practised locally for some years. Inspired by the liberal and progressive ideas of Judge John Altgeld, Darrow moved to

Chicago in 1887 where he and Altgeld became friends. Darrow became active in local democratic politics and in 1890 was appointed Chicago's corporation counsel. He later acted as general attorney to the Chicago and North Western Railway.

Darrow soon won a reputation as a labour lawyer, fighting many high-profile cases defending union leaders and miners. Following the complex McNamara brothers' case, in which Darrow was discredited by the defendants' sudden change of plea to guilty, he retired from labour law and moved into criminal law. Darrow was then involved in various headline-making cases. They included the 1924 Leopold–Loeb case, in which Darrow made innovative and successful use of psychiatric theories about determinism in human behaviour to have two teenagers' likely death sentences for murdering a young boy commuted to life imprisonment.

A lifelong agnostic, in 1925 Darrow took on the high-profile but ultimately unsuccessful defence of John Thomas Scopes for violating Tennessee's laws banning the teaching of the theory of evolution in public schools, the Scopes 'Monkey' trial. Darrow's cross-examination of the anti-scientific, fundamentalist side won national attention. In 1925–26 he fought segregation and intolerance in the Sweet trial.

Darrow was a prolific writer, speaker and lecturer, writing *Crime: Its Cause and Treatment* (1922) and *Infidels and Heretics* (1929), which argued the case for free thinking. Despising convention, he often appeared in court in shirtsleeves and braces. In more than 50 capital cases he lost only his first client to execution and was a strong opponent of capital punishment. After his death Darrow became a folk hero, the subject of various novels and plays, and still inspires a following today in the US Bar.

Now, gentlemen, just one more word, and I am through with this case. I do not live in Detroit. But I have no feeling against this city. In fact, I shall always have the kindest remembrance of it, especially if this case results as I think and feel that it will. I am the last one to come here to stir up race hatred, or any other hatred. I do not believe in the law of hate. I may not be true to my ideals always, but I believe in the law of love, and I believe you can do nothing with hatred. I would like to see a time when man loves his fellow man, and forgets his colour or his creed. We will never be civilized until that time comes.

I know the Negro race has a long road to go. I believe the life of the Negro race has been a life of tragedy, of injustice, of oppression. The law has made him equal, but man has not. And, after all, the last analysis is, what has man done? –

and not what has the law done? I know there is a long road ahead of him, before he can take the place which I believe he should take. I know that before him there is suffering, sorrow, tribulation and death among the blacks, and perhaps the whites. I am sorry. I would do what I could to avert it. I would advise patience; I would advise toleration; I would advise understanding; I would advise all of those things which are necessary for men who live together. Gentlemen, what do you think is your duty in this case? I have watched, day after day, these black, tense faces that have crowded this court. These black faces that now are looking to you twelve whites, feeling that the hopes and fears of a race are in your keeping.

‘I believe you can do nothing with hatred.’

This case is about to end, gentlemen. To them, it is life. Not one of their colour sits on this jury. Their fate is in the hands of twelve whites. Their eyes are fixed on you, their hearts go out to you, and their hopes hang on your verdict.

‘I would like to see a time when man loves his fellow man, and forgets his colour or his creed. We will never be civilized until that time comes.’

This is all. I ask you, on behalf of this defendant, on behalf of these helpless ones who turn to you, and more than that, – on behalf of this great state, and this great city which must face this problem, and face it fairly, – I ask you, in the name of progress and of the human race, to return a verdict of not guilty in this case!

‘Peace for our time.’

Neville Chamberlain

10 Downing Street, London, 30 September 1938

These were the words of Neville Chamberlain, Prime Minister of Great Britain, after returning from discussions with Adolf Hitler over German plans to annexe the Sudetenland in Czechoslovakia in September 1938. Chamberlain believed his agreement with Hitler meant war with Germany would be avoided.

Chamberlain is best remembered for his policy of appeasement towards the German leader Adolf Hitler. Appeasement was adopted partly because of the strong desire of Britain and France to avoid losses as terrible as those in World War I. Chamberlain felt that Europe's problems were the result of the over-harsh terms imposed on Germany in the Versailles Treaty at the end of World War I. He thought Hitler's complaints about the Treaty were justified and that the Sudetenland belonged to Germany. After the Munich conference, Chamberlain was less sure about appeasement and privately expressed his view that Hitler was half-mad. Eleven months after the Munich conference, Hitler invaded Poland. Britain and France declared war on Germany and World War II began.

Born 18 March 1869 in Birmingham, England. Elected to Parliament in 1918, Chamberlain held office as Chancellor of the Exchequer, Minister of Health and Prime Minister. In September 1938, Chamberlain flew to Germany for a series of meetings with Hitler. He returned from the final meeting on 30 September with the agreement he saw as **'peace for our time'.** Less than six months later, after Hitler's occupation of the Sudetenland, Chamberlain abandoned the policy of appeasement.
Died 9 November 1940 in London.

The son of Joseph Chamberlain, a radical statesman and member of Gladstone's cabinet, Neville Chamberlain came from good political stock. His half-brother Austen was British Foreign Secretary in 1924–27. Educated at Rugby School and at college in Birmingham, Neville managed his father's sisal plantation in the Bahamas before going into industry in Birmingham where he became Lord Mayor in 1915.

Chamberlain was drawn into politics and in 1916 joined Lloyd George's coalition government as the Director General of National Service. In 1918 he was elected to Parliament as a Conservative. He held a number of important posts, including Chancellor of the Exchequer. He was very industrious, a good administrator and a strong character and influence in Baldwin's cabinet. In 1937 he succeeded Baldwin as Prime Minister. Some argue that this had more to do with his prestigious political origins and faithful service than anything else and that he lacked the right knowledge and experience to carry out the foreign policy then needed in Europe.

In 1938, in an attempt to direct Fascist Italy away from Germany's influence, Chamberlain recognized Italian supremacy in Ethiopia. He also kept Britain out of the Spanish Civil

War of 1936–39. He was later widely condemned for his role in the Munich agreement in 1938, which gave Hitler what he wanted and left Czechoslovakia defenceless.

Despite declaring the achievement of peace, immediately after the Munich conference Chamberlain ordered the British rearmament programme to be speeded up. After Hitler invaded Prague in 1938, Chamberlain abandoned appeasement and made guarantees with France that they would give armed support for Poland if Hitler invaded the country. In April 1939, peacetime military conscription took place for the first time in British history. In September 1939 Chamberlain led the country into World War II.

Following a failed attempt by an Allied expedition to secure Norway against the Germans in 1940, Chamberlain lost the support of many Conservatives in Parliament and resigned as Prime Minister on 10 May in favour of Winston Churchill. Chamberlain served under Churchill as Lord President of the Council of War until September 1940 when he became ill and was forced to resign. He died a few weeks later and was buried in Westminster Abbey.

The following is the wording of the statement that Neville Chamberlain held when he stepped off the plane after the Berlin conference on 30 September, 1938.

We, the German Führer and Chancellor, and the British Prime Minister, have had a further meeting today and are agreed in recognizing that the question of Anglo–German relations is of the first importance for our two countries and for Europe.

We regard the agreement signed last night and the Anglo–German Naval Agreement as symbolic of the desire of our two peoples never to go to war with one another again.

We are resolved that the method of consultation shall be the method adopted to deal with any other questions that may concern our two countries, and we are determined to continue our efforts to remove possible sources of difference, and thus to contribute to assure the peace of Europe.

Later, in front of 10 Downing Street, he added:

My good friends, for the second time in our history, a British Prime Minister has returned from Germany bringing peace with honour. I believe it is peace for our time. Go home and get a nice quiet sleep.

‘My patience is now at an end.’

Adolf Hitler

Speech at the Sportpalast, Berlin, 26 September 1938

‘I am from now on just first soldier of the German Reich.’

Speech to the Reichstag, Berlin, 1 September 1939

In September 1938, a year before the outbreak of World War II, Adolf Hitler, Chancellor and Führer of the Third Reich in Germany, announced publicly that he would declare war if necessary in order to protect the Sudeten Germans in the west of Czechoslovakia. Hitler had always intended to create extra living space (*Lebensraum*) for Germans in Austria and Czechoslovakia and now used the three million Sudeten Germans as an excuse to further his plans, claiming that they were being persecuted.

Hitler stated this would be the last territorial claim he made in Europe. However, although he disavowed having any aggressive intent towards Europe, he had already broken the terms of the Versailles Treaty. In 1934 he had signed a non-aggression pact with Poland, but despite this he rearmed Germany in 1935, entered the demilitarized Rhineland in 1936 and in March 1938 annexed Austria. The Czechs, now almost surrounded by Germany, were worried about invasion. The Czech President, Eduard Benes, appealed to the French and British governments for support. Neville Chamberlain, Prime Minister of Great Britain, reassured him that Hitler had promised the Czechs had nothing to fear.

At that time Britain and France were still following their policy of appeasement of Hitler, though Winston Churchill was convinced that Germany would continue to find reasons for takeover in Europe until opposed. Chamberlain believed the German claim to the Sudetenland was reasonable. In September 1938 he agreed to let Hitler have the Sudetenland, believing that this would prevent war. Hitler entered Prague in March 1939 and invaded Poland in September. Britain and France then declared war on Germany.

Born 20 April 1889 in Braunau, Austria.
In 1920–21 Hitler became leader of the German National Socialist (Nazi) Party. In 1925 he published his autobiography, *Mein Kampf*, which set out his political philosophy and ambitions for the future of Germany. He became Chancellor (later *Führer*, or leader) in 1933. From 1935 Germany started to rearm, and began its rapid occupation of neighbouring countries. Hitler's declaration that **'my patience is now at an end'** over the Sudetenland preceded the signing of the Munich agreement with Britain and France, allowing the annexation of the Sudetenland to Germany, three days later. Within six months, German troops had occupied Czechoslovakia. In September 1939, Hitler's troops invaded Poland and Europe was at war. In the **speech to the Reichstag** in which he announced the invasion of Poland, Hitler challenged the 'neutrality' of Britain and France and celebrated Germany's non-aggression pact with the USSR, an agreement he was already intending to break.
Committed suicide 30 April 1945 in Berlin, Germany.

Alienated and unsuccessful as a young man, Hitler had found a niche during World War I in the comradeship of being a soldier. Decorated for bravery during the war, he was extremely bitter when it ended in defeat for Germany. As a result he became involved in politics and made his name as a speaker, becoming head of a political party called the National Socialists, or Nazis, in 1920. In 1923 he made an abortive attempt to overthrow the Weimar Republic in Germany and was imprisoned. While in prison he recorded his political philosophy in his book *Mein Kampf* ('my struggle'). In this he promised to bring under German rule all European peoples who spoke German and to seize extra living space for Germans from Russia and Poland. He also planned to eliminate the Slavs in Eastern Europe whom he considered 'sub-human'.

Though some thought Hitler half-mad, many were convinced by what he said. He gradually rose to power, aided by the Great Depression that had left millions of Germans unemployed. Once Chancellor of Germany, Hitler went about creating a one-party state of which he was dictator. Rule was maintained through a secret police, the Gestapo. Countless opponents of the regime were imprisoned or murdered and Jews lost citizenship in a law passed in 1935. Having brought economic recovery to the country, Hitler then pursued his foreign policy to unite all Germans in a greater single Germany, to destroy Communism and to conquer and colonize Eastern Europe, establishing a 'thousand-year Reich'.

World War II raged until 1945. The Russians invaded Germany in late January and on 7 March the Western Allies crossed the Rhine. The Russians stormed Berlin at the end of April, by which time Hitler had survived various assassination plots by his own countrymen but was a physical wreck. He was cut off from reality, bitter and isolated, living in a bunker in Berlin. On 30 April 1945 he and his wife Eva Braun, whom he had married hours previously, committed suicide, thus ending the Third Reich.

... I have really in these years pursued a practical peace policy. I have approached all apparently impossible problems with the firm resolve to solve them peacefully even when there was the danger of making more or less serious renunciations on Germany's part. I myself am a front-line soldier and I know how grave a thing war is. I wanted to spare the German people such an evil. Problem after problem I have tackled with the set purpose to make every effort to render possible a peaceful solution.

The most difficult problem which faced me was the relation between Germany and Poland. There was a danger that the conception of a 'heredity enmity' might take possession of our people and of the Polish people. That I wanted to prevent. I know quite well that I should not have succeeded if Poland at that time had had a democratic constitution. For these democracies which are overflowing with phrases about peace are the most bloodthirsty instigators of war. But Poland at that time was governed by no democracy but by a man. In the course of barely a year it was possible to conclude an agreement which, in the first instance for a period of ten years, on principle removed the danger of a conflict. We are all convinced that this agreement will bring with it a permanent pacification. We realize that here are two peoples which must live side by side and that neither of them can destroy the other. A state with a population of thirty-three millions will always strive for an access to the sea. A way to an understanding had therefore to be found. ...

‘He will either accept this offer and now at last give to the Germans their freedom, or we will go and fetch this freedom for ourselves.’

And now before us stands the last problem that must be solved and will be solved. It is the last territorial claim which I have to make in Europe, but it is the claim from which I will not recede and which, God willing, I will make good. ...

I have only a few statements still to make. I am grateful to Mr Chamberlain for all his efforts. I have assured him that the German people desires nothing else than peace, but I have also told him that I cannot go back behind the limits set to our patience. I have further assured him, and I repeat it here, that when this problem is solved there is for Germany no further territorial problem in Europe. And I have further assured him that at the moment when Czechoslovakia solves her problems, that means when the Czechs have come to terms with their other minorities, and that peaceably and not through oppression, then I have no further interest in the Czech state. And that is guaranteed to him! We want no Czechs!

But in the same way I desire to state before the German people that with regard to the problem of the Sudeten Germans my patience is now at an end! I have made Mr Benes an offer which is nothing but the carrying into effect of what he himself has promised. The decision now lies in his hands: peace or war. He will either accept this offer and now at last give to the Germans their freedom or we will go and fetch this freedom for ourselves.

On 1 September 1939, Hitler announced to the Reichstag his intention to invade Poland, knowing that this action would bring a declaration of war from Britain and France. In justification, he referred to the terms of the Versailles Treaty and duplicitously insisted he had no intention of invading countries to the west of Germany: 'I have declared that the frontier between France and Germany is a final one.' Nine months later, German troops had occupied Holland, Belgium and France and Britain was facing the threat of invasion. Even during the war, German industry flourished and productivity increased, helped by slave labour drawn from the occupied territories, including those beyond the 'western wall'.

I have declared that the frontier between France and Germany is a final one. I have repeatedly offered friendship and, if necessary, the closest cooperation to Britain, but this cannot be offered from one side only. It must find response on the other side. Germany has no interests in the West, and our western wall is for all time the frontier of the Reich on the west. Moreover, we have no aims of any kind there for the future. With this assurance we are in solemn earnest, and as long as others do not violate their neutrality we will likewise take every care to respect it.

'Germany has no interests in the West, and our western wall is for all time the frontier of the Reich on the west.'

I am happy particularly to be able to tell you of one event. You know that Russia and Germany are governed by two different doctrines. There was only one question that had to be cleared up. Germany has no intention of exporting its doctrine. Given the fact that Soviet Russia has no intention of exporting its doctrine to Germany, I no longer see any reason why we should still oppose one another. On both sides we are clear on that. Any struggle between our people would only be of advantage to others. We have, therefore, resolved to conclude a pact which rules out for ever any use of violence between us. It imposes the obligation on us to consult together in certain European questions. It makes possible for us economic cooperation, and above all it assures that the powers of both these powerful states are not wasted against one another. Every attempt of the West to bring about any change in this will fail.

At the same time I should like here to declare that this political decision means a tremendous departure for the future, and that it is a final one. Russia and Germany fought against one another in the World War. That shall and will not happen a second time. In Moscow, too, this pact was greeted exactly as you greet it. I can only endorse word for word the speech of the Russian Foreign Commissar, Molotov.

'My whole life has been nothing but one long struggle for my people.'

I am determined to solve the Danzig question; the question of the Corridor and to see to it that a change is made in the relationship between Germany and Poland that shall ensure a peaceful co-existence. In this I am resolved to continue to fight until either the present Polish government is willing to bring about this change or until another Polish government is ready to do so. I am resolved to remove from the German frontiers the element of uncertainty, the everlasting atmosphere of conditions resembling civil war. I will see to it that in the East there is, on the frontier, a peace precisely similar to that on our other frontiers.

In this I will take the necessary measures to see that they do not contradict the proposals I have already made known in the Reichstag itself to the rest of the world, that is to say, I will not war against women and children. I have ordered my air force to restrict itself to attacks on military objectives. If, however, the enemy thinks he can from that draw carte blanche on his side to fight by the other methods he will receive an answer that will deprive him of hearing and sight.

This night for the first time Polish regular soldiers fired on our own territory. Since 5.45 am we have been returning the fire, and from now on bombs will be met with bombs. Whoever fights with poison gas will be fought with poison gas. Whoever departs from the rules of humane warfare can only expect that we shall do the same. I will continue this struggle, no matter against whom, until the safety of the Reich and its rights are secured.

For six years now I have been working on the building up of the German defences. Over 90 milliards have in that time been spent on the building up of these defence forces. They are now the best equipped and are above all comparison with what they were in 1914. My trust in them is unshakeable. When I called up these forces and when I now ask sacrifices of the German people and if necessary every sacrifice, then I have a right to do so, for I also am today absolutely ready, just as we were formerly, to make every personal sacrifice.

'A November 1918 will never be repeated in German history.'

I am asking of no German man more than I myself was ready throughout four years at any time to do. There will be no hardships for Germans to which I myself will not submit. My whole life henceforth belongs more than ever to my people. I am from now on just first soldier of the German Reich. I have once more put on that coat that was the most sacred and dear to me. I will not take it off again until victory is secured, or I will not survive the outcome.

As a National Socialist and as a German soldier I enter upon this struggle with a stout heart. My whole life has been nothing but one long struggle for my people, for its restoration, and for Germany. There was only one watchword for that struggle: faith in this people. One word I have never learned: that is, surrender.

If, however, anyone thinks that we are facing a hard time, I should ask him to remember that once a Prussian king, with a ridiculously small state, opposed a stronger coalition, and in three wars finally came out successful because that state had that stout heart that we need in these times. I would, therefore, like to assure all the world that a November 1918 will never be repeated in German history. Just as I myself am ready at any time to stake my life – anyone can take it for my people and for Germany – so I ask the same of all others.

Whoever, however, thinks he can oppose this national command, whether directly or indirectly, shall fall. We have nothing to do with traitors. We are all faithful to our old principle. It is quite unimportant whether we ourselves live, but it is essential that our people shall live, that Germany shall live. The sacrifice that is demanded of us is not greater than the sacrifice that many generations have made. If we form a community closely bound together by vows, ready for anything, resolved never to surrender, then our will will master every hardship and difficulty. And I would like to close with the declaration that I once made when I began the struggle for power in the Reich. I then said: 'If our will is so strong that no hardship and suffering can subdue it, then our will and our German might shall prevail.'

'It is essential that the war continue for as long as possible.'

Joseph Stalin

Speech to the Politburo, 19 August 1939

Joseph Stalin's speech to the Soviet Politburo on 19 August 1939 reveals his deliberations prior to signing a pact with Nazi Germany on 22 August, in which the two countries agreed to divide Poland and not to fight each other. This was a duplicitous agreement between two dictators who mistrusted each other and hated each other's ideology. At that point, however, the pact was expedient to both.

Having successfully invaded Czechoslovakia in 1939, Hitler wanted to be able to invade Poland without the USSR coming to the aid of his enemies, the British and the French, and involving Germany in fighting on two fronts. Hitler knew it was unlikely Stalin would allow him to take Poland over without a fight. When negotiations for an alliance between Britain, France and Russia failed, Hitler spotted an opportunity. He offered the Soviets a treaty that would give Germany most of Poland, with Russia being left the eastern part of the country and given a free hand to take over Finland and the Baltic States.

Born Joseph Vissarionovich Dzhugashvili 21 December 1879 in Gori, Russia.
Stalin, the symbolically resonant name he adopted in 1910, means 'man of steel'. Twice exiled to Siberia for his revolutionary activity, Stalin took a leading part in the 1917 October revolution. From 1928 until his death, he was virtual dictator of the Union of Soviet Socialist Republics (USSR). His **speech to the Politburo** on 19 August 1939 was not published until 1991.
Died 5 March 1953 in Moscow.

This speech demonstrates Stalin's understanding of the possibilities open to him in the pact. Knowing that involvement in the war would at some point be inevitable, he wanted to choose the best time for it. He also knew the war could advance Soviet interests and was concerned that Germany might make peace (find a 'modus vivendi') with the Western powers. Stalin was also playing for time. Technologically backward and weakened by recent purges of its top military personnel, Russia was not yet ready to take on Germany. Stalin also argues in the speech that a long war would exhaust Britain, France and Germany and ultimately benefit Russia.

After the signing of the pact Hitler invaded Poland and in September 1939 Britain and France declared war against Germany. Despite the pact, Hitler was actually planning for war against the USSR and when he attacked them in 1941 the Soviets were totally unprepared. The brutality of the war waged by Germany against Russia brought some measure of reconciliation between the brutal Stalinist regime and its own people. This was not, however, to last and Stalin resumed his repressive measures in Russia after 1945.

Joseph Stalin, son of a cobbler and ex-serf, was born in Georgia in 1879. After training as a priest, in 1898 he became active in the revolutionary underground, and was twice exiled to Siberia (1902, 1913). He played an active role in the Russian Revolution in 1917 and in 1922 he became general secretary of the Party Central Committee. He held this post until his death and also had other important positions, through which he acquired great personal power in the party and government machine.

After Lenin's death (1924) he isolated and disgraced his political rivals, including Trotsky. In 1928 he began the collectivization of agriculture in which millions of peasants perished, and the first five-year plan for the forced industrialization of the economy. Between 1934 and 1938 he purged the party, government, armed forces and intelligentsia, imprisoning, exiling or shooting millions of so-called 'enemies of the people'.

At the end of World War II Stalin gained Soviet military and political control over the liberated countries of post-war Europe and Central Europe. From 1945 until his death his foreign policies contributed to the Cold War between the Soviet Union and the West. After his death Stalin was denounced by Khrushchev at the 20th Party Congress (1956) for crimes against the Party and under Gorbachev 'Stalinism' was officially condemned by the Soviet authorities.

The question of war and peace has entered a critical phase for us. Its solution depends entirely on the position which will be taken by the Soviet Union. We are absolutely convinced that if we conclude a mutual assistance pact with France and Great Britain, Germany will back off from Poland and seek a *modus vivendi* with the Western Powers. War would be avoided, but further events could prove dangerous for the USSR.

On the other hand, if we accept Germany's proposal, that you know, and conclude a non-aggression pact with her, she will certainly invade Poland, and the intervention of France and England is then unavoidable. Western Europe would be subjected to serious upheavals and disorder. In this case we will have a great opportunity to stay out of the conflict, and we could plan the opportune time for us to enter the war.

The experience of the last 20 years has shown that in peacetime the Communist movement is never strong enough for the Bolshevik Party to seize power. The dictatorship of such a Party will only become possible as the result of a major war.

Our choice is clear. We must accept the German proposal and, with a refusal, politely send the Anglo–French mission home.

It is not difficult to envisage the importance which we would obtain in this way of proceeding. It is obvious, for us, that Poland will be destroyed even before England and France are able to come to her assistance. In this case Germany will cede to us a part of Poland ... Our immediate advantage will be to take Poland all the way to the gates of Warsaw, as well as Ukrainian Galicia.

This is in the case that Germany would emerge victorious from the war. We must, however, envisage the possibilities that will result from the defeat as well as from the victory of Germany. In case of her defeat, a Sovietization of Germany will unavoidably occur and a Communist government will be created. We should not forget that a Sovietized Germany would bring about great danger, if this Sovietization is the result of German defeat in a transient war. England and France will still be strong enough to seize Berlin and to destroy a Soviet Germany. We would be unable to come effectually to the aid of our Bolshevik comrades in Germany.

‘Our goal is that Germany should carry out the war as long as possible so that England and France grow weary and become exhausted.’

Therefore, our goal is that Germany should carry out the war as long as possible so that England and France grow weary and become exhausted to such a degree that they are no longer in a position to put down a Sovietized Germany.

Our position is this. Maintaining neutrality and waiting for the right time, the USSR will presently assist Germany economically and supply her with raw materials and provisions. It goes without saying that our assistance should not exceed a certain limit; we must not send so much as to weaken our economy or the power of our army.

At the same time we must carry on active Communist propaganda in the Anglo–French bloc, and predominantly in France. We must expect that in that country in times of war, the Party should quit the legal means of warfare and turn underground. We know that their work will demand great sacrifices, but our French comrades will not hesitate. Their first task will be to decompose and demoralize the army and the police. If this preparatory work is fulfilled properly, the safety of Soviet Germany will be assured, and this will contribute to the Sovietization of France.

For the realization of these plans it is essential that the war continue for as long as possible, and all forces, which we have available in Western Europe and the Balkans, should be directed toward this goal.

Now let us consider the second possibility, a German victory. Some think that this would confront us with a serious danger. There is some truth in this, but it would be a mistake to regard the danger as so close at hand or as great as has been proposed.

If Germany should prove to be victorious, she will leave the war too weakened to start a war with the USSR within a decade at least. She will have to supervise the occupation of France and England and restore herself.

In addition, a victorious Germany will have vast colonies; the exploitation of those and their adaptation to German methods will also absorb Germany during several decades.

'We must strengthen our propaganda work in the belligerent countries, in order to be prepared when the war ends.'

Obviously, this Germany will be too busy elsewhere to turn against us. There is one additional thing that will strengthen our safety. In a conquered France, the French Communist Party will always be very strong. A Communist revolution will unavoidably break out, and we will be able to exploit the situation and to come to the aid of France and make her our ally. In addition, all the nations that fall under the 'protection' of a victorious Germany will become our allies. This presents for us a broad field of action for the initiation of world revolution.

Comrades, I have presented my considerations to you. I repeat that it is in the interest of the USSR, the workers' homeland, that a war breaks out between the Reich and the capitalist Anglo–French bloc. Everything should be done so that it drags out as long as possible with the goal of weakening both sides. For this reason, it is imperative that we agree to conclude the pact proposed by Germany, and then work in such a way that this war, once it is declared, will be prolonged maximally. We must strengthen our propaganda work in the belligerent countries, in order to be prepared when the war ends.

‘I have nothing to offer but blood, toil, tears, and sweat.’

Sir Winston Churchill

House of Commons, London, 13 May 1940

‘This was their finest hour.’

House of Commons, London, 18 June 1940

‘Never in the field of human conflict was so much owed by so many to so few.’

House of Commons, London, 20 August 1940

Winston Churchill was born in 1874 at Blenheim Palace, the son of Sir Randolph Churchill, second son of the Duke of Marlborough, and Jenny Jerome, daughter of an American tycoon. Although immensely privileged, he was not happy as a child. Like many Victorian parents, Churchill's were distant figures, and he was brought up by his nanny before being sent away to boarding school.

Born 30 November 1874, Blenheim Palace, Oxford, England.
Winston Churchill was a career soldier and war reporter before entering politics in 1901. He served in the War Cabinet in World War I and with British forces in France, 1915–17. Churchill was appointed Prime Minister of the British coalition government in World War II. **'I have nothing to offer but blood, toil, tears, and sweat'** was his first speech to the House of Commons after his appointment. Churchill was well aware of the power of the spoken word. His inspirational rhetoric was a feature of the first critical year of the war: **'their finest hour'** and **'the Few'** are his best-remembered wartime speeches. He was knighted in 1953.
Died 15 January 1965 in London.
In 2004, Churchill was voted 'greatest Briton' in a nationwide survey.

Churchill's school career at Harrow was undistinguished and he was only accepted at the Royal Military Academy at Sandhurst after one failed attempt. He felt intellectually inferior because of his lack of a university education and also regretted the lack of practice in public speaking that he would have gained at university debates.

Churchill also suffered from a slight lisp and a stammer, so from the beginning he set about drafting his speeches in such a way as to avoid many of the patterns of everyday speech that he found so difficult. He visited speech therapists and practised both words and gestures in front of a mirror until he had mastered his craft. He sometimes spent weeks constructing the speeches themselves, refining and improving them, and in this way came up with a style that was unique. His vocabulary was extremely large and he loved to fill his speeches with inventive word play, alliteration, vivid imagery and metaphors.

However, this style of speech and his manner of delivery did not always suit the mood of the times. His big set-piece speeches in the House of Commons, to which he was first elected in 1901, were often criticized as being out of touch and contributing little to the debate. He delivered apocalyptic messages so often that politicians and the public alike were tempted to believe that he was crying wolf. But in the period from 1938 leading up to World War II people began to take more notice of his message. Elected Prime Minister in 1940 he suddenly appeared to be the right man for the time, and he was finally able to use his remarkable powers of oratory to rally and uplift the whole British nation in its struggle against the Nazi threat.

It was in this context that Churchill delivered this short speech to the House of Commons just three days after being elected Prime Minister and forming his coalition cabinet.

On Friday evening last I received from His Majesty the mission to form a new administration. It was the evident will of Parliament and the nation that this should be conceived on the broadest possible basis and that it should include all parties. I have already completed the most important part of this task.

A war cabinet has been formed of five members, representing, with the Labour, Opposition, and Liberals, the unity of the nation. It was necessary that this should be done in one single day on account of the extreme urgency and rigour of events. Other key positions were filled yesterday. I am submitting a further list to the King tonight. I hope to complete the appointment of principal ministers during tomorrow.

'We have before us many, many months of struggle and suffering.'

The appointment of other ministers usually takes a little longer. I trust when Parliament meets again this part of my task will be completed and that the administration will be complete in all respects. I considered it in the public interest to suggest to the Speaker that the House should be summoned today. At the end of today's proceedings, the adjournment of the House will be proposed until Tuesday 21st May with provision for earlier meeting if need be. Business for that will be notified to MPs at the earliest opportunity.

I now invite the House by a resolution to record its approval of the steps taken and declare its confidence in the new government.

The resolution is:

'That this House welcomes the formation of a government representing the united and inflexible resolve of the nation to prosecute the war with Germany to a victorious conclusion.'

To form an administration of this scale and complexity is a serious undertaking in itself. But we are in the preliminary phase of one of the greatest battles in history. We are in action at many other points – in Norway and in Holland – and we have to be prepared in the Mediterranean. The air battle is continuing, and many preparations have to be made here at home.

In this crisis I think I may be pardoned if I do not address the House at any length today, and I hope that any of my friends and colleagues or former colleagues who are affected by the political reconstruction will make all allowances for any lack of ceremony with which it has been necessary to act.

I say to the House as I said to ministers who have joined this government, I have nothing to offer but blood, toil, tears, and sweat. We have before us an ordeal of the most grievous kind. We have before us many, many months of struggle and suffering.

You ask, what is our policy? I say it is to wage war by land, sea, and air. War with all our might and with all the strength God has given us, and to wage war against a monstrous tyranny never surpassed in the dark and lamentable catalogue of human crime. That is our policy.

'You ask, what is our aim? I can answer in one word. It is victory.'

You ask, what is our aim? I can answer in one word. It is victory. Victory at all costs – victory in spite of all terrors – victory, however long and hard the road may be, for without victory there is no survival.

Let that be realized. No survival for the British Empire, no survival for all that the British Empire has stood for, no survival for the urge, the impulse of the ages, that mankind shall move forward towards his goal.

I take up my task in buoyancy and hope. I feel sure that our cause will not be suffered to fail among men. I feel entitled at this juncture, at this time, to claim the aid of all and to say, 'Come then, let us go forward together with our united strength.'

In June 1940, France fell to the Germans and Britain was suddenly isolated, facing occupied Europe and the very real threat of invasion. On 18 June, a week after the French surrender, Churchill spoke to the House of Commons, warning that the coming summer would be critical to Britain's survival. He was convinced that the German invasion would come by air: 'I look forward confidently to the exploits of our fighter pilots – these splendid men, this brilliant youth – who will have the glory of saving their native land, their island home, and all they love, from the most deadly of all attacks.'

We do not yet know what will happen in France or whether the French resistance will be prolonged, both in France and in the French Empire overseas. The French Government will be throwing away great opportunities and casting adrift their future if they do not continue the war in accordance with their treaty obligations, from which we have not felt able to release them. The House will have read the historic declaration in which, at the desire of many Frenchmen – and of our own hearts – we have proclaimed our willingness at the darkest hour in French history to conclude a union of common citizenship in this struggle. However matters may go in France or with the French Government, or other French Governments, we in this island and in the British Empire will never lose our sense of comradeship with the French people. If we are now called upon to

'The Battle of France is over. I expect that the Battle of Britain is about to begin.'

endure what they have been suffering, we shall emulate their courage, and if final victory rewards our toils they shall share the gains, aye, and freedom shall be restored to all. We abate nothing of our just demands; not one jot or tittle do we recede. Czechs, Poles, Norwegians, Dutch, Belgians have joined their causes to our own. All these shall be restored.

What General Weygand called the Battle of France is over. I expect that the Battle of Britain is about to begin. Upon this battle depends the survival of Christian civilization. Upon it depends our own British life, and the long continuity of our institutions and our Empire. The whole fury and might of the enemy must very soon be turned on us.

'Hitler knows that he will have to break us in this island or lose the war.'

Hitler knows that he will have to break us in this island or lose the war. If we can stand up to him, all Europe may be free and the life of the world may move forward into broad, sunlit uplands. But if we fail, then the whole world, including the United States, including all that we have known and cared for, will sink into the abyss of a new Dark Age made more sinister, and perhaps more protracted, by the lights of perverted science.

Let us therefore brace ourselves to our duties, and so bear ourselves that if the British Empire and its Commonwealth last for a thousand years, men will still say, 'This was their finest hour'.

Two months later, with the summer of 1940 drawing to a close, Churchill reported that the immediate threat of invasion had receded. But when he gave this speech on 20 August the Battle of Britain, which was being fought in the air as he had predicted, had yet to reach its climax. Although hit hard, the German air force (Luftwaffe) had more planes than the RAF, particularly bombers. In the two weeks from 24 August until 6 September, German planes attacked London and airfields in the south of England by day and night with devastating effect. However, by 15 September it was clear that the British defence had worked. Churchill's simple description of the young RAF pilots who fought the Battle of Britain caught the imagination of the public, for whom they remained 'the Few'.

The gratitude of every home in our island, in our Empire, and indeed throughout the world, except in the abodes of the guilty, goes out to the British airmen who, undaunted by odds, unwearied in their constant challenge and mortal danger, are turning the tide of the World War by their prowess and by their devotion. Never in the field of human conflict was so much owed by so many to so few. All hearts go out to the fighter pilots, whose brilliant actions we see with our own eyes day after day. But we must never forget that all the time, night after night, month after month, our bomber squadrons travel far into Germany, find their targets in the darkness by the highest navigational skill, aim their attacks, often under the heaviest fire, often with serious loss, with deliberate careful discrimination, and inflict shattering blows upon the whole of the technical and war-making structure of the Nazi power.

'Perfidy unparalleled in the history of civilized nations.'

Vyacheslav Molotov

On the Nazi invasion of the Soviet Union, 22 June 1941

Despite signing a non-aggression pact with the USSR in 1939 prior to invading Poland, Hitler had always intended that Russia would provide Germany's future living space, or *Lebensraum*. Although Russia had kept to the terms of the pact, Hitler secretly prepared for invasion, and in summer 1941 Operation Barbarossa ('redbeard') took place. At 3 am on the morning of 22 June, three and a half million German, Romanian, Finnish and other Axis troops flooded across the Soviet borders. This speech was given in a radio broadcast by USSR Foreign Minister Vyacheslav Molotov on the same day as this crushing and unexpected event. At the time of the invasion Stalin disappeared from view, leaving Molotov to give the morale-rallying broadcast.

Born 9 March 1890 in Kukura.
His family name was Scriabin (they were related to the famous Russian composer Alexander Scriabin) but he adopted the pseudonym Molotov, meaning 'hammer', when he joined the Bolsheviks in 1906. Molotov's **speech on the Nazi invasion of the USSR** was broadcast on the day that 3.5 million German and Axis troops broke through the Russian borders. Coming into conflict with Krushchev in 1957, Molotov was dismissed from his posts and expelled from the Central Committee. He was later expelled from the Communist Party but afterwards reinstated.
Died 8 November 1986 in Moscow.
Molotov was the longest surviving participant in the events of 1917.

Within the first fortnight of the invasion Russia lost one million men, nearly all their planes and thousands of tanks. Stalin then ordered retreating Russians to 'scorch the earth', thereby rendering the country incapable of supporting the advancing German army. Through the summer the Germans gained rapid ground, taking Leningrad and Kiev and mercilessly killing thousands of men, women and children. The war in the East was fought with particular brutality, an outcome of the vehemently anti-Communist Nazi philosophy that viewed the Slavs as 'sub-human'.

Born in 1890 to a shop clerk with the family name of Scriabin, Vyacheslav Mikhailovich began his political activity while he was a student and joined the Bolsheviks in 1906. In 1909 Molotov was arrested for the first time and sent into exile in north Russia for two years. On his return he joined *Pravda*, the Bolshevik newspaper, where he met Stalin and became secretary of the editorial board. He was later part of the military revolutionary committee that planned the Bolshevik seizure of power in the Russian Revolution of 1917. In 1926 he earned promotion to full membership of the Politburo and during 1928–30 helped to purge the Moscow party of anti-Stalin membership. He served as Foreign Minister for two periods in 1939–49 and 1953–56.

On 23 August 1939 Molotov signed the Soviet–German non-aggression treaty together with Ribbentrop, the Nazi Foreign Minister. He later played a vital role in secret conferences with Roosevelt that led to the signing of the Lease-Lend agreements that supplied Russia with arms from America.

When Khrushchev came to power in 1957 Molotov was dismissed from government posts and the leading Party bodies. He was later appointed ambassador to Mongolia and in 1960–61 was representative to the International Atomic Energy Agency in Vienna. He was expelled from the Communist Party in 1962, but later reinstated in 1984. He died in 1986, aged 96.

Citizens of the Soviet Union:

The Soviet Government and its head, Comrade Stalin, have authorized me to make the following statement:

Today at 4 o'clock am, without any claims having been presented to the Soviet Union, without a declaration of war, German troops attacked our country, attacked our borders at many points and bombed from their airplanes our cities; Zhitomir, Kiev, Sevastopol, Kaunas and some others, killing and wounding over two hundred persons.

...This unheard of attack upon our country is perfidy unparalleled in the history of civilized nations. The attack on our country was perpetrated despite the fact that a treaty of non-aggression had been signed between the USSR and Germany and that the Soviet Government most faithfully abided by all provisions of this treaty.

'Napoleon suffered defeat and met his doom. It will be the same with Hitler.'

The attack upon our country was perpetrated despite the fact that during the entire period of operation of this treaty, the German Government could not find grounds for a single complaint against the USSR as regards observance of this treaty.

Entire responsibility for this predatory attack upon the Soviet Union falls fully and completely upon the German Fascist rulers.

At 5.30 am, that is, after the attack had already been perpetrated, Von der Schulenburg, the German Ambassador in Moscow, on behalf of his government made the statement to me as People's Commissar of Foreign Affairs to the effect that the German Government had decided to launch war against the USSR in connection with the concentration of Red Army units near the eastern German frontier.

In reply to this I stated on behalf of the Soviet Government that, until the very last moment, the German Government had not presented any claims to the Soviet Government, that Germany attacked the USSR despite the peaceable position of the Soviet Union, and that for this reason Fascist Germany is the aggressor.

On instruction of the government of the Soviet Union I also stated that at no point had our troops or our air force committed a violation of the frontier and therefore the statement made this morning by the Romanian radio to the effect that Soviet aircraft allegedly had fired on Romanian aerodromes is a sheer lie and provocation.

'Ours is a righteous cause. The enemy shall be defeated.'

...This war has been forced upon us, not by the German people, not by German workers, peasants and intellectuals, whose sufferings we well understand, but by the clique of bloodthirsty Fascist rulers of Germany who have enslaved Frenchmen, Czechs, Poles, Serbians, Norway, Belgium, Denmark, Holland, Greece and other nations.

...This is not the first time that our people have had to deal with an attack of an arrogant foe. At the time of Napoleon's invasion of Russia our people's reply was war for the fatherland, and Napoleon suffered defeat and met his doom.

It will be the same with Hitler, who in his arrogance has proclaimed a new crusade against our country. The Red Army and our whole people will again wage victorious war for the fatherland, for our country, for honour, for liberty.

...The government calls upon you, citizens of the Soviet Union, to rally still more closely around our glorious Bolshevist party, around our Soviet Government, around our great leader and comrade, Stalin. Ours is a righteous cause. The enemy shall be defeated. Victory will be ours.

'The only thing we have to fear is fear itself.'

Franklin D. Roosevelt

Inaugural address, 4 March 1933

'A date which will live in infamy.'

Speech to Congress, 8 December 1941

Franklin D. Roosevelt was born into a noted wealthy family and, despite having a privileged upbringing, developed a strong sense of social responsibility while at school. After attending law school and working in a Wall Street law firm, he married Anna Eleanor Roosevelt, a distant relative, in 1905. The couple were active in New York social circles but also concerned with the lot of the common people. Inspired by his uncle, US President Teddy Roosevelt, Franklin became involved in politics and won a seat as a Democrat in the New York State Senate in 1910. Between 1913 and 1920 he was Assistant Secretary of the Navy under President Woodrow Wilson.

Despite contracting polio in 1921 Franklin was elected President in 1932, pledging a 'New Deal' for the US people and galvanizing the country when the national banking system collapsed in March 1933. His famous speech assuring people that 'the only thing we have to fear is fear itself' demonstrated his considerable powers of leadership in a crisis. He then used federal government power to bring about the nation's economic recovery from the Great Depression. His popularity did not wane: he was overwhelmingly re-elected in 1936 and in 1940 won a third term.

Born 30 January 1882 in New York.
Roosevelt was first elected President in 1932 and re-elected in 1936, 1940 and 1944 – the only US President to win four consecutive elections. Roosevelt's **first inaugural speech** announced policies that re-established the US economy after the Depression. Having seen his country through economic recovery, Roosevelt then had to manage its response to war in Europe. Initially determined to keep America out of the conflict, Roosevelt nevertheless supplied Britain and the USSR with weapons to fight Hitler and in August 1941 signed the Atlantic Charter condemning Nazi tyranny. After the surprise Japanese attack on Pearl Harbor he did not hesitate and in his **speech to Congress** the following day took the US into World War II.
Died 12 April 1945 in Warm Springs, Georgia.

President Hoover, Mr Chief Justice, my friends: this is a day of national consecration, and I am certain that my fellow Americans expect that on my induction into the Presidency I will address them with a candour and a decision which the present situation of our nation impels.

This is pre-eminently the time to speak the truth, the whole truth, frankly and boldly. Nor need we shrink from honestly facing conditions in our country today. This great nation will endure as it has endured, will revive and will prosper.

So first of all let me assert my firm belief that the only thing we have to fear is fear itself – nameless, unreasoning, unjustified terror which paralyzes needed efforts to convert retreat into advance.

In every dark hour of our national life a leadership of frankness and vigour has met with that understanding and support of the people themselves which is essential to victory. I am convinced that you will again give that support to leadership in these critical days. In such a spirit on my part and on yours we face our common difficulties. They concern, thank God, only material things. Values have shrunken to fantastic levels. Taxes have risen, our ability to pay has fallen, government of all kinds is faced by serious curtailment of income, the means of exchange are frozen in the currents of trade, the withered leaves of industrial enterprise lie on every side, farmers find no markets for their produce, the savings of many years in thousands of families are gone.

More important, a host of unemployed citizens face the grim problem of existence, and an equally great number toil with little return. Only a foolish optimist can deny the dark realities of the moment.

Yet our distress comes from no failure of substance. We are stricken by no plague of locusts. Compared with the perils which our forefathers conquered because they believed and were not afraid, we have still much to be thankful for. Nature still offers her bounty and human efforts have multiplied it. Plenty is at our doorstep, but a generous use of it languishes in the very sight of the supply.

Primarily, this is because the rulers of the exchange of mankind's goods have failed through their own stubbornness and their own incompetence, have admitted their failures and abdicated. Practices of the unscrupulous money changers stand indicted in the court of public opinion, rejected by the hearts and minds of men.

‘Only a foolish optimist can deny the dark realities of the moment.’

True, they have tried, but their efforts have been cast in the pattern of an outworn tradition. Faced by failure of credit, they have proposed only the lending of more money.

Stripped of the lure of profit by which to induce our people to follow their false leadership, they have resorted to exhortations, pleading tearfully for restored conditions. They know only the rules of a generation of self-seekers.

They have no vision, and when there is no vision the people perish. ...

Happiness lies not in the mere possession of money, it lies in the joy of achievement, in the thrill of creative effort.

The joy and moral stimulation of work no longer must be forgotten in the mad chase of evanescent profits. These dark days will be worth all they cost us if they teach us that our true destiny is not to be ministered unto but to minister to ourselves and to our fellow-men.

‘When there is no vision the people perish.’

... This nation asks for action, and action now.

Our greatest primary task is to put people to work. This is no unsolvable problem if we face it wisely and courageously.

It can be accompanied in part by direct recruiting by the government itself, treating the task as we would treat the emergency of a war, but at the same time, through this employment, accomplishing greatly needed projects to stimulate and reorganize the use of our national resources.

Hand in hand with this, we must frankly recognize the over-balance of population in our industrial centres and, by engaging on a national scale in a redistribution, endeavour to provide a better use of the land for those best fitted for the land.

The task can be helped by definite efforts to raise the values of agricultural products and with this the power to purchase the output of our cities.

It can be helped by preventing realistically the tragedy of the growing loss, through foreclosure, of our small homes and our farms.

It can be helped by insistence that the Federal, State, and local governments act forthwith on the demand that their cost be drastically reduced.

It can be helped by the unifying of relief activities which today are often scattered, uneconomical and unequal. It can be helped by national planning for and supervision of all forms of transportation and of communications and other utilities which have a definitely public character.

There are many ways in which it can be helped, but it can never be helped merely by talking about it. We must act, and act quickly.

Finally, in our progress toward a resumption of work we require two safeguards against a return of the evils of the old order: there must be a strict supervision of all banking and credits and investments, there must be an end to speculation with other people's money, and there must be provision for an adequate but sound currency.

These are the lines of attack. I shall presently urge upon a new Congress in special session detailed measures for their fulfilment, and I shall seek the immediate assistance of the several States.

'This nation asks for action, and action now.'

... I am prepared under my constitutional duty to recommend the measures that a stricken nation in the midst of a stricken world may require.

But in the event that the Congress shall fail to take one of these courses, and in the event that the national emergency is still critical, I shall not evade the clear course of duty that will then confront me.

I shall ask the Congress for the one remaining instrument to meet the crisis ... broad executive power to wage a war against the emergency as great as the power that would be given to me if we were in fact invaded by a foreign foe.

For the trust reposed in me I will return the courage and the devotion that befit the time. I can do no less.

We face the arduous days that lie before us in the warm courage of national unity, with the clear consciousness of seeking old and precious moral values, with the clean satisfaction that comes from the stern performance of duty by old and young alike.

We aim at the assurance of a rounded and permanent national life.

We do not distrust the future of essential democracy. The people of the United States have not failed. In their need they have registered a mandate that they want direct, vigorous action.

They have asked for discipline and direction under leadership. They have made me the present instrument of their wishes. In the spirit of the gift I will take it.

In this dedication of a nation we humbly ask the blessing of God. May He protect each and every one of us! May He guide me in the days to come.

In November 1941 diplomatic negotiations between the US and Japan broke down and, although Japan had not declared war on the US, American spies indicated that Japanese naval forces were moving towards the oil-rich East Indies and Malaya. Reports that aircraft carriers were heading towards Hawaii were not taken seriously.

On 7 December 1941, Japan unexpectedly attacked the US Pacific fleet at its base in Pearl Harbor, Hawaii. By noon that day eight US battleships had been sunk or disabled and 2,403 Americans killed. The next day Roosevelt declared war on Japan. On 11 December Japan's allies, Germany and Italy, declared war against the US.

Once in the war, Roosevelt mobilized industry for military production, worked with Winston Churchill to determine military and naval policy and formed alliances with Churchill and Stalin at Tehran in 1943 and Yalta in 1944. Roosevelt won an unprecedented fourth term as President in 1945 but, exhausted by the pressures of wartime leadership, died soon afterwards.

Mr Vice President, Mr Speaker, Members of the Senate, and of the House of Representatives:

Yesterday, December 7th, 1941 – a date which will live in infamy – the United States of America was suddenly and deliberately attacked by naval and air forces of the Empire of Japan.

The United States was at peace with that nation and, at the solicitation of Japan, was still in conversation with its government and its emperor looking toward the maintenance of peace in the Pacific.

Indeed, one hour after Japanese air squadrons had commenced bombing in the American island of Oahu, the Japanese ambassador to the United States and his colleagues delivered to our Secretary of State a formal reply to a recent American message. And while this reply stated that it seemed useless to continue the existing diplomatic negotiations, it contained no threat or hint of war or of armed attack.

It will be recorded that the distance of Hawaii from Japan makes it obvious that the attack was deliberately planned many days or even weeks ago. During the intervening time, the Japanese government has deliberately sought to deceive the United States by false statements and expressions of hope for continued peace.

The attack yesterday on the Hawaiian islands has caused severe damage to

American naval and military forces. I regret to tell you that very many American lives have been lost. In addition, American ships have been reported torpedoed on the high seas between San Francisco and Honolulu.

Yesterday, the Japanese government also launched an attack against Malaya.

Last night, Japanese forces attacked Hong Kong.

Last night, Japanese forces attacked Guam.

Last night, Japanese forces attacked the Philippine Islands.

Last night, the Japanese attacked Wake Island.

And this morning, the Japanese attacked Midway Island.

Japan has, therefore, undertaken a surprise offensive extending throughout the Pacific area. The facts of yesterday and today speak for themselves. The people of the United States have already formed their opinions and well understand the implications to the very life and safety of our nation.

As commander in chief of the Army and Navy, I have directed that all measures be taken for our defence. But always will our whole nation remember the character of the onslaught against us.

No matter how long it may take us to overcome this premeditated invasion, the American people in their righteous might will win through to absolute victory.

I believe that I interpret the will of the Congress and of the people when I assert that we will not only defend ourselves to the uttermost, but will make it very certain that this form of treachery shall never again endanger us.

Hostilities exist. There is no blinking at the fact that our people, our territory, and our interests are in grave danger.

With confidence in our armed forces, with the unbounding determination of our people, we will gain the inevitable triumph – so help us God.

I ask that the Congress declare that since the unprovoked and dastardly attack by Japan on Sunday, December 7th, 1941, a state of war has existed between the United States and the Japanese empire.

‘The flame of French resistance must not and shall not die.’

Charles de Gaulle

Appeal of 18 June 1940

This speech was broadcast by General Charles de Gaulle after he fled to London following the German invasion of France in 1940. In it de Gaulle exhorted French people to continue the fight against Germany. Perhaps the most famous phrase associated with his appeal – 'France has lost a battle. But France has not lost the war!' – was never actually broadcast.

De Gaulle escaped to England after the head of the French government, Marshall Pétain, surrendered to the Germans on 22 June. The Germans took over the north of France, allowing Pétain to rule with his Vichy government in southern France until 1942. Over the next three years de Gaulle became a symbol of French resistance and worked to persuade the British, the Americans and French resistance groups to accept him as the head of the Free French forces.

Born in 1890 to patriotic and devoutly Catholic parents, de Gaulle entered military school in 1910. He served as a lieutenant in World War I, during which he was wounded several times and captured at Verdun. After the war he served in Poland as a major in the war against the USSR, took part in the occupation of Germany and studied and lectured at war college. However, de Gaulle became unpopular with the military establishment when his book *The Army of the Future* was published in 1934. In it he argued for the mechanization of the infantry and the widespread use of tanks – the very tactics used by the Germans to conquer France in 1940.

Born 22 November 1890 in Lille, France.
A career soldier, de Gaulle graduated from the Military Academy St Cyr in 1912 and joined an infantry regiment in 1913. His controversial military ideas were published in *The Army of the Future* in 1934. Shortly after arriving in Britain in 1940 he made his **appeal of 18 June**, one of the most important speeches in all of French history. He was elected unanimously as head of the French government in 1945 and as President in 1958, 1965 and 1968.
Died 9 November 1970 in Colombey-les-Deux-Eglises, France.

By 1944 de Gaulle had gained supreme control of the French war effort outside France and was increasingly recognized as their leader. On 26 August 1944 de Gaulle entered liberated Paris in triumph. During 1944–46 he worked with the Allies to defeat the Nazis, while drawing up a constitution for the Fourth Republic.

When France faced a crisis over war in Algeria in 1958 de Gaulle was invited to form a government and was elected President of the Fifth Republic. He embarked on a foreign policy designed to gain a new position for France more independent from America and Britain. After what he took to be a no-confidence vote in him, following a referendum, he resigned in 1969 and died the following year.

The leaders who, for many years past, have been at the head of the French armed forces, have set up a government.

Alleging the defeat of our armies, this government has entered into negotiations with the enemy with a view to bringing about a cessation of hostilities. It is quite true that we were, and still are, overwhelmed by enemy mechanized forces, both on the ground and in the air. It was the tanks, the planes and the tactics of the Germans, far more than the fact that we were outnumbered, that forced our armies to retreat. It was the German tanks, planes and tactics that provided the element of surprise which brought our leaders to their present plight.

'Must we abandon all hope ? Is our defeat final? ... No!'

But has the last word been said? Must we abandon all hope? Is our defeat final and irremediable? To these questions I answer – No!

Speaking in full knowledge of the facts, I ask you to believe me when I say that the cause of France is not lost. The very factors that brought about our defeat may one day lead us to victory.

For, remember this, France does not stand alone. She is not isolated. Behind her is a vast Empire, and she can make common cause with the British Empire, which commands the seas and is continuing the struggle. Like England, she can draw unreservedly on the immense industrial resources of the United States.

This war is not limited to our unfortunate country. The outcome of the struggle has not been decided by the Battle of France. This is a world war. Mistakes have been made, there have been delays and untold suffering, but the fact remains that there still exists in the world everything we need to crush our enemies some day. Today we are crushed by the sheer weight of mechanized force hurled against us, but we can still look to a future in which even greater mechanized force will bring us victory. The destiny of the world is at stake.

I, General de Gaulle, now in London, call on all French officers and men who are at present on British soil, or may be in the future, with or without their arms. I call on all engineers and skilled workmen from the armaments factories who are at present on British soil, or may be in the future, to get in touch with me.

Whatever happens, the flame of French resistance must not and shall not die.

'I am personally going to shoot that paper-hanging sonofabitch Hitler.'

General George S. Patton Jr

Speech to the US Third Army on the eve of D-Day, 5 June 1944

This speech was given by General Patton rallying his men in the US Third Army on the eve of the D-Day invasion of Normandy by the Allies during World War II. It is typical of Patton's forthright and frequently profane style. Never using notes, Patton always addressed his men in down-to-earth language, often giving commonsense advice they could follow to avoid being killed. Patton himself said of his swearing, 'You can't run an army without profanity; and it has to be eloquent profanity'. The Third Army was to be involved in 281 days of combat in France, during which it achieved a spectacular sweep across France and into Germany.

Born 11 November 1885 in San Gabriel, California.
In 1909 he graduated from West Point Military Academy and married Beatrice Ayer the following year. America entered World War II in December 1941 following the attack on Pearl Harbor, with Patton commanding the Western Task Force. In 1944 he was given command of the Third Army in France and successfully exploited German weakness. His plain-speaking **speech given 'somewhere in England'** on 5 June 1944, tells every soldier that he is crucial to the Allies' military success.
Died 21 December 1945 in Germany.

Following the meeting of Roosevelt, Churchill and Stalin at Tehran in 1943, it was agreed that a second front would now be opened up on Hitler by an invasion of Western Europe. 'Operation Overlord' had been years in the planning, with the accumulation of men and resources in south-east England, the feeding of misinformation to the Germans and air strikes on the French communication systems to disrupt German troop movements. The decision, which rested on the right weather conditions, was made by US General Dwight Eisenhower, Allied Supreme Commander in Europe, that D (for 'deliverance') Day would be 6 June 1944.

On D-Day a fleet of 5,000 crossed the English Channel carrying British, American, French and Canadian troops, vehicles and stores and towing artificially constructed harbours ('mulberries') to serve until a French port could be captured. After heavy bombardment by Allied planes and ships, the forces landed on five beaches in Normandy and airborne troops were also dropped. Expecting an assault further north, the Germans were taken by surprise and most beaches were taken swiftly, though there were heavy US losses at the beach code-named Omaha.

Born in 1885, George Smith Patton Jr grew up in an important military family from Virginia. He was keenly interested in the US Civil War, especially the great cavalry leaders. He graduated from West Point Military Academy in 1909, received a commission in the cavalry and saw tank service in World War I in France, becoming a vigorous advocate of tank warfare. Between the two wars he was active in the formation of tank units and in World War II became a supreme practitioner of mobile armoured warfare.

Patton played a key role in the invasion of North Africa in 1942 and the capture of Sicily in 1943, where he commanded the US Seventh Army.

The peak of his career came in 1944–45 with the Third Army's major thrust across France and into Germany, achieved despite logistical difficulties and demonstrating great drive and daring. Patton's great achievements led to authorities overlooking civilian criticism of his methods. However, when he criticized the Allied post-war denazification policies in Germany he was removed from command of the Third Army in 1945.

Nicknamed 'Old Blood and Guts' by his men, Patton was a colourful, controversial character. He was quick-tempered, tough-minded and outspoken as an officer. He was also a disciplinarian but his own self-sacrifice gained him loyalty from his men. Patton was fatally injured in a car accident in Mannheim in Germany and died in 1945. He is buried among the soldiers who died in the battle of the Bulge in Luxembourg.

... You are here today for three reasons. First, because you are here to defend your homes and your loved ones. Second, you are here for your own self respect, because you would not want to be anywhere else. Third, you are here because you are real men and all real men like to fight. When you, here, every one of you, were kids, you all admired the champion marble player, the fastest runner, the toughest boxer, the big league ball players, and the All-American football players. Americans love a winner. Americans will not tolerate a loser. Americans despise cowards. Americans play to win all of the time. I wouldn't give a hoot in hell for a man who lost and laughed. That's why Americans have never lost nor will ever lose a war; for the very idea of losing is hateful to an American.

'The very idea of losing is hateful to an American.'

You are not all going to die. Only two per cent of you right here today would die in a major battle. Death must not be feared. Death, in time, comes to all men. Yes, every man is scared in his first battle. If he says he's not, he's a liar. Some men are cowards but they fight the same as the brave men or they get the hell slammed out of them watching men fight who are just as scared as they are. The real hero is the man who fights even though he is scared. Some men get over their fright in a minute under fire. For some, it takes an hour. For some it takes days. But a real man will never let his fear of death overpower his honour, his sense of duty to his country and his innate manhood.

Battle is the most magnificent competition in which a human being can indulge. It brings out all that is best and removes all that is base. Americans pride themselves on being He Men and they ARE He Men. Remember that the enemy is just as frightened as you are, and probably more so. They are not supermen.

'The real hero is the man who fights even though he is scared.'

... All of the real heroes are not storybook combat fighters, either. Every single man in this army plays a vital role. Don't ever let up. Don't ever think that your job is unimportant. Every man has a job to do and he must do it. Every man is a vital link in the great chain. What if every truck driver suddenly decided that he didn't like the whine of those shells overhead, turned yellow, and jumped headlong into a ditch? The cowardly bastard could say, 'Hell, they won't miss me, just one man in thousands.' But, what if every man thought that way? Where in the hell would we be now? What would our country, our loved ones, our homes, even the world, be like? No, goddamnit, Americans don't think like that. Every man does his job. Every man serves the whole. Every department, every unit, is important in the vast scheme of this war.

... Sure, we want to go home. We want this war over with. The quickest way to get it over with is to go get the bastards who started it. The quicker they are whipped, the quicker we can go home. The shortest way home is through Berlin and Tokyo. And when we get to Berlin, I am personally going to shoot that paperhanging sonofabitch Hitler. Just like I'd shoot a snake!

... There is one great thing that you men will all be able to say after this war is over and you are home once again. You may be thankful that twenty years from now when you are sitting by the fireplace with your grandson on your knee and he asks you what you did in the great World War II, you won't have to cough, shift him to the other knee and say, 'Well, your granddaddy shovelled shit in Louisiana.' No, sir, you can look him straight in the eye and say, 'Son, your granddaddy rode with the great Third Army and a son-of-a-goddamned-bitch named Georgie Patton!'

‘The enemy has begun to employ a new and most cruel bomb.’

Emperor Hirohito

The surrender of Japan, August 1945

On 6 August 1945 an American aircraft dropped the first atomic bomb on the Japanese military base of Hiroshima, killing between 75,000 and 100,000 people and obliterating the city. The Japanese made no immediate response. Three days later a second bomb was dropped on Nagasaki causing comparable devastation. Shortly after, Emperor Hirohito of Japan broke imperial tradition by broadcasting a speech to his people announcing Japan's surrender in World War II.

America had been at war with Japan since the Japanese attack on the US Pacific fleet in Pearl Harbor, Hawaii, in 1941. Throughout their battles with the Americans, the Japanese demonstrated their commitment to death rather than surrender (which they considered dishonourable). Despite heavy bombing of Tokyo in March 1945, in which 83,000 Japanese civilians died, the Japanese continued to fight. Although the Americans were gradually winning the war they knew that there would be huge allied losses in trying to capture Japan.

Born 29 April 1901 in Tokyo.
Hirohito's chosen imperial name was Showa ('enlightened peace'). He very much wanted to avoid war but once Japan was involved in World War II he refused to leave the capital for safety, saying that he wished to share the experience of his subjects. The **surrender of Japan** was an unprecedented act in the country's history. The longest-reigning modern monarch, Hirohito oversaw the transformation of the Japanese throne from a divine to a symbolic institution.
Died 7 January 1989 in Tokyo.

President Truman, who had succeeded Roosevelt on his death in April 1945, argued that using the atomic bomb would prevent the massive loss of allied soldiers' lives, as well as saving the lives of thousands of captured soldiers and civilians being used as slave labour or dying of disease and starvation in Japanese prisons of war. Truman wanted to beat Japan without Russia's help and at the Potsdam Conference on 24 July mentioned only briefly to Stalin that the US had 'a new weapon of unusual destructive force'. In early August the bombs were dropped, forcing the Japanese to surrender, and the world entered a new phase of history.

Born in 1901, Michinomiya Hirohito was the 124th Emperor of Japan and the first Japanese Crown Prince to travel abroad when he visited Europe in 1921. As a young man he began a lifelong interest in marine biology and became a respected authority on the subject. Hirohito became Emperor in 1926 and opposed Japan's drift towards war through the invasion of Manchuria and alliance with Germany throughout the 1930s. Although the Japanese constitution gave him supreme authority (the Japanese Emperor was traditionally believed to be divine), in reality Hirohito was only able to ratify policies and was powerless against the Japanese army's increasing aggression.

In 1945 when Japanese leaders were divided between surrendering or fighting a desperate defence of their islands, Hirohito supported those urging peace.

After his broadcast accepting the Potsdam Declaration a new constitution was drafted by the occupying US forces and the Emperor's powers were entirely removed. Hirohito was allowed to keep his throne but in 1946 made a statement disclaiming his divinity. Increasingly, the Japanese royal family made attempts to become closer to its people and, in 1958, Hirohito's son married a commoner. In 1972 Hirohito visited Europe and briefly met President Nixon in Alaska. He made an official visit to the US in 1975. Emperor Hirohito died in the Imperial Palace in Tokyo in 1989 after a long illness.

To our good and loyal subjects. After pondering deeply the general trends of the world and the actual conditions obtaining in our empire today, we have decided to effect a settlement of the present situation by resorting to an extraordinary measure.

We have ordered our Government to communicate to the Governments of the United States, Great Britain, China and the Soviet Union that our empire accepts the provisions of their joint declaration.

To strive for the common prosperity and happiness of all nations as well as the security and well-being of our subjects is the solemn obligation which has been handed down by our imperial ancestors and which we lay close to the heart.

Indeed, we declared war on America and Britain out of our sincere desire to ensure Japan's self-preservation and the stabilization of East Asia, it being far from our thought either to infringe upon the sovereignty of other nations or to embark upon territorial aggrandizement.

But now the war has lasted for nearly four years. Despite the best that has been done by everyone – the gallant fighting of our military and naval forces, the diligence and assiduity of our servants of the State and the devoted service of our 100 million people – the war situation has developed not necessarily to Japan's advantage, while the general trends of the world have all turned against her interest.

Moreover, the enemy has begun to employ a new and most cruel bomb, the power of which to do damage is, indeed, incalculable, taking the toll of many innocent lives. Should we continue to fight, it would not only result in an ultimate collapse and obliteration of the Japanese nation, but also it would lead to the total extinction of human civilization.

Such being the case, how are we to save the millions of our subjects, nor to atone ourselves before the hallowed spirits of our imperial ancestors? This is the reason why we have ordered the acceptance of the provisions of the joint declaration of the powers.

'We have resolved to pave the way for a grand peace for all the generations to come.'

We cannot but express the deepest sense of regret to our allied nations of East Asia, who have consistently cooperated with the empire toward the emancipation of East Asia.

The thought of those officers and men as well as others who have fallen in the fields of battle, those who died at their posts of duty, or those who met with untimely death and all their bereaved families, pains our heart night and day.

The welfare of the wounded and the war sufferers, and of those who lost their homes and livelihood, are the object of our profound solicitude. The hardships and sufferings to which our nation is to be subjected hereafter will certainly be great.

We are keenly aware of the inmost feelings of all of you, our subjects. However, it is according to the dictates of time and fate that we have resolved to pave the way for a grand peace for all the generations to come by enduring the unendurable and suffering what is insufferable. Having been able to save and maintain the structure of the Imperial State, we are always with you, our good and loyal subjects, relying upon your sincerity and integrity.

Beware most strictly of any outbursts of emotion that may engender needless complications, or any fraternal contention and strife that may create confusion, lead you astray and cause you to lose the confidence of the world.

Let the entire nation continue as one family from generation to generation, ever firm in its faith of the imperishableness of its divine land, and mindful of its heavy burden of responsibilities, and the long road before it. Unite your total strength to be devoted to the construction for the future. Cultivate the ways of rectitude, nobility of spirit, and work with resolution so that you may enhance the innate glory of the Imperial State and keep pace with the progress of the world.

'At the stroke of the midnight hour, when the world sleeps, India will awake to life and freedom.'

Jawaharlal Nehru

Speech on the granting of Indian independence, 14 August 1947

On 14 August 1947, when Britain granted independence to India, the country's new leader, Jawaharlal Nehru, made this speech marking the end of a long struggle for freedom.

In 1885 various organizations seeking reform of British rule joined together in the Indian National Congress. At first, they simply wanted more schools and seats for Indians in the legislature. By 1907, however, the Congress was split between moderates seeking gradual dominion status for India and radicals wanting complete and immediate self-rule. An earlier split had occurred in 1906 when Muslim leaders, discontented with Hindu domination of the Congress, formed the Muslim League.

During World War I the various groups were temporarily united in supporting Britain. However, after the war Congress's militant faction was angered by Britain's slowness in responding to demands for self-rule and by the restrictions it imposed on political activity in India in 1919. Militant feelings were also stirred up by the Amritsar massacre, in which British troops attacked unarmed Indians assembled for a meeting, killing 379 people and wounding 1,200.

At an Indian National Congress Party meeting in 1916 Nehru met Mahatma Gandhi, whose campaign of non-violent resistance and civil disobedience against the British was beginning to develop. During World War II Congress passed the Quit India resolution in 1942, which led to imprisonment of Congress Party leaders including Gandhi and Nehru. However, by the end of the war popular support for the Congress was undeniable and Britain granted India self-rule. Gandhi could not prevent the Muslims forming their own state in Pakistan to be governed by Mohammed Jinnah. Nehru was made Prime Minister of the mainly Hindu country of India.

Born 14 November 1889 in Allahabad, India. The son of a wealthy lawyer, Nehru's life as a child was one of luxury. His family's first language was English and Nehru was educated in England. A close friend of Gandhi, he agreed with most of his principles, except Gandhi's ideal of the simple life: Nehru wanted to build modern India on the best aspects of both Indian and British traditions and make a place for the country in the international community. The version of his **speech on the granting of Indian independence** reproduced here is the one given to the Indian Parliament.
A second speech on the same theme was broadcast to the Indian people over the radio later that day. Nehru was popularly named Pandit ('wise man').
Died 27 May 1964 in Delhi, India.

Born in 1889, Nehru had a privileged childhood and was educated in Britain at Harrow and Trinity College, Cambridge. His father was a lawyer prominent in the nationalist movement and Jawaharlal was admitted to the English Bar and practised law on his return to India. However, he was more interested in politics, becoming leader of the radical wing of the Congress Party and Party President in 1929.

Like Gandhi, Nehru was repeatedly arrested by the British and imprisoned. He spent so much time in jail that he described this time as 'normal interludes in a life of abnormal political activity'.

Nehru was hugely popular in India where he was Prime Minister for 17 years. Determined to bring the country into the modern age of science and technology, he was the first important Indian leader to think about India in a world context. At home he raised people's awareness of the need for social concern about the poor and respect for democracy. He wrote many books, including his autobiography *Towards Freedom*. Nehru died from a stroke in 1964. His daughter Indira became Prime Minister of India two years later.

Long years ago we made a tryst with destiny, and now the time comes when we shall redeem our pledge, not wholly or in full measure, but very substantially. At the stroke of the midnight hour, when the world sleeps, India will awake to life and freedom. A moment comes, which comes but rarely in history, when we step out from the old to the new, when an age ends, and when the soul of a nation, long suppressed, finds utterance. It is fitting that at this solemn moment we take the pledge of dedication to the service of India and her people and to the still larger cause of humanity.

'Freedom and power bring responsibility.'

At the dawn of history India started on her unending quest, and trackless centuries are filled with her striving and the grandeur of her success and her failures. Through good and ill fortune alike she has never lost sight of that quest or forgotten the ideals which gave her strength. We end today a period of ill fortune and India discovers herself again. The achievement we celebrate today is but a step, an opening of opportunity, to the greater triumphs and achievements that await us. Are we brave enough and wise enough to grasp this opportunity and accept the challenge of the future?

Freedom and power bring responsibility. The responsibility rests upon this Assembly, a sovereign body representing the sovereign people of India. Before the birth of freedom we have endured all the pains of labour and our hearts are heavy with the memory of this sorrow. Some of those pains continue even now. Nevertheless, the past is over and it is the future that beckons to us now.

That future is not one of ease or resting but of incessant striving so that we may fulfil the pledges we have so often taken and the one we shall take today. The service of India means the service of the millions who suffer. It means the ending of poverty and ignorance and disease and inequality of opportunity. The ambition of the greatest man of our generation has been to wipe every tear from every eye. That may be beyond us, but as long as there are tears and suffering, so long our work will not be over.

‘The ambition of the greatest man of our generation has been to wipe every tear from every eye.’

And so we have to labour and to work, and work hard, to give reality to our dreams. Those dreams are for India, but they are also for the world, for all the nations and peoples are too closely knit together today for any one of them to imagine that it can live apart. Peace has been said to be indivisible; so is freedom, so is prosperity now, and so also is disaster in this one world that can no longer be split into isolated fragments.

‘The noble mansion of free India.’

To the people of India, whose representatives we are, we make an appeal to join us with faith and confidence in this great adventure. This is no time for petty and destructive criticism, no time for ill-will or blaming others. We have to build the noble mansion of free India where all her children may dwell.

‘The reason that we did this job is because it was an organic necessity.’

J. Robert Oppenheimer

Los Alamos, New Mexico, 2 November 1945

US physicist J. Robert Oppenheimer headed the American laboratory that built the atomic bomb. In this extract from a speech given four months after Hiroshima, Oppenheimer explored why Americans scientists created the bomb and considered the future cooperation between nations that would now be necessary.

Born 22 April 1904 in New York.
After studying at Harvard and the University of Cambridge, Oppenheimer took a PhD at the University of Göttingen in Germany. He was a brilliant scholar who had a gift for languages and a deep interest in Eastern religions and philosophy. Although he maintained that he felt no guilt for his work on atomic weapons, he never denied his sense of moral responsibility. His **speech at Los Alamos** sets out his beliefs in international collaboration and the duty of science.
Died 18 February 1967 in New York.

As early as 1939 Albert Einstein and Leo Szilard had outlined the dangers if Nazi laboratories were the first to develop an atomic bomb. Once America had entered the war, President Roosevelt set up a research centre and in 1942 Oppenheimer was asked to lead British and American physicists in finding a way to harness nuclear energy for military purposes.

The first atomic bomb was exploded at Alamogordo in New Mexico on 16 July 1945. Some years later, Oppenheimer described his reaction: 'We knew the world would not be the same. A few people laughed, a few people cried, most people were silent. I remembered the line from the Hindu scripture, the Bhagavad-Gita … "Now, I am become Death, the destroyer of worlds".' President Truman gave orders for a bomb to be dropped on Japan as soon as possible to bring a swift end to the war. The first bomb was dropped on Hiroshima on 6 August 1945 and a second on Nagasaki three days later. The devastation was far more horrifying than had been anticipated. Japan surrendered on 14 August 1945.

Robert Oppenheimer was born in 1904. He studied physics at Harvard and quantum mechanics and relativity theory at the Cavendish Laboratory at the University of Cambridge. From 1929 he held posts at the University of California in Berkeley and the California Institute of Technology, where he established large schools of theoretical physics. A whole generation of US physicists owed much to his intelligent and inspiring leadership.

In 1942, as part of the Manhattan Project's research and development work, Oppenheimer was asked to coordinate work on the atomic bomb. He was widely acknowledged as a brilliant director. In October 1945 he resigned and returned to California, although he continued to advise the government on the use and control of nuclear weapons.

Between 1947 and 1952 Oppenheimer was chairman of the board of scientific advisors of the Atomic Energy Commission. In 1949 the board refused to pass a proposal to start the manufacture of hydrogen bombs. This, together with his sharp tongue and views on arms control, made Oppenheimer military and political enemies. His opposition to the hydrogen bomb and alleged contacts with Communists led to his being denied security clearance in 1954. However, ten years later the AEC awarded him the prestigious Fermi Award, recognizing his scientific leadership and groundwork on many peaceful uses of atomic energy. Oppenheimer spent his last years exploring the relationship between science and society. He died of throat cancer in 1967.

I should like to talk tonight ... as a fellow scientist, and at least as a fellow worrier about the fix we are in.

... In considering what the situation of science is, it may be helpful to think a little of what people said and felt of their motives in coming into this job ... There was in the first place the great concern that our enemy might develop these weapons before we did, and the feeling – at least, in the early days, the very strong feeling – that without atomic weapons it might be very difficult, it might be an impossible, it might be an incredibly long thing to win the war. These things wore off a little as it became clear that the war would be won in any case. Some people, I think, were motivated by curiosity, and rightly so; and some by a sense of adventure, and rightly so. Others had more political arguments and said, 'Well, we know that atomic weapons are in principle possible, and it is not right that the threat of their unrealized possibility should hang over the world. It is right that the world should know what can be done in their field and deal with it.'... And there was finally, and I think rightly, the feeling that there was probably no place in the world where the development of atomic weapons would have a better chance of leading to a reasonable solution, and a smaller chance of leading to disaster, than within the United States. I believe all these things that people said are true, and I think I said them all myself at one time or another.

But when you come right down to it the reason that we did this job is because it was an organic necessity ... If you are a scientist you believe that it is good to find out how the world works; that it is good to find out what the realities are; that it is good to turn over to mankind at large the greatest possible power to control the world and to deal with it according to its lights and its values.

... It is not possible to be a scientist unless you believe that it is good to learn. It is not good to be a scientist, and it is not possible, unless you think that it is of the highest value to share your knowledge, to share it with anyone who is interested. It is not possible to be a scientist unless you believe that the knowledge of the world, and the power which this gives, is a thing which is of intrinsic value to humanity, and that you are using it to help in the spread of knowledge, and are willing to take the consequences.

'It is not possible to be a scientist unless you believe that it is good to learn.'

... I think it is true to say that atomic weapons are a peril which affect everyone in the world, and in that sense a completely common problem, as common a problem as it was for the Allies to defeat the Nazis. I think that in order to handle this common problem there must be a complete sense of community responsibility. I do not think that one may expect that people will contribute to the solution of the problem until they are aware of their ability to take part in the solution. I think that it is a field in which the implementation of such a common responsibility has certain decisive advantages. It is a new field, in which just the novelty and the special characteristics of the technical operations should enable one to establish a community of interest which might almost be regarded as a pilot plant for a new type of international collaboration. I speak of it as a pilot plant because it is quite clear that the control of atomic weapons cannot be in itself the unique end of such operation. The only unique end can be a world that is united, and a world in which war will not occur ... Now, this is not an easy thing, and the point I want to make, the one point I want to hammer home, is what an enormous change in spirit is involved. There are things which we hold very dear, and I think rightly hold very dear; I would say that the word democracy perhaps stood for some of them as well as any other word. There are many parts of the world in which there is no democracy. There are other things which we hold dear, and which we rightly should. And when I speak of a new spirit in international affairs I mean that even to these deepest of things which we cherish, and for which Americans have been willing to die – and certainly most of us would be willing to die – even in these deepest things, we realize that there is something more profound than that; namely, the common bond with other men everywhere.

... We are not only scientists; we are men, too. We cannot forget our dependence on our fellow men ... These are the strongest bonds in the world, stronger than those even that bind us to one another, these are the deepest bonds – that bind us to our fellow men.

‘I have just left your fighting sons in Korea. …They are splendid in every way.’

General Douglas MacArthur

Farewell address to Congress, Washington, 19 April 1951

In 1950 North Korea, backed by Russia, invaded South Korea. General Douglas MacArthur was appointed Commander of the United Nations forces sent to protect South Korea. MacArthur believed that a strongly aggressive strategy was needed, including bombardment of Chinese bases in Manchuria. When he communicated these beliefs he was charged with insubordination and relieved of command by President Truman, who feared his strategy would lead to war with China and the Soviet Union.

MacArthur immediately flew back to the United States and took up invitations to speak before both Houses of Congress, an unprecedented event in American history. In a dramatic address he repeated his demands for action against the Chinese to combat the Communist threat.

Born 28 January 1880 in Little Rock, Arkansas. The son of a general, MacArthur's military career was exemplary and he retired from active service shortly before World War II, when he was recalled. His fame rests on his brilliant wartime record but his televised **speech to Congress** revealed a talent for public speaking. Although he resisted Republican pressure to stand for President, he acted as a presidential adviser on many occasions. Died 5 April 1964 in New York.

Douglas MacArthur was born in Little Rock, Arkansas in 1880. After graduating first in his class at West Point military academy in 1903, Douglas became a second lieutenant and was stationed in the Philippines and Japan. During World War I he earned many combat decorations, while serving as Chief of Staff of the famous Rainbow Division and later as Commander of the 84th Infantry Brigade.

In 1919 MacArthur was appointed Superintendent of West Point where he broadened the curriculum and raised standards. Between 1922 and 1925 he was Commander in the Philippines and in 1930 was appointed Chief of Staff by President Hoover. In 1935 MacArthur returned to the Philippines to prepare the islands against possible Japanese aggression and in 1936 was appointed Field Marshall of the Philippine Army. He retired from the US army in December 1937.

In 1941 MacArthur was recalled to service when President Roosevelt gave him command of all the US army forces in the Far East, after the attack on Pearl Harbor. When Japan finally surrendered in 1945 MacArthur oversaw the signing of surrender documents on board the battleship *Missouri.*

After his service in South Korea and return to the US, MacArthur spent the last 12 years of his life in New York. He made periodic public speeches and was consulted by every US President. Although arrogant, aloof and egotistical, MacArthur was also warm-hearted, courageous, self-sacrificing and capable of inspiring loyalty. He had a brilliant mind but was convinced that America was menaced by a conspiracy of liberals and Communists.

I address you with neither rancour nor bitterness in the fading twilight of life, with but one purpose in mind: to serve my country.

... While I was not consulted prior to the President's decision to intervene in support of the Republic of Korea, that decision from a military standpoint, proved a sound one, as we hurled back the invader and decimated his forces. Our victory was complete, and our objectives within reach, when Red China intervened with numerically superior ground forces.

This created a new war and an entirely new situation, a situation not contemplated when our forces were committed against the North Korean invaders; a situation which called for new decisions in the diplomatic sphere to permit the realistic adjustment of military strategy.

Such decisions have not been forthcoming.

While no man in his right mind would advocate sending our ground forces into continental China, and such was never given a thought, the new situation did urgently demand a drastic revision of strategic planning if our political aim was to defeat this new enemy as we had defeated the old.

> 'I know war as few other men now living know it, and nothing to me is more revolting.'

Apart from the military need, as I saw it, to neutralize the sanctuary protection given the enemy north of the Yalu, I felt that military necessity in the conduct of the war made necessary: first, the intensification of our economic blockade against China; two, the imposition of a naval blockade against the China coast; three, removal of restrictions on air reconnaissance of China's coastal areas and of Manchuria; four, removal of restrictions on the forces of the Republic of China on Formosa, with logistical support to contribute to their effective operations against the common enemy.

For entertaining these views, all professionally designed to support our forces committed to Korea and bring hostilities to an end with the least possible delay and at a saving of countless American and allied lives, I have been severely criticized in lay circles, principally abroad, despite my understanding that from a military standpoint the above views have been fully shared in the past by practically every military leader concerned with the Korean campaign, including our own Joint Chiefs of Staff.

‘Old soldiers never die; they just fade away.’

I called for reinforcements but was informed that reinforcements were not available. I made clear that if not permitted to destroy the enemy built-up bases north of the Yalu, if not permitted to utilize the friendly Chinese Force of some 600,000 men on Formosa, if not permitted to blockade the China coast to prevent the Chinese Reds from getting succour from without, and if there were to be no hope of major reinforcements, the position of the command from the military standpoint forbade victory.

... Efforts have been made to distort my position. It has been said, in effect, that I was a warmonger. Nothing could be further from the truth. I know war as few other men now living know it, and nothing to me is more revolting. I have long advocated its complete abolition, as its very destructiveness on both friend and foe has rendered it useless as a means of settling international disputes.

There are some who, for varying reasons, would appease Red China. They are blind to history's clear lesson, for history teaches with unmistakeable emphasis that appeasement but begets new and bloodier war. ...

I have just left your fighting sons in Korea. They have met all tests there, and I can report to you without reservation that they are splendid in every way.

... I am closing my 52 years of military service. When I joined the army, even before the turn of the century, it was the fulfilment of all of my boyish hopes and dreams. The world has turned over many times since I took the oath on the plain at West Point, and the hopes and dreams have long since vanished, but I still remember the refrain of one of the most popular barrack ballads of that day which proclaimed most proudly that ‘old soldiers never die; they just fade away’.

And like the old soldier of that ballad, I now close my military career and just fade away, an old soldier who tried to do his duty as God gave him the light to see that duty.

Goodbye.

‘I am the First Accused.’

The first of these two speeches is an extract from Nelson Mandela's lengthy speech in his defence at his trial for sabotage and attempting violent overthrow of the South African state in 1964. Since 1960, Mandela had been the leader of *Umkhonto we Sizwe* ('Spear of the Nation'), the armed wing of the political party the African National Congress. The ANC had been banned for its opposition to the South African government's system of apartheid, a strict policy of racial segregation that repressed the black South African majority. In his defence, Mandela spoke both as an experienced lawyer and a political activist. He and his co-accused *Umkhonto we Sizwe* members received life sentences and Mandela was imprisoned from 1964 to 1990.

Born 18 July 1918 in Umtata, Transkei. During his early career as a lawyer, Mandela became a political activist with the banned political party, the African National Congress (ANC). In 1964 he was imprisoned for life for plotting violent revolution. **'I am the First Accused'** were the opening words of his speech in his own defence at his trial. Mandela became a symbolic figurehead for anti-apartheid and anti-racist campaigners throughout the world. In 1994, four years after his release from prison, the ANC won the South African election and Mandela became President. **'Free at last'** was his first official speech in his new political role.

Nelson Mandela was born in 1918, the eldest son of a Xhosa-speaking Tempu chief in the Transkei. He attended Methodist missionary school and later gained a law degree at Witwatersrand University, the only black student at the Law School. In 1952 he opened the first black law firm in Johannesburg with Oliver Tambo, later leader of the African National Congress in exile. In 1944 Mandela helped found the ANC Youth League.

During the 1970s and 1980s world protest against apartheid grew, with increased demands for Mandela's release. In 1989 newly elected President F. W. de Klerk accelerated the dismantling of apartheid. In 1990 the ban on the ANC was lifted and Mandela was released unconditionally. He was greeted rapturously by black and white South Africans and people throughout the world.

I am the First Accused.

I hold a Bachelor's Degree in Arts and practised as an attorney in Johannesburg for a number of years in partnership with Oliver Tambo. I am a convicted prisoner serving five years for leaving the country without a permit and for inciting people to go on strike at the end of May 1961.

... The lack of human dignity experienced by Africans is the direct result of the policy of white supremacy. White supremacy implies black inferiority.

Legislation designed to preserve white supremacy entrenches this notion. Menial tasks in South Africa are invariably performed by Africans. When anything has to be carried or cleaned the white man will look around for an African to do it for him, whether the African is employed by him or not. Because of this sort of attitude, whites tend to regard Africans as a separate breed. They do not look upon them as people with families of their own; they do not realize that they have emotions – that they fall in love like white people do; that they want to be

'Africans want to be paid a living wage.'

with their wives and children like white people want to be with theirs; that they want to earn enough money to support their families properly, to feed and clothe them and send them to school. And what 'house-boy' or 'garden-boy' or labourer can ever hope to do this?

Pass laws, which to the Africans are among the most hated bits of legislation in South Africa, render any African liable to police surveillance at any time. I doubt whether there is a single African male in South Africa who has not at some stage had a brush with the police over his pass. Hundreds and thousands of Africans are thrown into jail each year under pass laws. Even worse than this is the fact that pass laws keep husband and wife apart and lead to the breakdown of family life.

Poverty and the breakdown of family life have secondary effects. Children wander about the streets of the townships because they have no schools to go to, or no money to enable them to go to school, or no parents at home to see that they go to school, because both parents (if there be two) have to work to keep the family alive. This leads to a breakdown in moral standards, to an alarming rise in illegitimacy, and to growing violence which erupts not only politically, but everywhere. Life in the townships is dangerous. There is not a day that goes by without somebody being stabbed or assaulted. And violence is carried out of the townships in the white living areas. People are afraid to walk alone in the streets after dark. Housebreakings and robberies are increasing, despite the fact that the death sentence can now be imposed for such offences. Death sentences cannot cure the festering sore.

Africans want to be paid a living wage. Africans want to perform work which they are capable of doing, and not work which the Government declares them to be capable of. Africans want to be allowed to live where they obtain work, and not be endorsed out of an area because they were not born there. Africans want to be allowed to own land in places where they work, and not to be obliged to live in rented houses which they can never call their own. Africans want to be part of the general population, and not confined to living in their own ghettoes. African men want to have their wives and children to live with them where they work, and not be forced into an unnatural existence in men's hostels. African women want to be with their menfolk and not be left permanently widowed in the Reserves. Africans want to be allowed out after eleven o'clock at night and not to be confined to their rooms like little children. Africans want to be allowed to travel in their own country and to seek work where they want to and not where the Labour Bureau tells them to. Africans want a just share in the whole of South Africa; they want security and a stake in society.

Above all, we want equal political rights, because without them our disabilities will be permanent. I know this sounds revolutionary to the whites in this country, because the majority of voters will be Africans. This makes the white man fear democracy.

But this fear cannot be allowed to stand in the way of the only solution which will guarantee racial harmony and freedom for all. It is not true that the enfranchisement of all will result in racial domination. Political division, based on colour, is entirely artificial and, when it disappears, so will the domination of one colour group by another. The ANC has spent half a century fighting against racialism. When it triumphs it will not change that policy.

‘It is an ideal for which I am prepared to die.’

This then is what the ANC is fighting. Their struggle is a truly national one. It is a struggle of the African people, inspired by their own suffering and their own experience. It is a struggle for the right to live.

During my lifetime I have dedicated myself to this struggle of the African people. I have fought against white domination, and I have fought against black domination. I have cherished the ideal of a democratic and free society in which all persons live together in harmony and with equal opportunities. It is an ideal which I hope to live for and to achieve. But if needs be, it is an ideal for which I am prepared to die.

In 1991 Mandela succeeded Oliver Tambo as President of the ANC. He travelled widely to maintain international support for the total abolition of apartheid and in 1993 he and de Klerk won the Nobel Peace Prize for their reforming work. After elections in May 1994 the ANC were victorious and Nelson Mandela became President. The speech he gave on the evening of his victory is characteristic of his easy, mature political style.

In 1996, at the age of 81, Nelson Mandela stood down as President. He has been awarded honorary degrees from over 80 universities and numerous peace prizes. In 2004 his autobiography, *Long Walk to Freedom*, became a bestseller.

My fellow South Africans – the people of South Africa:

This is indeed a joyous night. Although not yet final, we have received the provisional results of the election, and are delighted by the overwhelming support for the African National Congress.

To all those in the African National Congress and the democratic movement who worked so hard these last few days and through these many decades, I thank you and honour you. To the people of South Africa and the world who are watching: this is a joyous night for the human spirit. This is your victory too. You helped end apartheid, you stood with us through the transition.

I watched, along with all of you, as the tens of thousands of our people stood patiently in long queues for many hours. Some sleeping on the open ground overnight waiting to cast this momentous vote.

South Africa's heroes are legend across the generations. But it is you, the people, who are our true heroes.

This is one of the most important moments in the life of our country. I stand here before you filled with deep pride and joy: pride in the ordinary, humble people of this country. ...

And joy that we can loudly proclaim from the rooftops – free at last!

I stand before you humbled by your courage, with a heart full of love for all of you. I regard it as the highest honour to lead the ANC at this moment in our history, and that we have been chosen to lead our country into the new century.

I pledge to use all my strength and ability to live up to your expectations of me as well as of the ANC.

I am personally indebted and pay tribute to some of South Africa's greatest leaders including John Dube, Josiah Gumede, GM Naicker, Dr Abdurahman, Chief Luthuli, Lilian Ngoyi, Helen Joseph, Yusuf Dadoo, Moses Kotane, Chris Hani and Oliver Tambo. They should have been here to celebrate with us, for this is their achievement too.

Tomorrow, the entire ANC leadership and I will be back at our desks. We are rolling up our sleeves to begin tackling the problems our country faces. We ask you all to join us – go back to your jobs in the morning. Let's get South Africa working.

For we must, together and without delay, begin to build a better life for all South Africans. This means creating jobs, building houses, providing education and bringing peace and security for all.

The calm and tolerant atmosphere that prevailed during the elections depicts the type of South Africa we can build. It set the tone for the future. We might have our differences, but we are one people with a common destiny in our rich variety of culture, race and tradition.

People have voted for the party of their choice and we respect that. This is democracy.

I hold out a hand of friendship to the leaders of all parties and their members, and ask all of them to join us in working together to tackle the problems we face as a nation. An ANC government will serve all the people of South Africa, not just ANC members.

We also commend the security forces for the sterling work done. This has laid a solid foundation for a truly professional security force, committed to the service of the people and loyalty to the new constitution.

Now is the time for celebration, for South Africans to join together to celebrate the birth of democracy. I raise a glass to you all for working so hard to achieve what can only be called a small miracle. Let our celebrations be in keeping with the mood set in the elections, peaceful, respectful and disciplined, showing we are a people ready to assume the responsibilities of government.

I promise that I will do my best to be worthy of the faith and confidence you have placed in me and my organization, the African National Congress. Let us build the future together, and toast a better life for all South Africans.

‘These were all good men.’

Eamon de Valera

Speech on the fiftieth anniversary of the Easter Rising, 10 April 1966

This speech concerns the Easter Rising in Dublin on 24 April 1916. Eamon de Valera was involved in the Irish rebellion against Great Britain and, unlike the other organizers captured with him, escaped execution, largely because he was born in America. In his subsequent career he played a major role in Ireland's fight for independence from British rule.

The Rising marked the beginning of the end of British power in Ireland and as the oldest survivor, de Valera gained a great deal of personal popularity.

The man regarded by many as the leading Irish statesman of the twentieth century was actually born in New York to a Spanish father and Irish mother. At the age of three, Eamon was sent to live in Ireland with his mother's relatives. After graduating from the Royal University of Dublin he became a mathematics teacher. He was a passionate supporter of Irish-language revival and in 1913 joined the Irish Volunteers, which led to his involvement in the Easter Rising.

Born 14 October 1882 in New York.
De Valera moved to Ireland while still a small child. Drawn initially to the priesthood, he remained a deeply religious man all his life. His greatest political achievement was probably the drafting of Eire's Constitution in 1937. The Constitution has been the inspiration for other countries, including South Africa's 1996 constitution. De Valera's **speech on the fiftieth anniversary of the Easter Rising** reiterates his commitment to the ideals of that time.
Died 29 August 1975 in Dublin.

De Valera was released in an amnesty in 1917 and then elected President of the illegal Sinn Féin government. In 1918 he was again imprisoned but escaped using a key smuggled to him in a cake. Disguised, he fled to America, where he raised $5 million for the cause of the non-existent Irish Republic.

On returning to Ireland de Valera led opposition to the Anglo-Irish treaty to create an Irish Free State with less than absolute independence. When the treaty was passed de Valera then assisted republican resistance in the following civil war. The anti-treaty forces were defeated and by 1927 de Valera had decided to take the oath to the British Crown required of all who sat in the Dáil, Parliament of the Irish Free State. His Fianna Fáil ('Soldiers of Destiny') party soon became the largest party in Irish politics. Between 1932 and 1948 de Valera was Prime Minister. He cut ties with Britain and developed national self-sufficiency in an Irish-speaking Ireland. In 1937 the Irish Free State virtually seceded from the British Commonwealth and became Ireland, or Eire. De Valera's strict Catholicism, neutrality during World War II (he refused to let Britain use Irish naval bases) and revival of the Irish language led to resistance by Northern Irish Protestants in Ulster to unification with Eire.

An extremely tall, gaunt, ascetic figure, de Valera could seem aloof. However, he maintained power as Prime Minister until 1948 when Fianna Fáil was defeated by John Costello's coalition goverment under which the Republic of Ireland left the British Commonwealth, a move de Valera had resisted, hoping eventually to unite Eire and Northern Ireland. De Valera returned as Prime Minister in 1951 and then again in 1957, by which time he was 74 and nearly blind. From 1959–73 he was President of the Republic of Ireland. In 1973 he retired to a nursing home where he died in 1975.

This Easter we are bringing back to our minds the Easter of fifty years ago and are seeking to honour the men who at that time gave or risked their lives that Ireland might be free.

We wish to honour, in particular, seven brave men who, despite all the deterrents, made the decision to assert, once more, in arms our nation's right to sovereign independence. It was a fateful decision which we now know to have been one of the boldest and most far-reaching in our history.

'Political freedom alone was not the ultimate goal.'

These were all good men, fully alive to their responsibilities, and it was only the firmest conviction, the fullest faith and love of country that prompted their action. Their singlemindedness and unselfishness, their sacrifice and the sacrifices of the others who gave the lives in the uprising inspired the national resurgence which followed. May the good God have them all in His keeping.

Time has proved these men to have been prophets. They foresaw what few could then have foreseen, and to their foresight and their insight into the hearts of our people, under God's favour, we owe the privileges we enjoy here today.

Political freedom alone was not the ultimate goal. It was to be, rather, the enabling condition for the gradual building up of a community in which an ever-increasing number of its members, relieved from the pressure of exacting economic demands, would be free to devote themselves more and more to the cultivation of the things of the mind and spirit and, so, able to have the happiness of a full life. Our nation could then become again, as it was for centuries in the past, a great intellectual and missionary centre from which would go forth the satisfying saving truths of Divine Revelation, as well as the fruits of the ripest secular knowledge.

'We can have our people reunited as a family.'

We cannot adequately honour the men of 1916 if we do not work and strive to bring about the Ireland of their desire. For this each one of us must do his part, and though the tasks immediately before us now are different from those of fifty years ago, we can have today, if we are sufficiently devoted and our will be firm, a national resurgence comparable to that which followed 1916: we can have our people reunited as a family – a nation of brothers – each working in industrial harmony, not for himself only, but for the good of all. We could then march forward confidently to that exaltation of our nation amongst the nations to which the men of 1916 pledged themselves.

'Language is a chief characteristic of nationhood.'

In the realization of all this our national language has a vital role. Language is a chief characteristic of nationhood – the embodiment, as it were, of the nation's personality and the closest bond between its people. No nation with a language of its own would willingly abandon it. The peoples of Denmark, Holland, Norway, for example, learn and know well one or more other languages, as we should, of course, for the sake of world communication, commerce and for cultural purposes; but they would never abandon their native language, the language of their ancestors, the language which enshrines all the memories of their past. They know that without it they would sink into an amorphous cosmopolitanism – without a past or a distinguishable future. To avoid such a fate, we of this generation must see to it that our language lives. That would be the resolve of the men and women of 1916. Will it not be the resolve of the young men and women of 1966?

‘Ask not what your country can do for you; ask what you can do for your country.’

John F. Kennedy

Inaugural address, Washington, 20 January 1961

‘Ich bin ein Berliner.’

Widely admired both at home and abroad, at 43 John F. Kennedy was the youngest man and the first Roman Catholic elected as US President. The eloquent speech he gave at his inauguration swept away many people's fears that he was too young and inexperienced for the job.

Born 29 May 1917 in Boston.
A glamorous figure, Kennedy was a war hero and Pulitzer Prize winner (for his biography *Profiles in Courage*, 1957). He entered the US Senate at the age of 25 and less than 20 years later was the youngest ever US President.
Kennedy was an admirer of fine oratory and refined and edited his **inaugural address** for two months before it was given. ***'Ich bin ein Berliner'***, given to an audience of Germans on either side of the newly-erected Berlin Wall, is credited as marking a turning point in the Cold War. The Berlin Wall finally came down in November 1989 and Germany was reunified the following year.
Assassinated 22 November 1963 in Dallas, Texas.

Kennedy's arrival in the White House on 20 January 1961 followed a narrow electoral victory over the Republican Richard Nixon, who had been Vice President for eight years. Kennedy promised tough defence policies but progressive health, housing and civil rights programmes and promoted his 'New Frontier' campaign to bring the nation out of economic slump. He participated in a series of TV debates with Nixon in which he appeared handsome and relaxed while Nixon looked tense and uneasy. Kennedy stressed the need for change to stop America's decline as a world power, which he claimed had occurred while Eisenhower was President. He also gained black support by helping to get Martin Luther King released from jail following his civil rights activities in Georgia.

Once in office as President, Kennedy appointed a cabinet of young able men, including some Republicans chosen on the basis of talent. He also appointed his brother Robert, whom he totally trusted, as Attorney General even though he was only 35. Together with his wife, Jacqueline, Kennedy revitalized the White House, encouraging intellectual and artistic activity.

It is hard to assess Kennedy's place in history as President because only 34 months after his election he was shot dead when in Dallas during his campaign for re-election in the 1964 presidential election. By then he had achieved political stature through his handling of the Cuban Missile Crisis in October 1962 and the signing of the nuclear test ban treaty with Russia in 1963. The American economy was greatly improving, civil rights laws were now on the agenda and the US space programme had begun. American involvement in Vietnam was becoming a major issue, which Kennedy referred to as 'the worst problem we've got'.

In the time since his death Kennedy has been widely discussed and seen either as a saintly hero or someone subject to considerable human weakness. Many people throughout the world were affected by his death because in life, Jack Kennedy's youth, good looks, energy and democratic aims had seemed to embody the optimism and sense of change that characterized the early 1960s.

Vice President Johnson, Mr Speaker, Mr Chief Justice, President Eisenhower, Vice President Nixon, President Truman, reverend clergy, fellow citizens: We observe today not a victory of party but a celebration of freedom, symbolizing an end as well as a beginning, signifying renewal as well as change. For I have sworn before you and Almighty God the same solemn oath our forebears prescribed nearly a century and three-quarters ago.

The world is very different now. For man holds in his mortal hands the power to abolish all forms of human poverty and all forms of human life. And yet the same revolutionary beliefs for which our forebears fought are still at issue around the globe – the belief that the rights of man come not from the generosity of the state but from the hand of God.

We dare not forget today that we are the heirs of that first revolution. Let the word go forth from this time and place, to friend and foe alike, that the torch has been passed to a new generation of Americans – born in this century, tempered by war, disciplined by a hard and bitter peace, proud of our ancient heritage – and unwilling to witness or permit the slow undoing of those human rights to which this nation has always been committed, and to which we are committed today at home and around the world.

Let every nation know, whether it wishes us well or ill, that we shall pay any price, bear any burden, meet any hardship, support any friend, oppose any foe to assure the survival and the success of liberty.

This much we pledge – and more.

To those old allies whose cultural and spiritual origins we share, we pledge the loyalty of faithful friends. United there is little we cannot do in a host of cooperative ventures. Divided there is little we can do, for we dare not meet a powerful challenge at odds and split asunder.

To those new states whom we welcome to the ranks of the free, we pledge our word that one form of colonial control shall not have passed away merely to be replaced by a far more iron tyranny. We shall not always expect to find them supporting our view. But we shall always hope to find them strongly supporting their own freedom – and to remember that, in the past, those who foolishly sought power by riding the back of the tiger ended up inside.

To those people in the huts and villages of half the globe struggling to break the bonds of mass misery, we pledge our best efforts to help them help themselves, for whatever period is required – not because the Communists may be doing it, not because we seek their votes, but because it is right.

If a free society cannot help the many who are poor, it cannot save the few who are rich.

‘The torch has been passed to a new generation of Americans.’

To our sister republics south of our border, we offer a special pledge: to convert our good words into good deeds, in a new alliance for progress, to assist free men and free governments in casting off the chains of poverty. But this peaceful revolution of hope cannot become the prey of hostile powers. Let all our neighbours know that we shall join with them to oppose aggression or subversion anywhere in the Americas.

And let every other power know that this hemisphere intends to remain the master of its own house.

To that world assembly of sovereign states, the United Nations, our last best hope in an age where the instruments of war have far outpaced the instruments of peace, we renew our pledge of support – to prevent it from becoming merely a forum for invective, to strengthen its shield of the new and the weak, and to enlarge the area in which its writ may run.

Finally, to those nations who would make themselves our adversary, we offer not a pledge but a request: that both sides begin anew the quest for peace – before the dark powers of destruction unleashed by science engulf all humanity in planned or accidental self-destruction.

We dare not tempt them with weakness. For only when our arms are sufficient beyond doubt can we be certain beyond doubt that they will never be employed.

But neither can two great and powerful groups of nations take comfort from our present course – both sides overburdened by the cost of modern weapons, both rightly alarmed by the steady spread of the deadly atom, yet both racing to alter that uncertain balance of terror that stays the hand of mankind's final war. So let us begin anew – remembering on both sides that civility is not a sign of weakness, and sincerity is always subject to proof.

'Let us never negotiate out of fear. But let us never fear to negotiate.'

Let us never negotiate out of fear. But let us never fear to negotiate.

Let both sides explore what problems unite us instead of belabouring those problems which divide us.

Let both sides, for the first time, formulate serious and precise proposals for the inspection and control of arms, and bring the absolute power to destroy other nations under the absolute control of all nations.

Let both sides seek to invoke the wonders of science instead of its terrors. Together let us explore the stars, conquer the deserts, eradicate disease, tap the ocean depths, and encourage the arts and commerce.

Let both sides unite to heed, in all corners of the earth, the command of Isaiah – to 'undo the heavy burdens ... and let the oppressed go free'.

And if a beachhead of cooperation may push back the jungle of suspicion, let both sides join in creating a new endeavour – not a new balance of power, but a new world of law – where the strong are just, and the weak secure, and the peace preserved.

All this will not be finished in the first one hundred days. Nor will it be finished in the first one thousand days; nor in the life of this Administration; nor even perhaps in our lifetime on this planet. But let us begin.

In your hands, my fellow citizens, more than mine, will rest the final success or failure of our course. Since this country was founded, each generation of Americans has been summoned to give testimony to its national loyalty. The graves of young Americans who answered the call to service surround the globe.

Now the trumpet summons us again – not as a call to bear arms, though arms we need – not as a call to battle, though embattled we are – but a call to bear the burden of a long twilight struggle, year in and year out, rejoicing in hope, patient in tribulation, a struggle against the common enemies of man: tyranny, poverty, disease and war itself.

Can we forge against these enemies a grand and global alliance, North and South, East and West, that can assure a more fruitful life for all mankind? Will you join in that historic effort?

In the long history of the world, only a few generations have been granted the role of defending freedom in its hour of maximum danger. I do not shrink from this responsibility – I welcome it. I do not believe that any of us would exchange places with any other people or any other generation. The energy, the faith, the devotion which we bring to this endeavour will light our country and all who serve it. And the glow from that fire can truly light the world.

‘Ask not what your country can do for you; ask what you can do for your country.’

And so, my fellow Americans, ask not what your country can do for you; ask what you can do for your country.

My fellow citizens of the world, ask not what America will do for you, but what together we can do for the freedom of man.

Finally, whether you are citizens of America or citizens of the world, ask of us here the same high standards of strength and sacrifice which we ask of you. With a good conscience our only sure reward, with history the final judge of our deeds, let us go forth to lead the land we love, asking His blessing and His help, but knowing that here on earth God's work must truly be our own.

When the Russians built the Berlin Wall in August 1961 to stem the flow of emigrants from East Berlin, Kennedy rejected advice to smash it down through force. On visiting West Berlin in 1963 he delivered a rousing speech (*'Ich bin ein Berliner'*, I am a Berliner) in which he cited the Wall as the 'most obvious and vivid demonstration of the failure of the Communist system' and 'an offence against humanity'. West Berliners loved the speech and Kennedy is widely remembered for it, but the problem of the Wall remained for another 26 years.

I am proud to come to this city as the guest of your distinguished Mayor, who has symbolized throughout the world the fighting spirit of West Berlin. And I am proud to visit the Federal Republic with your distinguished Chancellor who for so many years has committed Germany to democracy and freedom and progress, and to come here in the company of my fellow American, General Clay, who has been in this city during its great moments of crisis and will come again if ever needed.

Two thousand years ago, the proudest boast was '*civis Romanus sum*'. Today, in the world of freedom, the proudest boast is '*Ich bin ein Berliner*'.

I appreciate my interpreter translating my German.

There are many people in the world who really don't understand, or say they don't, what is the great issue between the free world and the Communist world.

Let them come to Berlin.

There are some who say that Communism is the wave of the future.

Let them come to Berlin.

And there are some who say, in Europe and elsewhere, we can work with the Communists.

Let them come to Berlin.

'Freedom is indivisible, and when one man is enslaved, all are not free.'

And there are even a few who say that it is true that Communism is an evil system, but it permits us to make economic progress.

Lass' sie nach Berlin kommen. Let them come to Berlin.

Freedom has many difficulties and democracy is not perfect. But we have never had to put a wall up to keep our people in – to prevent them from leaving us. I want to say on behalf of my countrymen who live many miles away on the other side of the Atlantic, who are far distant from you, that they take the greatest pride, that they have been able to share with you, even from a distance, the story of the last 18 years. I know of no town, no city, that has been besieged for 18 years that still lives with the vitality and the force, and the hope, and the determination of the city of West Berlin.

'All free men, wherever they may live, are citizens of Berlin.'

While the wall is the most obvious and vivid demonstration of the failures of the Communist system – for all the world to see – we take no satisfaction in it; for it is, as your Mayor has said, an offence not only against history but an offence against humanity, separating families, dividing husbands and wives and brothers and sisters, and dividing a people who wish to be joined together.

What is true of this city is true of Germany: real, lasting peace in Europe can never be assured as long as one German out of four is denied the elementary right of free men, and that is to make a free choice. In 18 years of peace and good faith, this generation of Germans has earned the right to be free, including the right to unite their families and their nation in lasting peace, with good will to all people.

You live in a defended island of freedom, but your life is part of the main. So let me ask you, as I close, to lift your eyes beyond the dangers of today, to the hopes of tomorrow, beyond the freedom merely of this city of Berlin, or your country of Germany, to the advance of freedom everywhere, beyond the wall to the day of peace with justice, beyond yourselves and ourselves to all mankind.

Freedom is indivisible, and when one man is enslaved, all are not free. When all are free, then we can look forward to that day when this city will be joined as one and this country and this great Continent of Europe in a peaceful and hopeful globe. When that day finally comes, as it will, the people of West Berlin can take sober satisfaction in the fact that they were in the front lines for almost two decades.

All free men, wherever they may live, are citizens of Berlin.

And, therefore, as a free man, I take pride in the words '*Ich bin ein Berliner*'.

'I have a dream.'

Martin Luther King, Jr

Lincoln Memorial, Washington DC, 28 August 1963

'I've seen the promised land.'

Memphis, Tennessee, 3 April 1968

Martin Luther King's famous speech 'I have a dream', was delivered to 250,000 civil rights supporters on the steps of the Lincoln Memorial in Washington, at the culmination of the 'March on Washington for Jobs and Freedom', in August 1963. The speech is credited with mobilizing supporters of desegregation and prompting the 1964 Civil Rights Act.

Born 15 January 1929 in Atlanta, Georgia. Martin Luther King Jr was an outstanding student and academic theologian, who was ordained as a Baptist minister at the age of 19 and awarded a PhD in systematic theology by the University of Boston in 1955 and the Nobel Peace Prize in 1964. King was a major figure in the US Civil Rights Movement. His speech **'I have a dream'** was delivered during a civil rights march on Washington DC in 1963. **'I've seen the promised land'**, King's final speech, was given the night before his death.
Assassinated 4 April 1968 in Memphis, Tennessee. Martin Luther King Day is observed every year in the United States on the third Monday in January.

Martin Luther King Jr was born in 1929 in Atlanta, Georgia to the Reverend and Mrs Martin Luther King. In 1947 he decided to follow his father and become a Baptist minister, delivering his first sermon in his father's church in the summer of that year. The following year he was ordained as a Baptist minister and received his BA degree in sociology from Moorhouse College.

The event that is credited with starting King on his civil rights crusade occurred in 1955. Rosa Parks, a black seamstress, took a seat in the section of a Montgomery bus reserved for whites. When the driver asked her to move to the back under the state's segregation law, she refused and was arrested. Shortly after this, King arrived in town and launched the Montgomery Bus Boycott. After deliberating for over a year, the Supreme Court ruled that Montgomery's segregation laws were unconstitutional and ordered the integration of the city's buses.

The Lincoln Memorial crowd, and the country, were already in ferment because of the issue of the bus ruling so King's speech was bound to stoke the fires of opposition further. Whether he understood this and had a sense of his place in history is something that later commentators would speculate about. What is clear is that his speech was timely, adding exactly the right note to the debate at the right time. Sadly, his blend of moral indignation and Christian values was soon to cost him his life.

Martin Luther King was awarded the Nobel Peace Prize on 14 October 1964 in recognition of his status as both a symbol of the civil rights movement and of America itself.

Five score years ago, a great American, in whose symbolic shadow we stand today, signed the Emancipation Proclamation. This momentous decree came as a great beacon light of hope to millions of Negro slaves, who had been seared in the flames of withering injustice. It came as a joyous daybreak to end the long night of their captivity.

But one hundred years later, the Negro still is not free. One hundred years later, the life of the Negro is still sadly crippled by the manacles of segregation and the chains of discrimination. One hundred years later, the Negro lives on a lonely island of poverty in the midst of a vast ocean of material prosperity. One hundred years later, the Negro is still languished in the corners of American society and finds himself an exile in his own land. And so we've come here today to dramatize a shameful condition.

'One hundred years later, the Negro still is not free.'

In a sense we have come to our nation's capital to cash a cheque. When the architects of our republic wrote the magnificent words of the Constitution and the Declaration of Independence, they were signing a promissory note to which every American was to fall heir. This note was a promise that all men, yes, black men as well as white men, would be guaranteed the unalienable rights of life, liberty, and the pursuit of happiness. It is obvious today that America has defaulted on this promissory note, insofar as her citizens of colour are concerned. Instead of honouring this sacred obligation, America has given the Negro people a bad cheque, a cheque which has come back marked 'insufficient funds'.

But we refuse to believe that the bank of justice is bankrupt. We refuse to believe that there are insufficient funds in the great vaults of opportunity of this nation. And so we have come to cash this cheque, a cheque that will give us upon demand the riches of freedom and the security of justice.

We have also come to this hallowed spot to remind America of the fierce urgency of Now. This is no time to engage in the luxury of cooling off or to take the tranquillizing drug of gradualism. Now is the time to make real the promises of democracy. Now is the time to rise from the dark and desolate valley of segregation to the sunlit path of racial justice. Now is the time to lift our nation from the quicksands of racial injustice to the solid rock of brotherhood. Now is the time to make justice a reality for all of God's children.

It would be fatal for the nation to overlook the urgency of the moment. This sweltering summer of the Negro's legitimate discontent will not pass until there is an invigorating autumn of freedom and equality. Nineteen sixty-three is not an end but a beginning. Those who hope that the Negro needed to blow off steam and will now be content will have a rude awakening if the nation returns to business as usual. There will be neither rest nor tranquillity in America until the Negro is granted his citizenship rights. The whirlwinds of revolt will continue to shake the foundations of our nation until the bright day of justice emerges.

But there is something that I must say to my people who stand on the warm threshold which leads into the palace of justice. In the process of gaining our rightful place we must not be guilty of wrongful deeds. Let us not seek to satisfy our thirst for freedom by drinking from the cup of bitterness and hatred. We must ever conduct our struggle on the high plane of dignity and discipline. We must not allow our creative protest to degenerate into physical violence. Again and again we must rise to the majestic heights of meeting physical force with soul force.

The marvellous new militancy which has engulfed the Negro community must not lead us to a distrust of all white people, for many of our white brothers, as evidenced by their presence here today, have come to realize that their destiny is tied up with our destiny. And they have come to realize that their freedom is inextricably bound to our freedom. We cannot walk alone.

And as we walk, we must make the pledge that we shall always march ahead. We cannot turn back. There are those who are asking the devotees of civil rights, 'When will you be satisfied?' We can never be satisfied as long as the Negro is the victim of the unspeakable horrors of police brutality. We can never be satisfied as long as our bodies, heavy with the fatigue of travel, cannot gain lodging in the motels of the highways and the hotels of the cities. We cannot be satisfied as long as a Negro in Mississippi cannot vote and a Negro in New York believes he has nothing for which to vote. No, no, we are not satisfied and we will not be satisfied until justice rolls down like waters and righteousness like a mighty stream.

I am not unmindful that some of you have come here out of great trials and tribulations. Some of you have come fresh from narrow jail cells. Some of you have come from areas where your quest for freedom left you battered by the storms of persecutions and staggered by the winds of police brutality. You have been the veterans of creative suffering. Continue to work with the faith that unearned suffering is redemptive. Go back to Mississippi, go back to Alabama, go back to South Carolina, go back to Georgia, go back to Louisiana, go back to the slums and ghettos of our northern cities, knowing that somehow this situation can and will be changed. Let us not wallow in the valley of despair, I say to you today, my friends. And so even though we face the difficulties of today and tomorrow, I still have a dream. It is a dream deeply rooted in the American dream.

'I have a dream today.'

I have a dream that one day this nation will rise up and live out the true meaning of its creed: We hold these truths to be self-evident that all men are created equal.

I have a dream that one day on the red hills of Georgia the sons of former slaves and the sons of former slave owners will be able to sit down together at the table of brotherhood.

I have a dream that one day even the state of Mississippi, a state sweltering with the heat of injustice, sweltering with the heat of oppression, will be transformed into an oasis of freedom and justice.

I have a dream that my four little children will one day live in a nation where they will not be judged by the colour of their skin but by the content of their character. I have a dream today!

I have a dream that one day, down in Alabama, with its vicious racists, with its governor having his lips dripping with the words of interposition and nullification; one day right down in Alabama little black boys and black girls will be able to join hands with little white boys and white girls as sisters and brothers. I have a dream today!

I have a dream that one day every valley shall be exalted, and every hill and mountain shall be made low, the rough places will be made plain, and the crooked places will be made straight, and the glory of the Lord shall be revealed and all flesh shall see it together.

This is our hope. This is the faith that I will go back to the South with. With this faith we will be able to hew out of the mountain of despair a stone of hope. With this faith we will be able to transform the jangling discords of our nation into a beautiful symphony of brotherhood. With this faith we will be able to work together, to pray together, to struggle together, to go to jail together, to stand up for freedom together, knowing that we will be free one day. And this will be the day, this will be the day when all of God's children will be able to sing with new meaning, 'My country 'tis of thee, sweet land of liberty, of thee I sing. Land where my fathers died, land of the Pilgrim's pride, from every mountainside, let freedom ring!' And if America is to be a great nation, this must become true.

'From every mountainside, let freedom ring!'

And so let freedom ring from the prodigious hilltops of New Hampshire.

Let freedom ring from the mighty mountains of New York.

Let freedom ring from the heightening Alleghenies of Pennsylvania.

Let freedom ring from the snow-capped Rockies of Colorado.

Let freedom ring from the curvaceous slopes of California.

But not only that. Let freedom ring from Stone Mountain of Georgia.

Let freedom ring from Lookout Mountain of Tennessee.

Let freedom ring from every hill and molehill of Mississippi, from every mountainside, let freedom ring!

And when this happens, when we allow freedom to ring, when we let it ring from every village and every hamlet, from every state and every city, we will be able to speed up that day when all of God's children, black men and white men, Jews and Gentiles, Protestants and Catholics, will be able to join hands and sing in the words of the old Negro spiritual, 'Free at last, free at last. Thank God Almighty, we are free at last.'

Four years later, on 4 April 1968, Martin Luther King, Jr was killed by a sniper's bullet while standing on the balcony of the Lorraine Motel in Memphis, Tennessee, where he was to lead a protest march in sympathy with striking garbage workers in the city. The day before, he had given a speech in which he recalled an earlier assassination attempt and mentioned threats that he had recently received. His prophetic speech ended on a note of serenity: 'I'm happy, tonight. I'm not worried about anything. I'm not fearing any man.'

You know, several years ago, I was in New York City autographing the first book that I had written. And while sitting there autographing books, a demented black woman came up. The only question I heard from her was, 'Are you Martin Luther King?'

And I was looking down writing, and I said yes. And the next minute I felt something beating on my chest. Before I knew it I had been stabbed by this demented woman. I was rushed to Harlem Hospital. It was a dark Saturday afternoon. And that blade had gone through, and the X-rays revealed that the tip of the blade was on the edge of my aorta, the main artery. And once that's punctured, you drown in your own blood – that's the end of you.

It came out in the New York Times the next morning, that if I had sneezed, I would have died. Well, about four days later, they allowed me, after the operation, after my chest had been opened, and the blade had been taken out, to move around in the wheel chair in the hospital. They allowed me to read some of the mail that came in, and from all over the states, and the world, kind letters came in. I read a few, but one of them I will never forget. I had received one from the President and the Vice President. I've forgotten what those telegrams said. I'd received a visit and a letter from the Governor of New York, but I've forgotten what the letter said. But there was another letter that came from a little girl, a young girl who was a student at the White Plains High School. And I looked at that letter, and I'll never forget it. It said simply, 'Dear Dr King: I am a ninth-grade student at the White Plains High School.' She said, 'While it should not matter, I would like to mention that I am a white girl. I read in the paper of your misfortune, and of your suffering. And I read that if you had sneezed, you would have died. And I'm simply writing you to say that I'm so happy that you didn't sneeze.'

> 'Whenever men and women straighten their backs up, they are going somewhere, because a man can't ride your back unless it is bent.'

And I want to say tonight, I want to say that I am happy that I didn't sneeze. Because if I had sneezed, I wouldn't have been around here in 1960, when students all over the South started sitting-in at lunch counters. And I knew that as they were sitting in, they were really standing up for the best in the American dream. And taking the whole nation back to those great wells of democracy which were dug deep by the Founding Fathers in the Declaration of Independence and the Constitution. If I had sneezed, I wouldn't have been around in 1962, when Negroes in Albany, Georgia, decided to straighten their backs up. And whenever men and women straighten their backs up, they are going somewhere, because a man can't ride your back unless it is bent. If I had sneezed, I wouldn't have been here in 1963, when the black people of Birmingham, Alabama, aroused the conscience of this nation, and brought into being the Civil Rights Bill. If I had sneezed, I wouldn't have had a chance later that year, in August, to try to tell America about a dream that I had had. If I had sneezed, I wouldn't have been down in Selma, Alabama, to see the great movement there. If I had sneezed, I wouldn't have been in Memphis to see a community rally around those brothers and sisters who are suffering. I'm so happy that I didn't sneeze.

‘I've been to the mountaintop. …And I've seen the promised land.’

And they were telling me, now it doesn't matter now. It really doesn't matter what happens now. I left Atlanta this morning, and as we got started on the plane, there were six of us, the pilot said over the public address system, 'We are sorry for the delay, but we have Dr Martin Luther King on the plane. And to be sure that all of the bags were checked, and to be sure that nothing would be wrong with the plane, we had to check out everything carefully. And we've had the plane protected and guarded all night.'

And then I got into Memphis. And some began to say that threats, or talk about the threats that were out. What would happen to me from some of our sick white brothers?

Well, I don't know what will happen now. We've got some difficult days ahead. But it doesn't matter with me now. Because I've been to the mountaintop. And I don't mind. Like anybody, I would like to live a long life. Longevity has its place. But I'm not concerned about that now. I just want to do God's will. And He's allowed me to go up to the mountain. And I've looked over. And I've seen the promised land. I may not get there with you. But I want you to know tonight, that we, as a people will get to the promised land. And I'm happy, tonight. I'm not worried about anything. I'm not fearing any man. Mine eyes have seen the glory of the coming of the Lord.

‘You can’t hate the roots of a tree, and not hate the tree.’

Malcolm X

Detroit, 14 February 1965

Malcolm X, the American black nationalist leader, gave inspiring and powerful speeches, full of strong imagery and cogent reasoning. A week after he delivered this speech Malcolm X was assassinated by a member of the Nation of Islam, a group in which he had been a leading figure. However, in 1964 Malcolm X had changed his position on how to achieve black goals and become a figure of hate for the Nation of Islam.

This change of heart was the last of many radical changes during Malcolm X's short but highly influential life. Born in Nebraska in 1925 as Malcolm Little, his father was a radical black Baptist minister. While Malcolm was quite young his family moved several times because of threats from Ku Klux Klansmen, who burned down the family home in Michigan and, when Malcolm was six, murdered his father.

Born 19 May 1925 in Omaha, Nebraska.
After the murder of his father and mental breakdown of his mother, Malcolm slid into a life of crime. His conversion to Islam in jail changed the direction of his life. Although he initially preached radical ideas of black supremacy, Malcolm X came to reject them towards the end of his life and became an orthodox Muslim. **'More African than American'** illustrates his later statement of belief.
Murdered 21 February 1965 in Harlem, New York.

Malcolm's mother became mentally ill and the family of eight children was split up. Malcolm left school at 15 and moved in with his sister in Boston where he gradually became involved in criminal activities. In 1946 he was jailed for drug-pushing and burglary. In prison he was drawn to the ascetic ideas of the Nation of Islam movement, led by Elijah Muhammad.

On his release in 1953 Malcolm Little joined the movement. He studied personally with Muhammad and by 1954 was leader of the mosque in Harlem. He changed his name to Malcolm X, symbolizing his new life as an 'ex-smoker, ex-drinker, ex-Christian, ex-slave'. During the ten years he spent promoting the Nation of Islam Malcolm X became their most powerful spokesperson. However, his extreme ideas frightened many whites and were out of keeping with the views of black civil rights leaders then advocating non-violent resistance. The Nation of Islam wanted black separatism, and taught that blacks should vigorously defend themselves in the face of white violence.

In 1964, Malcolm X visited Mecca. He converted to orthodox Islam and began to believe in the possibility of brotherhood between blacks and whites. On his return he founded the Organization of Afro–American unity and began holding meetings in Harlem to promote its policies. A week before he gave this speech his house was bombed by the Nation of Islam. He was preaching at his base at Harlem's Audubon Ballroom when he was assassinated.

... I am not a racist in any form whatsoever. I don't believe in any form of racism. I don't believe in any form of discrimination or segregation. I believe in Islam.

... Elijah Muhammad had taught us that the white man could not enter into Mecca in Arabia and all of us who followed him, we believed it ... When I got over there and went to Mecca and saw these people who were blond and blue-eyed and pale-skinned and all those things, I said 'Well,' but watched them closely. And I noticed that though they were white, and they would call themselves white, there was a difference between them and the white ones over here. And that basic difference was this: In Asia or the Arab world or in Africa, where the Muslims are, if you find one who says he's white, all he's doing is using an adjective to describe something that's incidental about him, one of his incidental characteristics; there is nothing else to it, he's just white.

But when you get the white man over here in America and he says he's white, he means something else. You can listen to the sound of his voice – when he says he's white, he means he's boss. That's right. That's what white means in this language. You know the expression 'free, white and twenty-one'. He made that up. He's letting you know that white means free, boss. He's up there, so that when he says he's white he has a little different sound in his voice. I know you know what I'm talking about ...

Despite the fact that I saw that Islam was a religious brotherhood, I also had to face reality. And when I got back into this American society, I'm not in a society that practises brotherhood. I'm in a society that might preach it on Sunday, but they don't practise it on any day. America is a society where there is no brotherhood. This society is controlled primarily by the racists and segregationists who are from Washington, DC, in positions of power.

... Now what effect does the struggle over Africa have on us? Why should the black man in America concern himself since he's been away from the African continent for three or four hundred years? Why should we concern ourselves? What impact does what happens to them have upon us? Number one, you have to realize that up until 1959 Africa was dominated by the colonial powers. Having complete control over Africa, the colonial powers of Europe projected the image of Africa negatively. They always project Africa in a negative light: jungle savages, cannibals, nothing civilized. Why then naturally it was so negative that it was negative to you and me, and you and I began to hate it. We didn't want anybody telling us anything about Africa, much less calling us Africans. In hating Africa and in hating the Africans, we ended up hating ourselves, without even realizing it. Because you can't hate the roots of a tree, and not hate the tree. You can't hate your origin and not end up hating yourself. You can't hate Africa and not hate yourself.

'Deep within the subconscious of the black man in this country, he is still more African than he is American.'

You show me one of these people over here who has been thoroughly brainwashed and has a negative attitude toward himself. You can't have a positive attitude toward yourself and a negative attitude toward Africa at the same time. To the same degree that your understanding of and attitude toward Africa become positive, you'll find your understanding of and your attitude toward yourself will also become positive. And this is what the white man knows. So they very skilfully make you and me hate our African identity, our African characteristics.

... One of the things that made the Black Muslim movement grow was its emphasis upon things African. This was the secret to the growth of the Black Muslim movement. African blood, African origin, African culture, African ties. And you'd be surprised – we discovered that deep within the subconscious of the black man in this country, he is still more African than he is American. He thinks that he's more American than African, because the man is jiving him, the man is brainwashing him every day.

... Just because you're in this country doesn't make you an American. No, you've got to go farther than that before you can become an American. You've got to enjoy the fruits of Americanism. You haven't enjoyed those fruits. You've enjoyed the thorns. You've enjoyed the thistles.

... I say again that I am not a racist. I don't believe in any form of segregation or anything like that. I'm for brotherhood for everybody, but I don't believe in forcing brotherhood upon people who don't want it. Let us practise brotherhood among ourselves, and then if others want to practise brotherhood with us, we're for practising it with them also. But I don't think that we should run around trying to love somebody who doesn't love us.

‘I have been far oftener discriminated against because I am a woman than because I am black.’

Shirley Chisholm

Speech to Congress, Washington, 21 May 1969

The oldest of four girls, Shirley Chisholm was born in November 1924, in Brooklyn, New York, into a poor family. Her parents were immigrants from the West Indies who worked as cleaners and factory workers. They sent their daughters to live with their maternal grandmother in Barbados, where they benefited from education in local British schools.

At the age of ten Chisholm returned to Brooklyn and continued to study. She majored in sociology at Brooklyn College and joined the debating society, learning techniques of oratory that would serve her well in her future career. She also became active in the National Association for the Advancement of Colored People (NAACP), in which she debated vigorously for minority rights.

Born 30 November 1924 in New York. After studying sociology and child education, Chisholm became Director of the Hamilton-Madison Child Care Center in New York before going into politics. In 1969 she became the first black Congresswoman (Democrat) and sponsored the **Equal Rights Amendment** through Congress. Shirley Chisholm competed unsuccessfully for nomination as the Democrat presidential candidate in 1972. She published two books, *Unbought and Unbossed* (1970) and *The Good Fight* (1973), and in 1993 she was inducted into the National Women's Hall of Fame. Died 1 January 2005 in Florida.

After college she took a master's degree in child education and taught at a nursery school in Harlem, before becoming director of the largest nursery school network in New York. In 1953 she was instrumental in a successful campaign to elect an eminent black lawyer to the municipal court.

In 1964 Chisholm won a seat in the New York State Assembly. She was very active, bringing in laws that provided funding for the education of disadvantaged youths, and unemployment insurance for those providing day-care and domestic duties.

As the first black Congresswoman she served on several committees, notably labour and education, and campaigned for increases in federal funding for day-care and a higher minimum wage. Her famous address to the House of Representatives in May 1969 articulates her passionate belief in improving the lot of the socially disadvantaged and highlights the unfair treatment of women. She proposed the Equal Rights Amendment, which would guarantee equal rights for all, regardless of colour or gender.

In 1972 Chisholm became the first African-American woman to seek nomination for the Presidency. Although unsuccessful, she continued to be politically active, especially speaking out for women's rights, and served on the Advisory Council of the National Organization for Women and on the National Political Congress of Black Women. She died on New Year's Day 2005.

Mr Speaker, when a young woman graduates from college and starts looking for a job, she is likely to have a frustrating and even demeaning experience ahead of her. If she walks into an office for an interview, the first question she will be asked is, 'Do you type?'

There is a calculated system of prejudice that lies unspoken behind that question. Why is it acceptable for women to be secretaries, librarians, and teachers, but totally unacceptable for them to be managers, administrators, doctors, lawyers and Members of Congress?

The unspoken assumption is that women are different. They do not have executive ability, orderly minds, stability, leadership skills and they are too emotional.

It has been observed before, that society for a long time discriminated against another minority, the blacks, on the same basis – that they were different and inferior. The happy little homemaker and the contented 'old darkey' on the plantation were both produced by prejudice.

As a black person, I am no stranger to race prejudice. But the truth is that in the political world I have been far oftener discriminated against because I am a woman than because I am black.

Prejudice against blacks is becoming unacceptable although it will take years to eliminate it. But it is doomed because, slowly, white America is beginning to admit that it exists. Prejudice against women is still acceptable. There is very little understanding yet of the immorality involved in double pay scales and the classification of most of the better jobs as 'for men only'.

'... I have been far oftener discriminated against because I am a woman than because I am black.'

More than half of the population of the United States is female. But women occupy only two per cent of the managerial positions. They have not even reached the level of tokenism yet. No women sit on the AFL–CIO council or Supreme Court. There have been only two women who have held Cabinet rank, and at present there are none. Only two women now hold ambassadorial rank in the diplomatic corps. In Congress, we are down to one Senator and ten Representatives.

Considering that there are about $3\frac{1}{2}$ million more women in the United States than men, this situation is outrageous.

... It is for this reason that I wish to introduce today a proposal that has been before every Congress for the last 40 years and that sooner or later must become part of the basic law of the land – the equal rights amendment.

'The unspoken assumption is that women are different.'

Let me note and try to refute two of the commonest arguments that are offered against this amendment. One is that women are already protected under the law and do not need legislation. Existing laws are not adequate to secure equal rights for women. Sufficient proof of this is the concentration of women in lower paying, menial, unrewarding jobs and their incredible scarcity in the upper level jobs. If women are already equal, why is it such an event whenever one happens to be elected to Congress?

It is obvious that discrimination exists. Women do not have the opportunities that men do. And women that do not conform to the system, who try to break with the accepted patterns, are stigmatized as 'odd' and 'unfeminine.' The fact is that a woman who aspires to be chairman of the board, or a Member of the House, does so for exactly the same reasons as any man. Basically, these are that she thinks she can do the job and she wants to try.

A second argument often heard against the equal rights amendment is that it would eliminate legislation that many States and the Federal Government have enacted giving special protection to women and that it would throw the marriage and divorce laws into chaos.

As for the marriage laws, they are due for a sweeping reform, and an excellent beginning would be to wipe the existing ones off the books. Regarding special protection for working women, I cannot understand why it should be needed. Women need no protection that men do not need. What we need are laws to protect working people, to guarantee them fair pay, safe working conditions, protection against sickness and layoffs, and provision for dignified, comfortable retirement. Men and women need these things equally. That one sex needs protection more than the other is a male supremacist myth as ridiculous and unworthy of respect as the white supremacist myths that society is trying to cure itself of at this time.

'Who are the kidnap victims?'

Pierre Trudeau

Pierre Trudeau gave this impassioned broadcast during a period that came to be known as the 'October crisis' – the effects of which are still felt in Canada today.

Pierre Elliott Trudeau was one of Canada's most popular leaders – bilingual, cultured, suave and stylish, he had wide appeal. However, he was often accused of arrogance and his occasional flippant remarks were infamous. Addressing agriculture students in 1979, he said: 'Farmers are professional complainers. When there is too much sun, they complain. When there is too much rain, they complain. A farmer is a complainer.'

Born 18 October 1919 in Montreal, Quebec. Trudeau was the youngest Canadian Prime Minister. In 1970 he faced his greatest challenge when the *Front de Libération du Québec* kidnapped a diplomat and a cabinet minister. Trudeau's **national broadcast during this 'October crisis'** was characteristically robust and the actions he took highly controversial.
Died 28 September 2000 in Montreal.

Trudeau was born in 1919 in Montreal, Quebec and studied at Montreal, Harvard and London before becoming a lawyer. From 1961 until 1965 he was Professor of Law at the University of Montreal. He then entered politics, becoming an MP in 1965.

In February 1968, as Minister of Justice, he introduced a Bill of Rights, aimed at guaranteeing the protection of language rights for French-speaking citizens throughout Canada. In April of the same year, he succeeded Lester Pearson as party leader.

In June 1968, under Trudeau's leadership, the Liberal Party was swept to power with 155 seats and the new Prime Minister began to introduce what he referred to as the 'Just Society', creating new departments to deal with urgent problems, including Environment, Science and Technology, Communications and Urban Affairs. His key aims were to meet the needs of society through innovation, and also to strengthen the sense of national unity.

Despite his Quebec origins, Trudeau was a firm opponent of nationalism and had no sympathies for those promoting secession for Quebec, a conflict that was to come to a head during his time in office in the 'October crisis' of 1970. At the height of this struggle he took charge of a hostage incident when Quebec Nationalists captured a British diplomat and a Quebecois minister. Trudeau's response was to invoke the War Measures Act and suspend civil liberties. In his famous speech at this time he took a very firm line, refusing to bow to the demands of the kidnappers, who eventually released their British captive, although the minister was murdered.

Trudeau's death on 28 September 2000 was followed by a general state of mourning for a genuinely popular leader who inspired respect and a sense of national pride in the majority of Canadians.

I am speaking to you at a moment of grave crisis, when violent and fanatical men are attempting to destroy the unity and the freedom of Canada. One aspect of that crisis is the threat which has been made on the lives of two innocent men. These are matters of the utmost gravity and I want to tell you what the Government is doing to deal with them.

What has taken place in Montreal in the past two weeks is not unprecedented. It has happened elsewhere in the world on several recent occasions; it could happen elsewhere within Canada. But Canadians have always assumed that it could not happen here and as a result we are doubly shocked that it has.

Our assumption may have been naive, but it was understandable; understandable because democracy flourishes in Canada; understandable because individual liberty is cherished in Canada.

Notwithstanding these conditions – partly because of them – it has now been demonstrated to us by a few misguided persons just how fragile a democratic society can be, if democracy is not prepared to defend itself, and just how vulnerable to blackmail are tolerant, compassionate people.

‘Democracy flourishes in Canada; ... individual liberty is cherished in Canada.’

The governments of Canada and Quebec have been told by groups of self-styled revolutionaries that they intend to murder in cold blood two innocent men unless their demands are met. The kidnappers claim they act as they do in order to draw attention to instances of social injustice. But I ask them whose attention are they seeking to attract. The Government of Canada? The Government of Quebec? Every government in this country is well aware of the existence of deep and important social problems. And every government to the limit of its resources and ability is deeply committed to their solution. But not by kidnappings and bombings. By hard work. And if any doubt exists about the good faith or the ability of any government, there are opposition parties ready and willing to be given an opportunity to govern. In short there is available everywhere in Canada an effective mechanism to change governments by peaceful means. It has been employed by disenchanted voters again and again.

Who are the kidnap victims? To the victims' families they are husbands and fathers. To the kidnappers their identity is immaterial. The kidnappers' purposes would be served equally well by having in their grip you or me, or perhaps some child. Their purpose is to exploit the normal, human feelings of Canadians and to bend those feelings of sympathy into instruments for their own violent and revolutionary ends.

'Freedom and personal security are safeguarded by laws; those laws must be respected.'

What are the kidnappers demanding in return for the lives of these men? Several things. For one, they want their grievances aired by force in public on the assumption, no doubt, that all right-thinking persons would be persuaded that the problems of the world can be solved by shouting slogans and insults.

They want more, they want the police to offer up as a sacrificial lamb a person whom they assume assisted in the lawful arrest and proper conviction of certain of their criminal friends.

They also want money. Ransom money.

They want still more. They demand the release from prison of 17 criminals, and the dropping of charges against six other men, all of whom they refer to as 'political prisoners'. Who are these men who are held out as latter-day patriots and martyrs? Let me describe them to you.

Three are convicted murderers; five others were jailed for manslaughter; one is serving a life imprisonment after having pleaded guilty to numerous charges related to bombings; another has been convicted of 17 armed robberies; two were once paroled but are now back in jail awaiting trial on charges of robberies.

Yet we are being asked to believe that these persons have been unjustly dealt with, that they have been imprisoned as a result of their political opinions, and that they deserve to be freed immediately, without recourse to due process of law.

The responsibility of deciding whether to release one or other of these criminals is that of the Federal Government. It is a responsibility that the Government will discharge according to law. To bow to the pressures of these kidnappers who demand that the prisoners be released would be not only an abdication of responsibility, it would lead to an increase in terrorist activities in Quebec. It would be as well an invitation to terrorism and kidnapping across the country. We might well find ourselves facing an endless series of demands for the release of criminals from jails, from coast to coast, and we would find that the hostages could be innocent members of your family or mine.

At the moment the FLQ is holding hostage two men in the Montreal area, one a British diplomat, the other a Quebec cabinet minister. They are threatened with murder. Should governments give in to this crude blackmail we would be facing the breakdown of the legal system, and its replacement by the law of the jungle. The Government's decision to prevent this from happening is not taken just to defend an important principle, it is taken to protect the lives of Canadians from dangers of the sort I have mentioned. Freedom and personal security are safeguarded by laws; those laws must be respected in order to be effective.

‘The criminal law as it stands is simply not adequate to deal with systematic terrorism.’

If it is the responsibility of Government to deny the demands of the kidnappers, the safety of the hostages is without question the responsibility of the kidnappers. Only the most twisted form of logic could conclude otherwise. Nothing that either the Government of Canada or the Government of Quebec has done or failed to do, now or in the future, could possibly excuse any injury to either of these two innocent men. The guns pointed at their heads have FLQ fingers on the triggers. Should any injury result, there is no explanation that could condone the acts. Should there be harm done to these men, the Government promises unceasing pursuit of those responsible.

During the past 12 days, the Governments of Canada and Quebec have been engaged in constant consultations. The course followed in this matter had the full support of both governments, and of the Montreal municipal authorities. In order to save the lives of Mr Cross and Mr Laporte, we have engaged in communications with the kidnappers.

... If a democratic society is to continue to exist, it must be able to root out the cancer of an armed, revolutionary movement that is bent on destroying the very basis of our freedom. For that reason the Government, following an analysis of the facts, including requests of the Government of Quebec and the City of

Montreal for urgent action, decided to proclaim the War Measures Act. It did so at 4.00 am this morning, in order to permit the full weight of Government to be brought quickly to bear on all those persons advocating or practising violence as a means of achieving political ends.

The War Measures Act gives sweeping powers to the Government. It also suspends the operation of the Canadian Bill of Rights. I can assure you that the Government is most reluctant to seek such powers, and did so only when it became crystal clear that the situation could not be controlled unless some extraordinary assistance was made available on an urgent basis.

The authority contained in the Act will permit Governments to deal effectively with the nebulous yet dangerous challenge to society represented by the terrorist organizations. The criminal law as it stands is simply not adequate to deal with systematic terrorism.

The police have therefore been given certain extraordinary powers necessary for the effective detection and elimination of conspiratorial organizations which advocate the use of violence. These organizations, and membership in them, have been declared illegal. The powers include the right to search and arrest without warrant, to detain suspected persons without the necessity of laying specific charges immediately, and to detain persons without bail.

These are strong powers and I find them as distasteful as I am sure do you. They are necessary, however, to permit the police to deal with persons who advocate or promote the violent overthow of our democratic system. In short, I assure you that the Government recognizes its grave responsibilities in interfering in certain cases with civil liberties, and that it remains answerable to the people of Canada for its actions. The Government will revoke this proclamation as soon as possible.

As I said in the House of Commons this morning, the government will allow sufficient time to pass to give it the necessary experience to assess the type of statute which may be required in the present circumstances.

It is my firm intention to discuss then with the leaders of the Opposition parties the desirability of introducing legislation of a less comprehensive nature. In this respect I earnestly solicit from the leaders and from all Honourable members constructive suggestions for the amendment of the regulations. Such suggestions will be given careful consideration for possible inclusion in any new statute.

'Stop the killing.'

Golda Meir

Address to the Knesset, Jerusalem, 26 May 1970

Golda Mabovitz was born in Kiev, Ukraine in 1898. Her parents emigrated with their family to the United States in 1906 where she attended school and teacher training college in Milwaukee. She joined the Labour Zionist Party in 1915, an early indication of her political interest.

Born 3 May 1898 in Kiev, Ukraine.
After a childhood in the US, Golda Meir and her husband emigrated to Palestine where she became a member of the Israeli government in 1948 and, in 1969, Prime Minister. Meir's **address to the Knesset** warned of the dangers of increased Soviet influence in the Middle East: it was given less than two years after the Soviet invasion of Czechoslovakia, when the world was nervous about the spread of Communism. In the event, the USSR was keen to improve relations with the US and refused to supply Egypt with additional weapons and military support. In 1973 President Sadat, Nasser's successor, expelled 20,000 Soviet advisers from Egypt.
Died 8 December 1978 in Jerusalem.

In 1917 she married Morris Myerson and later changed her married name to Meir. As a qualified teacher she taught in local schools for several years, but in 1921 she and Morris went to live in Palestine, joining a kibbutz where they helped with farm work, before moving to Tel Aviv where Golda Meir worked as a treasurer in the Office of Public Works of the Histadruth (Trades Union Federation).

From 1928, as secretary of the Working Women's Council in Palestine, she became its representative on the executive of the Histadruth. From the following year she acted as a delegate to congresses of the World Zionist Organization and became increasingly involved with politics as a member of the executive of the Jewish National Council in Palestine.

In 1948 Golda Meir was appointed a member of the Provisional Government and became Israel's Ambassador to the Soviet Union. She joined the Knesset in 1949, serving as Minister of Labour and National Insurance until 1956, when she became Foreign Minister, a post she held for ten years. In this period, she came to international prominence, continuing a close relationship with the United States, and also forging links with South America and the newly independent countries of Africa.

This was a difficult period for the young state of Israel. It featured armed struggles with nearby Arab countries, including the Six-Day War in June 1967 when Israel attacked Egypt, Syria and Jordan, gaining much territory, including East Jerusalem, the West Bank, Sinai and the Golan Heights, and causing simmering Arab resentment.

Golda Meir finally become Prime Minister in March 1969, at the age of 71. In a famous address to the Knesset in May the following year, she offered to extend the hand of peace to Israel's Arab neighbours but also voiced her fears about their aggressive intentions, warning in particular of Egypt's military relationship with the Soviet Union.

Sadly, her worst fears were to come true with the outbreak of the Yom Kippur War on 6 October 1973, when Egypt and Syria combined forces against Israel. Meir and her Labour Party won the election of December 1973 but in 1974 she resigned, in the aftermath of the war.

... In recent months, and in the past weeks especially, the security situation has worsened seriously on the southern front in particular, and the harmful effect of that is felt on the other fronts also.

The main feature of this escalation and tension is an advanced and dangerous stage of Soviet involvement in Egypt, at the beck and call of Egyptian aggression and infractions of the ceasefire. There is no precedent for this involvement in the history of Soviet penetration into the Middle East, and it is encouraging Egypt in its plan to renew the war of attrition and so move further along the path of its vaulting ambition to vanquish Israel. ...

The Israel Defence Forces have punished this vainglorious aggression. I shall not retell the tale of their courage and resource: the digging in, the daring operations of the Air Force, the power of the armour. Aggression has been repelled, the enemy's timetable upset and the pressure on our front line eased by our striking at vital enemy military targets along the Canal and far behind it and confounding his plans for all-out war. True, to our great sorrow, we have suffered losses in killed and wounded, but our vigorous self-defence has thwarted Egypt's scheming and stultified its endeavours to wear us down and shake our southern front.

'No small nation, no minor nation, can any longer dwell in safety within its frontiers.'

Thus bankrupt, the Cairo regime had only the choice between accepting Israel's constant call to return to reciprocal observance of the ceasefire, as a stepping-stone to peace, or leaning more heavily still on the Soviet Union to the point of asking it to become operationally involved, so that Egypt might carry on the war of attrition, notwithstanding the unpleasant repercussions of that involvement.

Egypt chose the second course.

... We have informed Governments of the ominous significance of this new phase in Soviet involvement. We have explained that a situation has developed which ought to perturb not only Israel, but every state in the free world. The lesson of Czechoslovakia must not be forgotten. If the free world – and particularly the United States, its leader – can pass on to the next item on its agenda without any effort to deter the Soviet Union from selfishly involving itself so largely in a quarrel with which it has no concern, then it is not Israel alone that is imperilled, but no small nation, no minor nation, can any longer dwell in safety within its frontiers.

'The aspiration to peace is ... the cornerstone of our pioneering life and labour.'

... Three years after the Six-Day War, we can affirm that two fundamental principles have become a permanent part of the international consciousness: Israel's right to stand fast on the ceasefire lines, not budging until the conclusion of peace that will fix secure and recognized boundaries; and its right to self-defence and to acquire the equipment essential to defence and deterrence.

... The aspiration to peace is not only the central plank in our platform, it is the cornerstone of our pioneering life and labour. Ever since renewal of independence, we have based all our undertakings of settlement and creativity on the fundamental credo that we did not come to dispossess the Arabs of the land but to work together with them in peace and prosperity, for the good of all.

... We have not wearied of reiterating, day in, day out, our preparedness for peace: we have not abandoned hopes of finding a way into the hearts of our neighbours, though they yet dismiss our appeals with open animosity.

Today again, as the guns thunder, I address myself to our neighbours: Stop the killing, end the fire and bloodshed which bring tribulation and torment to all the peoples of the region! End rejection of the ceasefire, end bombardment and raids, end terror and sabotage!

To attain peace, I am ready to go at any hour to any place, to meet any authorized leader of any Arab state – to conduct negotiations with mutual respect, in parity and without pre-conditions, and with a clear recognition that the problems under controversy can be solved. For there is room to fulfil the national aspirations of all the Arab states and of Israel as well in the Middle East, and progress, development and cooperation can be hastened among all its nations, in place of barren bloodshed and war without end.

‘There can be no whitewash at the White House.’

Richard M. Nixon

Address to the nation, 30 April 1973

Richard Milhous Nixon was born into a Quaker family in Yorba Linda, California. He studied at Whittier College and at Duke University Law School, where he excelled, going on to practise law in Whittier. During World War II, he enlisted in the US Navy, serving in the Pacific as a Lieutenant Commander.

After the war Nixon entered politics, winning a seat as a Republican in the House of Representatives and playing a prominent role as a member of the House Committee on Un-American Activities. From 1951–53 he served on the US Senate.

In 1952 President Eisenhower chose Nixon as his Vice-President. In 1960, Nixon himself received the Republican nomination for President but lost the election by a narrow margin to John F. Kennedy. Nixon finally triumphed and became President in 1969. In his 1972 run for a second term in the White House, Nixon defeated the Democrat candidate George McGovern by one of the widest margins recorded.

Born 9 January 1913 in California..
Nixon is the only person to have served two terms as both Vice-President and President. His second term as President was overshadowed by the Watergate scandal. In his **address to the nation** in April 1973, he denied any involvement while accepting responsibility for dealing with the crisis. Despite the disgrace of Watergate, Nixon's reputation as an expert in foreign policy was acknowledged by later Presidents, who regularly consulted him.
Died 22 April 1994 in Yorba Linda, California.

During his presidency, Nixon undertook a quest for global stability. In 1972 he visited Moscow and Beijing and succeeded in reducing tensions with both the Soviet Union and China. With the USSR Premier Leonid Brezhnev, he drew up a treaty aimed at limiting strategic nuclear weapons. In 1973 Nixon arrived at an accord with North Vietnam that ended America's long and bloody involvement in the Indochina conflict. Henry Kissinger, his Secretary of State, was a tireless ambassador who successfully brokered disengagement agreements between Israel, Egypt and Syria.

But despite his achievements, Nixon is chiefly remembered for the greatest scandal to implicate a US President – the Watergate affair. During the 1972 presidential campaign there was a break-in at the offices of the Democratic National Committee. It was revealed that the perpetrators had been commissioned by high-ranking Republican officials. Despite his public declaration that there could be 'no whitewash at the White House', Nixon's attempt to cover up the full facts of the Watergate affair was exposed. Facing impeachment, he resigned in August 1974.

Good evening.

I want to talk to you tonight from my heart on a subject of deep concern to every American.

In recent months, members of my Administration and officials of the Committee for the Re-Election of the President – including some of my closest friends and most trusted aides – have been charged with involvement in what has come to be known as the Watergate affair. These include charges of illegal activity during and preceding the 1972 presidential election and charges that responsible officials participated in efforts to cover up that illegal activity.

The inevitable result of these charges has been to raise serious questions about the integrity of the White House itself. Tonight I wish to address those questions.

Last June 17, while I was in Florida trying to get a few days rest after my visit to Moscow, I first learned from news reports of the Watergate break-in. I was appalled at this senseless, illegal action, and I was shocked to learn that employees of the Re-Election Committee were apparently among those guilty. I immediately ordered an investigation by appropriate Government authorities. On September 15, as you will recall, indictments were brought against seven defendants in the case.

As the investigations went forward, I repeatedly asked those conducting the investigation whether there was any reason to believe that members of my Administration were in any way involved. I received repeated assurances that there were not. Because of these continuing reassurances, because I believed the reports I was getting, because I had faith in the persons from whom I was getting them, I discounted the stories in the press that appeared to implicate members of my Administration or other officials of the campaign committee.

‘The truth should be fully brought out – no matter who was involved.’

Until March of this year, I remained convinced that the denials were true and that the charges of involvement by members of the White House Staff were false. The comments I made during this period, and the comments made by my Press Secretary on my behalf, were based on the information provided to us at the time we made those comments. However, new information then came to me which persuaded me that there was a real possibility that some of these charges were true, and suggesting further that there had been an effort to conceal the facts both from the public, from you, and from me.

As a result, on March 21, I personally assumed the responsibility for coordinating intensive new inquiries into the matter, and I personally ordered those conducting the investigations to get all the facts and to report them directly to me, right here in this office.

‘Justice will be pursued fairly, fully and impartially.’

I again ordered that all persons in the Government or at the Re-Election Committee should cooperate fully with the FBI, the prosecutors and the grand jury. I also ordered that anyone who refused to cooperate in telling the truth would be asked to resign from Government service. And, with ground rules adopted that would preserve the basic constitutional separation of powers between the Congress and the Presidency, I directed that members of the White House Staff should appear and testify voluntarily under oath before the Senate committee which was investigating Watergate.

I was determined that we should get to the bottom of the matter, and that the truth should be fully brought out – no matter who was involved.

At the same time, I was determined not to take precipitate action and to avoid, if at all possible, any action that would appear to reflect on innocent people. I wanted to be fair. But I knew that in the final analysis, the integrity of this office – public faith in the integrity of this office – would have to take priority over all personal considerations.

Today, in one of the most difficult decisions of my Presidency, I accepted the resignations of two of my closest associates in the White House – Bob Haldeman, John Ehrlichman – two of the finest public servants it has been my privilege to know.

I want to stress that in accepting these resignations, I mean to leave no implication whatever of personal wrongdoing on their part, and I leave no implication tonight of implication on the part of others who have been charged in this matter. But in matters as sensitive as guarding the integrity of our democratic process, it is essential not only that rigorous legal and ethical standards be observed but also that the public, you, have total confidence that they are both being observed and enforced by those in authority and particularly by the President of the United States. They agreed with me that this move was necessary in order to restore that confidence.

'This office is a sacred trust and I am determined to be worthy of that trust.'

... Whatever may appear to have been the case before, whatever improper activities may yet be discovered in connection with this whole sordid affair, I want the American people, I want you to know beyond the shadow of a doubt that during my term as President, justice will be pursued fairly, fully and impartially, no matter who is involved. This office is a sacred trust and I am determined to be worthy of that trust.

In any organization, the man at the top must bear the responsibility. That responsibility, therefore, belongs here, in this office. I accept it. And I pledge to you tonight, from this office, that I will do everything in my power to ensure that the guilty are brought to justice and that such abuses are purged from our political processes in the years to come, long after I have left this office.

... Since March, when I first learned that the Watergate affair might in fact be far more serious than I had been led to believe, it has claimed far too much of my time and my attention. Whatever may now transpire in the case, whatever the actions of the grand jury, whatever the outcome of any eventual trials, I must now turn my full attention – and I shall do so – once again to the larger duties of this office. I owe it to this great office that I hold, and I owe it to you – to my country. ... There is vital work to be done toward our goal of a lasting structure of peace in the world – work that cannot wait, work that I must do. ...

There is also vital work to be done right here in America: to ensure prosperity, and that means a good job for everyone who wants to work; to control inflation, that I know worries every housewife, everyone who tries to balance a family budget in America; to set in motion new and better ways of ensuring progress toward a better life for all Americans.

When I think of this office – of what it means – I think of all the things that I want to accomplish for this Nation, of all the things I want to accomplish for you.

On Christmas Eve, during my terrible personal ordeal of the renewed bombing of North Vietnam, which after 12 years of war finally helped to bring America peace with honour, I sat down just before midnight. I wrote out some of my goals for my second term as President. Let me read them to you:

To make it possible for our children, and for our children's children, to live in a world of peace.

To make this country be more than ever a land of opportunity – of equal opportunity, full opportunity for every American.

To provide jobs for all who can work, and generous help for those who cannot work.

To establish a climate of decency and civility, in which each person respects the feelings and the dignity and the God-given rights of his neighbour.

To make this a land in which each person can dare to dream, can live his dreams – not in fear, but in hope – proud of his community, proud of his country, proud of what America has meant to himself and to the world.

'There is vital work to be done ... work that cannot wait, work that I must do.'

These are great goals. I believe we can, we must work for them. We can achieve them. But we cannot achieve these goals unless we dedicate ourselves to another goal.

We must maintain the integrity of the White House, and that integrity must be real, not transparent. There can be no whitewash at the White House.

‘Women’s education is almost more important than the education of boys and men.’

Indira Gandhi

New Delhi, India, 23 November 1974

Indira Gandhi was the only child of Kamala and Jawaharlal Nehru. She received a good education, first at Visva-Bharati University in Bengal and then at Oxford. Politics was in her blood and on returning to India she joined the National Congress Party, which was at the forefront of the struggle for independence.

An accomplished politician, Indira Gandhi rose in the party and was elected President in 1959. After the death of Nehru in 1964, Bahadur Shastri became Prime Minister and appointed her as Minister of Information. But Shastri died only two years later and at this point Gandhi became Prime Minister, suddenly finding herself running the world's largest democracy.

She was re-elected narrowly in 1967, and decisively in 1971. In the same year she gave India's military support to what was then East Pakistan (East Bengal), leading to the creation of the independent state of Bangladesh. In 1972 she led the Congress Party to a landslide victory. However, this was followed by a difficult period in which she was accused of violating election laws and faced being barred from politics. In response she declared a state of emergency and imprisoned her opponents.

Born 19 November 1917 in Allahabad.
The daughter of one Indian Prime Minister and the mother of another, Indira Gandhi was India's first female leader. Nationalization of India's banks, a programme for self-sufficiency and environmental policies contributed to her popularity. Initially nicknamed *goongi gudiya* ('dumb doll'), opinion was swiftly revised as she proved herself one of India's strongest leaders. Indira Gandhi strove to increase the participation of women in politics and society, as her **speech at Indraprastha College for Women** illustrates.
Assassinated 31 October 1984 in New Delhi.

Although inspired by the teachings of her pacifist namesake, Indira Gandhi did not shrink from extreme measures. On 6 June 1984 she sent the army to quell a Sikh occupation of the Golden Temple at Amritsar, an action that resulted in more than 1,000 deaths and simmering Sikh resentment.

Her political career was to end in tragedy. In October 1984 she was assassinated by two of her Sikh bodyguards, an eventuality she had previously considered: 'If I die a violent death as some fear and a few are plotting, I know the violence will be in the thought and the action of the assassin, not in my dying'. A similar fate awaited her son and successor Rajiv in 1991.

An ancient Sanskrit saying says, woman is the home and the home is the basis of society. It is as we build our homes that we can build our country. If the home is inadequate – either inadequate in material goods and necessities or inadequate in the sort of friendly, loving atmosphere that every child needs to grow and develop – then that country cannot have harmony and no country which does not have harmony can grow in any direction at all.

That is why women's education is almost more important than the education of boys and men. We – and by 'we' I do not mean only we in India but all the world – have neglected women's education. It is fairly recent. Of course, not to you but when I was a child, the story of early days of women's education in England, for instance, was very current. Everybody remembered what had happened in the early days.

'All that is modern is not good just as all that is old is neither all good nor all bad.'

... Now, we have got education and there is a debate all over the country whether this education is adequate to the needs of society or the needs of our young people. I am one of those who always believe that education needs a thorough overhauling. But at the same time, I think that everything in our education is not bad, that even the present education has produced very fine men and women, specially scientists and experts in different fields, who are in great demand all over the world and even in the most affluent countries. Many of our young people leave us and go abroad because they get higher salaries, they get better conditions of work.

... One of the biggest responsibilities of the educated women today is how to synthesize what has been valuable and timeless in our ancient traditions with what is good and valuable in modern thought. All that is modern is not good just as all that is old is neither all good nor all bad. We have to decide, not once and for all but almost every week, every month what is coming out that is good and useful to our country and what of the old we can keep and enshrine in our society. To be modern, most people think that it is something of a manner of dress or a manner of speaking or certain habits and customs, but that is not really being modern. It is a very superficial part of modernity.

... Now, for India to become what we want it to become with a modern, rational society and firmly based on what is good in our ancient tradition and in our soil, for this we have to have a thinking public, thinking young women who are not content to accept what comes from any part of the world but are willing to listen to it, to analyze it and to decide whether it is to be accepted or whether it is to be thrown out and this is the sort of education which we want, which enables our young people to adjust to this changing world and to be able to contribute to it.

Some people think that only by taking up very high jobs, you are doing something important or you are doing national service. But we all know that the most complex machinery will be ineffective if one small screw is not working as it should and that screw is just as important as any big part. It is the same in national life. There is no job that is too small; there is no person who is too small. Everybody has something to do. And if he or she does it well, then the country will run well.

In our superstition, we have thought that some work is dirty work. For instance, sweeping has been regarded as dirty. Only some people can do it; others should not do it. Now we find that manure is the most valuable thing that the world has today and many of the world's economies are shaking because there is not enough fertilizer – and not just the chemical fertilizer but the ordinary manure, night-soil and all that sort of thing, things which were considered dirty.

Now it shows how beautifully balanced the world was with everything fitted in with something else. Everything, whether dirty or small, had a purpose.

'There is no job that is too small; there is no person who is too small.'

... So, I hope that all of you who have this great advantage of education will not only do whatever work you are doing keeping the national interests in view, but you will make your own contribution to creating peace and harmony, to bringing beauty in the lives of our people and our country. I think this is the special responsibility of the women of India. We want to do a great deal for our country, but we have never regarded India as isolated from the rest of the world. What we want to do is to make a better world. So, we have to see India's problems in the perspective of the larger world problems.

‘Hate, ignorance and evil.’

Chaim Herzog

Address to UN General Assembly, 10 November 1975

Destined to become Israel's sixth President, Chaim Herzog was born in Belfast, Northern Ireland, in 1918, the son of the Chief Rabbi of Ireland. The family lived in Belfast and Dublin and in 1935 moved to Palestine where Yitzhak Herzog became Chief Rabbi in 1937.

In Palestine Chaim served in the *Haganah*, the Jewish underground, during the Arab Revolt of 1936–38. He then continued his studies at the Government of Palestine Law School in Jerusalem, then Cambridge and London, taking a degree in Law.

At the outbreak of World War II Herzog joined the British Army, serving as a tank commander. He was later involved with intelligence, directing operations in Germany, and becoming head of intelligence in the north of the country. One of his notable achievements was to identify a captured German soldier as the top Nazi Heinrich Himmler. He was also involved in the liberation of a number of concentration camps, from which he gained first-hand knowledge of the horrors of the Holocaust.

Born 17 September 1918 in Belfast, Ireland. **'Hate, ignorance and evil'** was given early in Herzog's term as Israeli ambassador to the UN, when he denounced an infamous resolution seeking to equate Zionism with racism. Chaim Herzog was a noted military historian, publishing several books on modern conflicts in the Middle East. Best remembered in Ireland for many years as a champion bantam-weight boxer, Herzog revisited his Irish roots, returning to Belfast and Dublin before his death.
Died 17 April 1997 in Tel Aviv, Israel.

As soon as the war ended, Herzog returned to Palestine and began working for the formation of a separate Jewish state, subsequently created in the UN Partition Plan of 1947. He saw military action again as an officer during the 1948 Arab–Israeli War.

From 1948 until 1950, and later from 1959 to 1962, Herzog was head of the Military Intelligence Branch of the Israeli Defence Force (IDF), and between 1950–54 he was Israeli Defence Attaché at the US Israeli Embassy. During the Six-Day War in 1967 he was a military commentator broadcasting on the radio and after Israel had captured the West Bank he became the first Military Governor of that territory.

From 1975 until 1978 he was Israel's Ambassador to the United Nations. However, it was not until 1981 that Chaim Herzog entered the Knesset as a representative of the Labour Party. In 1983 he was elected the sixth President of Israel, serving two consecutive five-year terms.

His experiences of Nazi atrocities in Europe, and the struggles of the fledgling Jewish homeland during the early years of the State of Israel, help to explain the anger apparent in his 1975 address to the United Nations.

Mr President.

It is symbolic that this debate, which may well prove to be a turning point in the fortunes of the United Nations and a decisive factor in the possible continued existence of this organization, should take place on November 10. Tonight, thirty-seven years ago, has gone down in history as *Kristallnacht*, the Night of the Crystals. This was the night in 1938 when Hitler's Nazi stormtroopers launched a coordinated attack on the Jewish community in Germany, burned the synagogues in all its cities and made bonfires in the streets of the Holy Books and the Scrolls of the Holy Law and Bible. It was the night when Jewish homes were attacked and heads of families taken away, many of them never to return. It was the night when the windows of all Jewish businesses and stores were smashed, covering the streets in the cities of Germany with a film of broken glass which dissolved into the millions of crystals which gave that night its name. It was the night which led eventually to the crematoria and the gas chambers, Auschwitz, Birkenau, Dachau, Buchenwald, Theresienstadt and others. It was the night which led to the most terrifying holocaust in the history of man.

... I do not come to this rostrum to defend the moral and historical values of the Jewish people. They do not need to be defended. They speak for themselves. They have given to mankind much of what is great and eternal. They have done for the spirit of man more than can readily be appreciated by a forum such as this one.

‘I come here to denounce the two great evils which menace society in general and a society of nations in particular. These two evils are hatred and ignorance.’

I come here to denounce the two great evils which menace society in general and a society of nations in particular. These two evils are hatred and ignorance. These two evils are the motivating force behind the proponents of this resolution and their supporters. These two evils characterize those who would drag this world organization, the ideals of which were first conceived by the prophets of Israel, to the depths to which it has been dragged today.

We are seeing here today but another manifestation of the bitter anti-Semitic, anti-Jewish hatred which animates Arab society. Who would have believed that in this year, 1975, the malicious falsehoods of the 'elders of Zion' would be distributed officially by Arab governments? Who would have believed that we would today contemplate an Arab society which teaches the vilest anti-Jewish hate in the kindergartens?... We are being attacked by a society which is motivated by the most extreme form of racism known in the world today. This is the racism which was expressed so succinctly in the words of the leader of the PLO, Yassir Arafat, in his opening address at a symposium in Tripoli, Libya: 'There will be no presence in the region other than the Arab presence...'. In other words, in the Middle East from the Atlantic Ocean to the Persian Gulf only one presence is allowed, and that is Arab presence. No other people, regardless of how deep are its roots in the region, is to be permitted to enjoy its right to self-determination.

As I stand on this rostrum, the long and proud history of my people unravels itself before my inward eye. I see the oppressors of our people over the ages as they pass one another in evil procession into oblivion. I stand here before you as the representative of a strong and flourishing people which has survived them all and which will survive this shameful exhibition and the proponents of this resolution.

The great moments of Jewish history come to mind as I face you, once again outnumbered and the would-be victim of hate, ignorance and evil. I look back on those great moments. I recall the greatness of a nation which I have the honour to represent in this forum. I am mindful at this moment of the Jewish people throughout the world wherever they may be, be it in freedom or in slavery, whose prayers and thoughts are with me at this moment.

I stand here not as a supplicant. Vote as your moral conscience dictates to you. For the issue is neither Israel nor Zionism. The issue is the continued existence of this organization, which has been dragged to its lowest point of discredit by a coalition of despots and racists.

The vote of each delegation will record in history its country's stand on anti-Semitic racism and anti-Judaism. You yourselves bear the responsibility for your stand before history, for as such will you be viewed in history. We, the Jewish people, will not forget.

For us, the Jewish people, this is but a passing episode in a rich and event-filled history. We put our trust in our Providence, in our faith and beliefs, in our time-hallowed tradition, in our striving for social advance and human values, and in our people wherever they may be. For us, the Jewish people, this resolution based on hatred, falsehood and arrogance, is devoid of any moral or legal value.

'Love begins at home.'

Mother Teresa

Speech on receiving the Nobel Peace Prize,*
Oslo, Norway, 11 December 1979

Mother Teresa was a Roman Catholic nun, famous for her work among the poor and dying of Calcutta in India. In 1979 she won the Nobel Prize for Peace.

Born in 1910 into an Albanian grocer's family, Agnes Gonxha Bojaxhiu attended the local school, where her religious interests were already forming. At 18 she left home to join the Sisters of Loreto, an Irish community where she received the name Sister Mary Teresa. She made her first vows in Calcutta in 1929, and from 1937, after taking her final vows, was known as Mother Teresa. After a period teaching at a girls' high school, in 1946 she followed an inner urge, her 'inspiration', to leave convent life and work with the poor. In 1948 the Vatican gave her permission to leave the Sisters of Loreto and to start new work under the guidance of the Archbishop of Calcutta. Her newly formed group, the Missionaries of Charity, took the usual vows of poverty, chastity and obedience, plus a fourth vow, to give free help to the poorest people. They began ministering to the dying in 1952.

In 1957 the Missionaries began to work with lepers and expanded their educational work. They also opened a home for orphans and abandoned children and in 1959 they began to expand, starting work in other Indian cities. Before long they had a presence in more than 22 Indian cities, and Mother Teresa had visited Australia, Africa and South America to establish foundations.

The Missionaries of Charity and affiliated lay groups expanded throughout the 1970s and Mother Teresa received increasing recognition and financial support. By 1979, when she accepted the Nobel Prize for Peace, she and her affiliated groups had more than 200 different operations in over 25 countries around the world. Later she sent her Missionaries of Charity into Russia, China and Cuba.

Born 27 August 1910 in Skopje, Macedonia. Mother Teresa famously described herself: 'By blood I am Albanian. By citizenship an Indian. By faith, I am a Catholic nun. As to my calling, I belong to the world. As to my heart, I belong entirely to the heart of Jesus.' Her **speech accepting the Nobel Peace Prize** in 1979, which was also the International Year of the Child, affirms her belief in the value of every human life, including the unborn. Died 5 September 1997 in Calcutta.

Tiny but energetic, in old age her wrinkled face familiar through the media, Mother Teresa maintained an aura of sanctity, little changed by the worldwide attention she received. Known as the 'saint of the gutters', her practical nature was combined with a complete lack of cynicism and absolute belief in the love of God for his poorest creatures. Long before her death in September 1997, books and articles started to canonize her and in October 2003 she was beatified.

* Mother Teresa made two speeches at the Nobel Prize Convention. This speech, made on 11 December 1979, is from a prepared text that was later published. She also made a similar speech on the previous day which addressed the same concerns.

Today the greatest means – the greatest destroyer of peace is abortion. And we who are standing here – our parents wanted us. We would not be here if our parents would do that to us. Our children, we want them, we love them, but what of the millions. Many people are very, very concerned with the children in India, with the children in Africa where quite a number die, maybe of malnutrition, of hunger and so on, but millions are dying deliberately by the will of the mother. And this is what is the greatest destroyer of peace today. Because if a mother can kill her own child – what is left for me to kill you and you kill me – there is nothing between. And this I appeal in India, I appeal everywhere: Let us bring the child back, and this year being the child's year: What have we done for the child? At the beginning of the year I told, I spoke everywhere and I said: Let us make this year that we make every single child born, and unborn, wanted. And today is the end of the year, have we really made the children wanted?

... I believe that we are not real social workers. We may be doing social work in the eyes of the people, but we are really contemplatives in the heart of the world. For we are touching the Body of Christ 24 hours. We have 24 hours in his presence, and so you and I. You too must try to bring that presence of God in your family, for the family that prays together stays together. And I think that we in our family don't need bombs and guns, to destroy to bring peace – just get together, love one another, bring that peace, that joy, that strength of presence of each other in the home. And we will be able to overcome all the evil that is in the world.

There is so much suffering, so much hatred, so much misery, and we with our prayer, with our sacrifice are beginning at home. Love begins at home, and it is not how much we do, but how much love we put in the action that we do. It is to God Almighty – how much we do it does not matter, because He is infinite, but how much love we put in that action. How much we do to Him in the person that we are serving.

‘The greatest destroyer of peace is abortion.’

... And with this prize that I have received as a prize of peace, I am going to try to make the home for many people that have no home. Because I believe that love begins at home, and if we can create a home for the poor – I think that more and more love will spread. And we will be able through this understanding love to bring peace, be the good news to the poor. The poor in our own family first, in our country and in the world.

To be able to do this, our Sisters, our lives have to be woven with prayer. They have to be woven with Christ to be able to understand, to be able to share. Because today there is so much suffering – and I feel that the passion of Christ is being relived all over again. Are we there to share that passion, to share that suffering of people? Around the world, not only in the poor countries, but I found the poverty of the West so much more difficult to remove. When I pick up a person from the street, hungry, I give him a plate of rice, a piece of bread, I have satisfied. I have removed that hunger. But a person that is shut out, that feels unwanted, unloved, terrified, the person that has been thrown out from society – that poverty is so hurtful and so much, and I find that very difficult. Our Sisters are working amongst that kind of people in the West. So you must pray for us that we may be able to be that good news, but we cannot do that without you. You have to do that here in your country. You must come to know the poor, maybe our people here have material things, everything, but I think that if we all look into our own homes, how difficult we find it sometimes to smile at each other, and that the smile is the beginning of love.

‘We are touching the body of Christ 24 hours.’

... I never forget some time ago about fourteen professors came from the United States from different universities. And they came to our house and we talked of love, of compassion, and then one of them asked me: Say, Mother, please tell us something that we will remember, and I said to them: Smile at each other, make time for each other in your family. Smile at each other. And then another one asked me: Are you married? and I said: Yes, and I find it sometimes very difficult to smile at Jesus because he can be very demanding sometimes. This is really something true, and there is where love comes – when it is demanding, and yet we can give it to Him with joy. Just as I have said today, I have said that if I don't go to Heaven for anything else I will be going to Heaven for all the publicity because it has purified me and sacrificed me and made me really ready to go to Heaven. I think that this is something, that we must live life beautifully, we have Jesus with us and He loves us. If we could only remember that God loves us, and we have an opportunity to love others as he loves us, not in big things, but in small things with great love, then Norway becomes a nest of love. And how beautiful it will be that from here a centre for peace has been given. That from here the joy of life of the unborn child comes out. If you become a burning light of peace in the world, then really the Nobel Peace Prize is a gift of the Norwegian people. God bless you!

'Our Polish freedom costs so much.'

Pope John Paul II

Speech at Jasna Góra Monastery, Poland, 18 June 1983

In 1978 Cardinal Karol Wojtyla became John Paul II, the first-ever Polish pope and the first non-Italian to hold office in 455 years. He was also the first pope from a Communist country. His appointment was a great boost to the Catholic faithful in his native land, for whom allegiance to the Church was one of few available means of protest against the Communist government. John Paul II delivered these words at the Jasna Góra monastery in June 1983 in front of a million young people. Carefully embedded in the speech were certain words – 'workers' and 'solidarity' – recognized by the listening crowd as acknowledging the banned Solidarity movement. On hearing these, the crowd raised many Solidarity banners and the end of the speech was greeted by tumultuous applause.

Born 18 May 1920 in Wadowice, Poland.
It is unclear why the authorities granted permission for John Paul II's second visit to Poland in 1983. The visit, and his **speech at Jasna Góra** in particular, is seen as critical in maintaining the movement of defiance that eventually toppled the Communist stronghold in Eastern Europe in 1989.
Died 2 April 2005 in Rome.

The son of an army officer, Karol Wojtyla lost his mother while still a child and grew up close to his father. He was an outstanding student and sportsman, showing an early love of poetry and acting. He was at Jagiellonian University in September 1938 when the Germans invaded Poland. The university was closed down but Karol and many others continued to study clandestinely. He graduated with distinction in theology in 1946 and the same year was ordained as a priest.

After serving as a parish priest and studying in Rome, in 1954 Karol was appointed Professor of Social Ethics at the Catholic University of Lublin. In 1963 he became Archbishop of Krakow, a role in which he demonstrated political astuteness and acted as a strong adversary of the Communist government. He became an international figure during the 2nd Vatican Council of 1962–65 and was appointed a cardinal in 1967. In 1978, at the relatively young age of 58, he was elected Pope by an overwhelming majority. His papacy was to last 26 years, during which he survived two assassination attempts.

John Paul II made jet travel the hallmark of his papacy, visiting more than 120 countries and preaching to millions of people across six continents. The third-longest reigning pope in history, John Paul II enjoyed extraordinary popularity throughout the world's Catholic community. He continued to travel widely even as his health declined. He died in April 2005, aged 85.

Our Lady of Jasna Góra is the teacher of true love for all. And this is particularly important for you, dear young people. In you, in fact, is decided that form of love which all of your life will have and, through you, human life on Polish soil: the matrimonial, family, social and national form – but also the priestly, religious and missionary one. Every life is determined and evaluated by the interior form of love. Tell me what you love, and I will tell you who you are.

'Tell me what you love, and I will tell you who you are.'

I watch! How beautiful it is that this word is found in the call of Jasna Góra. It possesses a profound evangelical ancestry: Christ says many times 'watch'... Perhaps also from the Gospel it passes into the tradition of scouting. In the call of Jasna Góra it is the essential element of the reply that we wish to give to the love by which we are surrounded in the sign of the Sacred Icon.

The response to this love must be precisely the fact that I watch!

What does it mean, 'I watch'?

It means that I make an effort to be a person with a conscience. I do not stifle this conscience and I do not deform it; I call good and evil by name, and I do not blur them; I develop in myself what is good, and I seek to correct what is evil, by overcoming it in myself. This is a fundamental problem which can never be minimized or put on a secondary level. No! It is everywhere and always a matter of the first importance. Its importance is all the greater in proportion to the increase of circumstances which seem to favour our tolerance of evil and the fact that we easily excuse ourselves from this, especially if adults do so.

My dear friends! It is up to you to put up a firm barrier against immorality, a barrier – I say – to those social vices which I will not here call by name but which you yourselves are perfectly aware of. You must demand this of yourselves, even if others do not demand it of you. Historical experiences tell us how much the immorality of certain periods cost the whole nation. Today when we are fighting for the future form of our social life, remember that this form depends on what people will be like. Therefore: watch!

...'I watch' also means: I see another. I do not close in on myself, in a narrow search for my own interests, my own judgements. 'I watch' means: love of neighbour, it means: fundamental interhuman solidarity.

Before the Mother of Jasna Góra I wish to give thanks for all the proofs of this solidarity which have been given by my compatriots, including Polish youth, in the difficult period of not many months ago. It would be difficult for me to enumerate here all the forms of this solicitude which surrounded those who were interned, imprisoned, dismissed from work, and also their families. You know this better than I. I received only sporadic news about it.

... 'I watch' also means: I feel responsible for this great common inheritance whose name is Poland. This name defines us all. This name obliges us all. This name costs us all.

Perhaps at times we envy the French, the Germans or the Americans because their name is not tied to such a historical price and because they are so easily free: while our Polish freedom costs so much.

'On you depends tomorrow.'

My dear ones, I will not make a comparative analysis. I will only say that it is what costs that constitutes value. It is not, in fact, possible to be truly free without an honest and profound relationship with values. We do not want a Poland which costs us nothing. We watch, instead, beside all that makes up the authentic inheritance of the generations, seeking to enrich it. A nation, then, is first of all rich in its people. Rich in man. Rich in youth. Rich in every individual who watches in the name of truth: it is truth, in fact, that gives form to love.

... Even if I am not among you every day, as was the case for many years in the past, nevertheless I carry in my heart a great solicitude. A great, enormous solicitude. A solicitude for you. Precisely because on you depends tomorrow.

I pray for you every day.

'Mr Gorbachev, tear down this wall!'

Ronald Reagan

Speech at the Brandenburg Gate, West Berlin, Germany, 12 June 1987

Ronald Wilson Reagan was born in 1911, in Tampico, Illinois. After attending school in Dixon he studied sociology and economics at Eureka College where he was also active in both drama and sport, taking the lead role in plays and playing in the college football team. He was also a lifeguard at Rock River and saved many swimmers who got into difficulties there.

After he graduated, Reagan worked as a sports announcer on the radio but his career really took off when he passed a Hollywood screen test in 1937. He appeared in no fewer than 53 films, becoming a familiar face to cinema audiences throughout the United States.

Born 6 February 1911 in Tampico, Illinois.
Reagan was a moving and effective speaker. He would brief his speechwriter, Peggy Noonan, on what he wanted to say and she crafted his speeches to suit his ability to deliver ideas with simple sincerity. His **speech at the Brandenburg Gate**, given in 1987 acknowledges John Kennedy's historic speech nearly a quarter of a century earlier, when the Berlin Wall was first erected, and deliberately echoes Kennedy's famous phrases in demanding its demolition.
Died 5 June 2004 in Los Angeles, California.

Reagan's speaking skills and friendly demeanour stood him in good stead for future public office. He became politically active when, as President of the Screen Actors Guild, he was involved in discussions about Communism in the film industry and his personal views changed from liberal to conservative.

In 1966 Reagan entered politics and was elected by a large majority as Governor of California, winning re-election in 1970. After two failed bids, in 1980 he won the Republican nomination as presidential candidate. He easily beat incumbent President Jimmy Carter, taking office as the 40th US President in January 1981. He won a second term four years later.

Reagan's first term in office was dramatically interrupted when he was shot on 30 March 1981, a bullet narrowly missing his heart. He apologized stoically to his wife Nancy afterwards, 'Honey, I forgot to duck'.

The Reagan years in the White House saw reductions in taxation and government regulations and increased military spending, but critics pointed to a spiralling national debt, and benefits for the wealthy rather than the poor. In foreign policy Reagan focused on the evils of the Soviet Union, which he saw as a threat to freedom across the globe. Liberal opinion was horrified when he called for a build-up of nuclear arms to match and exceed the Soviet arsenal. Nevertheless his robust foreign policy saw a gradual improvement in relations with the Soviet Union and the negotiation of a treaty eliminating mid-range nuclear missiles.

In June 1987, Reagan called for the removal of the Berlin Wall, appealing directly to Soviet Premier Mikhail Gorbachev to remove the physical and symbolic barrier between the two Germanys and the Eastern and Western blocs of Europe. In the year Reagan left office, the Berlin Wall was demolished, followed by the unravelling of the Soviet Union itself.

The last years of Reagan's life were overshadowed by Alzheimer's Disease, a condition he acknowledged publicly, hoping to raise awareness of the illness, and faced with characteristic courage: 'I now begin the journey that will lead me into the sunset of my life.'

Twenty-four years ago, President John F. Kennedy visited Berlin, speaking to the people of this city and the world at the City Hall. Well, since then two other Presidents have come, each in his turn, to Berlin. And today I, myself, make my second visit to your city.

We come to Berlin, we American Presidents, because it's our duty to speak, in this place, of freedom. But I must confess, we're drawn here by other things as well: by the feeling of history in this city, more than 500 years older than our own nation; by the beauty of the Grünewald and the Tiergarten; most of all, by your courage and determination. Perhaps the composer Paul Lincke understood something about American Presidents. You see, like so many Presidents before me, I come here today because wherever I go, whatever I do, *Ich hab noch einen Koffer in Berlin*, I still have a suitcase in Berlin.

Our gathering today is being broadcast throughout Western Europe and North America. I understand that it is being seen and heard as well in the East. To those listening throughout Eastern Europe, a special word: Although I cannot be with you, I address my remarks to you just as surely as to those standing here before me. For I join you, as I join your fellow countrymen in the West, in this firm, this unalterable belief: *Es gibt nur ein Berlin*, there is only one Berlin.

Behind me stands a wall that encircles the free sectors of this city, part of a vast system of barriers that divides the entire continent of Europe. From the Baltic, south, those barriers cut across Germany in a gash of barbed wire, concrete, dog runs, and guard towers. Farther south, there may be no visible, no obvious wall. But there remain armed guards and checkpoints all the same – still a restriction on the right to travel, still an instrument to impose upon ordinary men and women the will of a totalitarian state. Yet it is here in Berlin where the wall emerges most clearly; here, cutting across your city, where the news photo and the television screen have imprinted this brutal division of a continent upon the mind of the world. Standing before the Brandenburg Gate, every man is a German, separated from his fellow men. Every man is a Berliner, forced to look upon a scar.

President von Weizsacker has said, 'The German question is open as long as the Brandenburg Gate is closed'. Today I say: As long as the gate is closed, as long as this scar of a wall is permitted to stand, it is not the German question alone that remains open, but the question of freedom for all mankind. Yet I do not come here to lament. For I find in Berlin a message of hope, even in the shadow of this wall, a message of triumph.

... Where four decades ago there was rubble, today in West Berlin there is the greatest industrial output of any city in Germany – busy office blocks, fine homes and apartments, proud avenues and the spreading lawns of parkland. Where a city's culture seemed to have been destroyed, today there are two great universities, orchestras and an opera, countless theatres and museums. Where there was want, today there's abundance – food, clothing, automobiles – the wonderful goods of the *Ku'damm*. From devastation, from utter ruin, you Berliners have, in freedom, rebuilt a city that once again ranks as one of the greatest on earth. The Soviets may have had other plans. But my friends, there were a few things the Soviets didn't count on – *Berliner Herz, Berliner Humor, ja, und Berliner Schnauze*, Berliner heart, Berliner humour, yes, and Berliner *Schnauze*.

‘Wherever I go, whatever I do, I still have a suitcase in Berlin.’

In the 1950s, Khrushchev predicted: 'We will bury you.' But in the West today, we see a free world that has achieved a level of prosperity and well-being unprecedented in all human history. In the Communist world, we see failure, technological backwardness, declining standards of health, even want of the most basic kind – too little food. Even today, the Soviet Union still cannot feed itself. After these four decades, then, there stands before the entire world one great and inescapable conclusion: Freedom leads to prosperity. Freedom replaces the ancient hatreds among the nations with comity and peace. Freedom is the victor.

And now the Soviets themselves may, in a limited way, be coming to understand the importance of freedom. We hear much from Moscow about a new policy of reform and openness. Some political prisoners have been released. Certain foreign news broadcasts are no longer being jammed. Some economic enterprises have been permitted to operate with greater freedom from state control.

‘Freedom leads to prosperity. ... Freedom is the victor.’

Are these the beginnings of profound changes in the Soviet state? Or are they token gestures, intended to raise false hopes in the West, or to strengthen the Soviet system without changing it? We welcome change and openness; for we believe that freedom and security go together, that the advance of human liberty can only strengthen the cause of world peace. There is one sign the Soviets can make that would be unmistakeable, that would advance dramatically the cause of freedom and peace.

General Secretary Gorbachev, if you seek peace, if you seek prosperity for the Soviet Union and Eastern Europe, if you seek liberalization: come here to this gate! Mr Gorbachev, open this gate! Mr Gorbachev, tear down this wall!

‘No one could live long in Berlin without being completely disabused of illusions.’

... In these four decades, as I have said, you Berliners have built a great city. You've done so in spite of threats – the Soviet attempts to impose the East-mark, the blockade. Today the city thrives in spite of the challenges implicit in the very presence of this wall. What keeps you here? Certainly there's a great deal to be said for your fortitude, for your defiant courage. But I believe there's something deeper, something that involves Berlin's whole look and feel and way of life – not mere sentiment. No one could live long in Berlin without being completely disabused of illusions. Something instead, that has seen the difficulties of life in Berlin but chose to accept them, that continues to build this good and proud city in contrast to a surrounding totalitarian presence that refuses to release human energies or aspirations. Something that speaks with a powerful voice of affirmation, that says yes to this city, yes to the future, yes to freedom. In a word, I would submit that what keeps you in Berlin is love – love both profound and abiding.

Perhaps this gets to the root of the matter, to the most fundamental distinction of all between East and West. The totalitarian world produces backwardness because it does such violence to the spirit, thwarting the human impulse to create, to enjoy, to worship. The totalitarian world finds even symbols of love and of worship an affront. Years ago, before the East Germans began rebuilding their churches, they erected a secular structure: the television tower at Alexander Platz. Virtually ever since, the authorities have been working to correct what they view as the tower's one major flaw, treating the glass sphere at the top with paints and chemicals of every kind. Yet even today when the sun strikes that sphere – that sphere that towers over all Berlin – the light makes the sign of the cross. There in Berlin, like the city itself, symbols of love, symbols of worship, cannot be suppressed.

'The wall cannot withstand freedom.'

As I looked out a moment ago from the Reichstag, that embodiment of German unity, I noticed words crudely spray-painted upon the wall, perhaps by a young Berliner: 'This wall will fall. Beliefs become reality.' Yes, across Europe, this wall will fall. For it cannot withstand faith; it cannot withstand truth. The wall cannot withstand freedom.

And I would like, before I close, to say one word. I have read, and I have been questioned since I've been here about certain demonstrations against my coming. And I would like to say just one thing, and to those who demonstrate so. I wonder if they have ever asked themselves that if they should have the kind of government they apparently seek, no one would ever be able to do what they're doing again.

Thank you and God bless you all.

'Freedom of choice is a universal principle to which there should be no exceptions.'

Mikhail Gorbachev

Speech to the United Nations, New York, 7 December 1988

Mikhail Gorbachev was General Secretary of the Soviet Communist Party (1985–91) and President of the Soviet Union from 1988 until 1991. He is most famous for his liberalizing policies, which effectively ended the Cold War by opening up the Soviet Union to freer interaction with the West.

Born 2 March 1931 Provolnoye, North Caucasus.
He became Soviet leader in 1985. Mikhail Gorbachev's **speech to the United Nations** in December 1988 amounted to an official declaration of the end to the Cold War. The Soviets' unilateral decision to reduce their armed forces, independent of any international agreement, marked the beginning of a new era in world politics. As well as the Gorbachev Foundation, he is the founder of the global conservation organization, Green Cross International.

Mikhail Sergeievich Gorbachev was born in 1931 in the North Caucasus to a peasant family on a collective farm. His father was a mechanic and Mikhail worked on the farm from the age of 13. He studied diligently and earned a degree in law at Moscow University, joining the Communist Party and becoming Secretary of the Young Communist League in the Law Department. In due course he became an agricultural administrator in the Stavropol region and rose to the rank of Regional Secretary of the League. He gained a reputation for honesty and innovation and quickly ascended the political ladder.

In 1970 Gorbachev was elected to the Supreme Soviet. By 1980 he was the youngest full member of the Politburo, the USSR's governing body. After Konstantin Chernenko's death in 1985, Gorbachev became leader of the Soviet Union.

The rapid pace of reform that followed was largely due to Gorbachev's vision and international outlook. His 1988 address to the UN General Assembly embeds many of his aims, outlining initiatives unthinkable just a short period before. At home, he allowed freedom of expression and beliefs that had been long suppressed, and abroad he established friendly relations with traditional enemies in the western capitalist world, most notably the United States.

Gorbachev's reforming ideas were soon matched by actions, including the withdrawal of Soviet forces from Central Europe. Reformist ideas and energies soon flowed to the Soviet satellite states of Central Europe, including East Germany. The change from Communist dictatorships to western-style democracies was rapid. In 1990, Gorbachev received the Nobel Peace Prize, mainly for his foreign policy initiatives. However, he resigned in 1991 following the disintegration of the Soviet Union.

Since 1992, Gorbachev has run his own foundation for social, economic and political research (the Gorbachev Foundation) and he is internationally recognized as a highly influential statesman.

Freedom of choice is a universal principle to which there should be no exceptions. We have not come to the conclusion of the immutability of this principle simply through good motives. We have been led to it through impartial analysis of the objective processes of our time.

... Our country is undergoing a truly revolutionary upsurge. The process of restructuring is gaining pace. ... Under the badge of democratization, restructuring has now encompassed politics, the economy, spiritual life and ideology. We have unfolded a radical economic reform, we have accumulated experience, and from the new year we are transferring the entire national economy to new forms and work methods. Moreover, this means a profound reorganization of production relations and the realization of the immense potential of socialist property.

... We are more than fully confident. We have both the theory, the policy and the vanguard force of restructuring a party which is also restructuring itself in accordance with the new tasks and the radical changes throughout society. And the most important thing: all peoples and all generations of citizens in our great country are in favour of restructuring.

'Freedom of choice is a universal principle to which there should be no exceptions.'

... Today I can inform you of the following. The Soviet Union has made a decision on reducing its armed forces. In the next two years, their numerical strength will be reduced by 500,000 persons, and the volume of conventional arms will also be cut considerably. These reductions will be made on a unilateral basis, unconnected with negotiations on the mandate for the Vienna meeting. By agreement with our allies in the Warsaw Pact, we have made the decision to withdraw six tank divisions from the GDR, Czechoslovakia, and Hungary, and to disband them by 1991. Assault landing formations and units, and a number of others, including assault river-crossing forces, with their armaments and combat equipment, will also be withdrawn from the groups of Soviet forces situated in those countries. The Soviet forces situated in those countries will be cut by 50,000 persons, and their arms by 5,000 tanks. All remaining Soviet divisions on the territory of our allies will be reorganized. They will be given a different structure from today's which will become unambiguously defensive, after the removal of a large number of their tanks.

... Finally, being on US soil, but also for other, understandable reasons, I cannot but turn to the subject of our relations with this great country. ... Relations between the Soviet Union and the United States of America span 5½ decades. The world has changed, and so have the nature, role and place of these relations in world politics. For too long they were built under the banner of confrontation, and sometimes of hostility, either open or concealed. But in the last few years, throughout the world people were able to heave a sigh of relief, thanks to the changes for the better in the substance and atmosphere of the relations between Moscow and Washington.

'We have already graduated from the primary school of instruction in mutual understanding.'

No one intends to underestimate the serious nature of the disagreements, and the difficulties of the problems which have not been settled. However, we have already graduated from the primary school of instruction in mutual understanding and in searching for solutions in our and in the common interests. The USSR and the United States created the biggest nuclear missile arsenals, but after objectively recognizing their responsibility, they were able to be the first to conclude an agreement on the reduction and physical destruction of a proportion of these weapons, which threatened both themselves and everyone else.

Both sides possess the biggest and the most refined military secrets. But it is they who have laid the basis for and are developing a system of mutual verification with regard to both the destruction and the limiting and banning of armaments production. It is they who are amassing experience for future bilateral and multilateral agreements. We value this.

... I finish my first speech at the United Nations with the same feeling with which I began it: a feeling of responsibility to my own people and to the world community. We have met at the end of a year that has been so significant for the United Nations, and on the threshold of a year from which all of us expect so much. One would like to believe that our joint efforts to put an end to the era of wars, confrontation and regional conflicts, aggression against nature, the terror of hunger and poverty, as well as political terrorism, will be comparable with our hopes. This is our common goal, and it is only by acting together that we may attain it. Thank you.

'The time for negotiation has arrived.'

F. W. de Klerk

Speech at the opening of Parliament, Pretoria, South Africa, 2 February 1990

Frederik Willem de Klerk was born in 1936 in Johannesburg, South Africa. He was from a prominent Afrikaaner family, and his father, Senator Jan de Klerk, was a senior Cabinet Minister.

He studied law and for 11 years was a lawyer in the Transvaal. He entered Parliament in 1972 and was appointed to the South African Cabinet in 1978. In February 1989 he became leader of the National Party and in the autumn of that year was unanimously elected President of the Republic.

A particular feature of de Klerk's presidency was his openness. In sharp contrast to his predecessors, he made frequent television appearances and welcomed the media. This was a difficult time for South Africa, with apartheid (enforced racial segregation) being widely condemned, and de Klerk gradually gained global respect for his calm negotiations in what was to become a period of important transition towards a non-racial democracy.

Born 18 March 1936 in Johannesburg.
He became President of the Republic of South Africa in 1989. Nine days after the changes announced in de Klerk's **speech at the opening of Parliament** in February 1990, Nelson Mandela was released from prison. In 1993, de Klerk was awarded the Nobel Peace Prize jointly with Nelson Mandela. Although de Klerk ran against Mandela in the general election the following year, his opposition was only nominal and the ANC won a conclusive victory.
In 2004, de Klerk established the Global Leadership Foundation, which promotes peace, democracy and development.

The opening of Parliament in February 1990 marked a sea change in South Africa's history, and de Klerk used the occasion to announce remarkable changes that signalled the end of apartheid. He announced that many illegal organizations, including the African National Congress (ANC), would be unbanned and stunned and delighted people around the world by declaring that the ANC leader Nelson Mandela would be released from prison, where he had been held for 26 years.

In 1993, de Klerk described how he would like to be remembered: 'I would hope that history will recognize that I, together with all those who supported me, have shown courage, integrity, honesty at the moment of truth in our history. That we took the right turn.'

South Africa's first ever racially inclusive election was held in April 1994 and on 10 May that year de Klerk became one of two Deputy Presidents in South Africa's new Government of National Unity under the leadership of President Nelson Mandela.

In May 1996 de Klerk resigned his post, having transformed his country's political system and succeeded in re-integrating South Africa internationally.

Mr Speaker, Members of Parliament.

The general elections on September the 6th, 1989, placed our country irrevocably on the road of drastic change. Underlying this is the growing realization by an increasing number of South Africans that only a negotiated understanding among the representative leaders of the entire population is able to ensure lasting peace.

The alternative is growing violence, tension and conflict. That is unacceptable and in nobody's interest. The well-being of all in this country is linked inextricably to the ability of the leaders to come to terms with one another on a new dispensation. No-one can escape this simple truth.

... Our country and all its people have been embroiled in conflict, tension and violent struggle for decades. It is time for us to break out of the cycle of violence and break through to peace and reconciliation. The silent majority is yearning for this. The youth deserve it.

With the steps the Government has taken it has proven its good faith and the table is laid for sensible leaders to begin talking about a new dispensation, to reach an understanding by way of dialogue discussion.

'Our country and all its people have been embroiled in conflict, tension and violent struggle for decades.'

The agenda is open and the overall aims to which we are aspiring should be acceptable to all reasonable South Africans.

Among other things, those aims include a new, democratic constitution; universal franchise; no domination; equality before an independent judiciary; the protection of minorities as well as of individual rights; freedom of religion; a sound economy based on proven economic principles and private enterprise; dynamic programmes directed at better education, health services, housing and social conditions for all.

In this connection Mr Nelson Mandela could play an important part. The Government has noted that he has declared himself to be willing to make a constructive contribution to the peaceful political process in South Africa.

I wish to put it plainly that the Government has taken a firm decision to release

Mr Mandela unconditionally. I am serious about bringing this matter to finality without delay. The Government will take a decision soon on the date of his release.

Unfortunately, a further short passage of time is unavoidable.

Normally there is a certain passage of time between the decision to release and the actual release because of logistical and administrative requirements. In the case of Mr Mandela there are factors in the way of his immediate release, of which his personal circumstances and safety are not the least. He has not been an ordinary prisoner for quite some time. Because of that, his case requires particular circumspection.

Today's announcements, in particular, go to the heart of what Black leaders – also Mr Mandela – have been advancing over the years as their reason for having resorted to violence. The allegation has been that the Government did not wish to talk to them and that they were deprived of their right to normal political activity by the prohibition of their organizations.

Without conceding that violence has ever been justified, I wish to say today to those who argued in this manner: the Government wishes to talk to all leaders who seek peace. The unconditional lifting of the prohibition on the said organizations places everybody in a position to pursue politics freely. The justification for violence which was always advanced, no longer exists.

These facts place everybody in South Africa before a *fait accompli*. On the basis of numerous previous statements there is no longer any reasonable excuse for the continuation of violence. The time for talking has arrived and whoever still makes excuses does not really wish to talk.

‘The time for negotiation has arrived.’

Therefore, I repeat my invitation with greater conviction than ever:

Walk through the open door, take your place at the negotiating table together with the Government and other leaders who have important power bases inside and outside of Parliament.

Henceforth, everybody's political points of view will be tested against their realism, their workability and their fairness. The time for negotiation has arrived.

‘We live in a contaminated moral environment.’

Vaclav Havel

Broadcast to the people of Czechoslovakia, 1 January 1990

Vaclav Havel (born 1936) is a playwright and former President of the Czech Republic. At the age of 19 Havel began publishing magazine articles, later working in the theatre as a stagehand. For the Theatre on the Balustrade he wrote witty plays expressing dissent against the Czech Communist suppression of artistic and literary freedoms. Havel's plays were critically acclaimed throughout Europe.

When Czechoslovakia fell under Soviet domination in 1968, there were severe consequences for Havel's once-wealthy family, who were now classified as 'class enemies'. Havel's plays were banned, although they continued to be performed outside Czechoslovakia and Havel continued to write for underground publications. He was offered the chance to leave the country several times, but he declined: 'The solution of this human situation does not lie in leaving it.'

In 1977 Havel, supported by hundreds of Czech intellectuals, helped to draw up the Charter 77 human rights document. His essay *The Power of the Powerless* (1978) accused the Communist regime of creating a society of morally corrupt individuals. Havel was imprisoned for subversion. He was released in 1983 but continued to criticize the government in the press and in 1989 was imprisoned for a further nine months. In the same year an opposition movement called Civic Forum, which Havel helped to found, gained momentum and culminated in the bloodless 'Velvet Revolution', which overthrew Communism in Czechoslovakia.

Born 5 October 1936 in Prague.
As a writer and playwright, Havel wrote with no regard to Communist censorship and was imprisoned several times. He was elected President of Czechoslovakia in 1989. His presidential speeches became another kind of literary genre for him. His speech '**a contaminated moral environment**' shocked his listeners with his insistence that the people should accept part-responsibility for the corruption of the previous regime. His moral authority was widely admired by the leaders of most of the major world powers but irritated his political opponents.
Havel has recovered from lung cancer and continues to write.

In December 1989 Havel was elected President of Czechoslovakia. He resigned in 1992 when the Slovak Parliament passed its own constitution and Czechoslovakia split into two new states – the Republic of Slovakia and the Czech Republic. Havel was elected the first President of the Czech Republic in 1993.

Despite ill health, Havel continued to write and received many awards for his literary as well as his human rights achievements, becoming an inspiration to fighters for democracy, symbolizing the ability of one person to change the course of history through non-violent means. He retired at the end of his second term as President.

We live in a contaminated moral environment. We fell morally ill because we became used to saying something different from what we thought. We learned not to believe in anything, to ignore each other, to care only about ourselves. Concepts such as love, friendship, compassion, humility or forgiveness lost their depth and dimensions, and for many of us they represented only psychological peculiarities, or they resembled gone-astray greetings from ancient times, a little ridiculous in the era of computers and spaceships. Only a few of us were able to cry out loud that the powers that be should not be all-powerful, and that special farms, which produce ecologically pure and top-quality food just for them, should send their produce to schools, children's homes and hospitals if our agriculture was unable to offer them to all. The previous regime – armed with its arrogant and intolerant ideology – reduced man to a force of production and nature to a tool of production. In this it attacked both their very substance and their mutual relationship. It reduced gifted and autonomous people, skilfully working in their own country, to nuts and bolts of some monstrously huge, noisy and stinking machine, whose real meaning is not clear to anyone. It cannot do more than slowly but inexorably wear down itself and all its nuts and bolts.

'We fell morally ill because we became used to saying something different from what we thought.'

When I talk about contaminated moral atmosphere, I am not talking just about the gentlemen who eat organic vegetables and do not look out of the plane windows. I am talking about all of us. We had all become used to the totalitarian system and accepted it as an unchangeable fact and thus helped to perpetuate it. In other words, we are all – though naturally to differing extents – responsible for the operation of the totalitarian machinery; none of us is just its victim: we are all also its co-creators.

Why do I say this? It would be very unreasonable to understand the sad legacy of the last forty years as something alien, which some distant relative bequeathed us. On the contrary, we have to accept this legacy as a sin we committed against ourselves. If we accept it as such, we will understand that it is up to us all, and up to us only, to do something about it. We cannot blame the previous rulers for everything, not only because it would be untrue but also because it could blunt the duty that each of us faces today, namely, the obligation to act independently, freely, reasonably and quickly. Let us not be mistaken: the best government in the world, the best Parliament and the best President, cannot achieve much on their own. And it would also be wrong to expect a general remedy from them only. Freedom and democracy include participation and therefore responsibility from us all.

'We are all responsible for the operation of the totalitarian machinery.'

If we realize this, then all the horrors that the new Czechoslovak democracy inherited will cease to appear so terrible. If we realize this, hope will return to our hearts.

... In conclusion, I would like to say that I want to be a President who will speak less and work more. To be a President who will not only look out of the windows of his aeroplane but who, first and foremost, will always be present among his fellow citizens and listen to them well.

You may ask what kind of republic I dream of. Let me reply: I dream of a republic independent, free and democratic, of a republic economically prosperous and yet socially just, in short, of a humane republic which serves the individual and which therefore holds the hope that the individual will serve it in turn. Of a republic of well-rounded people, because without such it is impossible to solve any of our problems, human, economic, ecological, social or political.

The most distinguished of my predecessors opened his first speech with a quotation from the great Czech educator Comenius. Allow me to round off my first speech with my own paraphrase of the same statement:

People, your government has returned to you!

'The perils of indifference.'

Elie Wiesel

Seventh White House Millennium Evening, Washington, 12 April 1999

Elie Wiesel is a writer famous for his witness to the sufferings endured by Jews in the concentration camps of Nazi Germany. He was born in 1928 in Sighet, Transylvania, now part of Romania, and grew up in a Jewish community where Yiddish was his first language. Elie studied classical Hebrew from a very early age and religion was central to his life.

In 1944 the Nazis arrived and 'cleansed' Sighet of its Jews, deporting them *en masse* to concentration camps. On arrival at Auschwitz, he was separated from his mother and younger sister and never saw them again. He and his father managed to stay together but suffered terrible hardship, being used as slave labour, and starved and beaten. They were moved to Buchenwald where Elie's father perished from malnutrition, exposure and dysentery just before Buchenwald was liberated by the Allies in 1945.

Elie was taken to Paris, where he studied philosophy at the Sorbonne and worked as a Hebrew teacher and choirmaster. He became a professional journalist, writing articles for French and Israeli newspapers. For ten years he wrote nothing about the war but eventually he drew on the experiences of his early life in his writing.

In 1956 an accident changed the course of his life. Wiesel was knocked down by a taxi in New York and suffered injuries that confined him to a wheelchair for nearly a year. He applied for American citizenship and stayed in New York, becoming a feature writer for *Der Forverts*, a Yiddish newspaper.

Born 30 September 1928 in Transylvania. Elie Wiesel is Andrew W. Mellon Professor in the Humanities at Boston University and has served as Chairman of the US Holocaust Memorial Council. In 1986, he was awarded the Nobel Peace Prize. With his wife Marion he founded the Elie Wiesel Foundation for Humanity. **'The perils of indifference'** was given to an invited audience at the White House. Hillary Clinton, wife of President Bill Clinton, introduced Wiesel, saying, 'You have taught us never to forget. You have made sure that we always listen to the victims of indifference, hatred and evil.'

His first book, *La Nuit*, published in 1958, recounts his experience of life in the concentration camps. Other books were to follow: *L'Aube* ('Dawn'), *Le Jour* (translated as 'The Accident'), and *La Ville de la Chance* ('The Town Beyond the Wall'). He also published plays, several other novels, essays and short stories.

As well as being a devoted supporter of Israel, Elie Wiesel has spoken out for oppressed minorities elsewhere, including the Soviet Jews, the 'disappeared' of Argentina, refugees from Cambodia, the Kurds, native Indians in Nicaragua and famine victims.

In this speech, addressing President Clinton and the US Congress in April 1999, he drew on his own experiences to highlight the plight of oppressed and disadvantaged people throughout the world.

Fifty-four years ago to the day, a young Jewish boy from a small town in the Carpathian Mountains woke up, not far from Goethe's beloved Weimar, in a place of eternal infamy called Buchenwald. He was finally free, but there was no joy in his heart. He thought there never would be again. Liberated a day earlier by American soldiers, he remembers their rage at what they saw. And even if he lives to be a very old man, he will always be grateful to them for that rage, and also for their compassion. Though he did not understand their language, their eyes told him what he needed to know – that they, too, would remember, and bear witness. ...

We are on the threshold of a new century, a new millennium. What will the legacy of this vanishing century be? How will it be remembered in the new millennium? Surely it will be judged, and judged severely, in both moral and metaphysical terms. These failures have cast a dark shadow over humanity: two World Wars, countless civil wars, the senseless chain of assassinations (Gandhi, the Kennedys, Martin Luther King, Sadat, Rabin), bloodbaths in Cambodia and Nigeria, India and Pakistan, Ireland and Rwanda, Eritrea and Ethiopia, Sarajevo and Kosovo; the inhumanity in the gulag and the tragedy of Hiroshima. And, on a different level, of course, Auschwitz and Treblinka. So much violence; so much indifference.

What is indifference? Etymologically, the word means 'no difference'. A strange and unnatural state in which the lines blur between light and darkness, dusk and dawn, crime and punishment, cruelty and compassion, good and evil. What are its courses and inescapable consequences? Is it a philosophy? Is there a philosophy of indifference conceivable? Can one possibly view indifference as a virtue? Is it necessary at times to practise it simply to keep one's sanity, live normally, enjoy a fine meal and a glass of wine, as the world around us experiences harrowing upheavals?

'Indifference is always the friend of the enemy.'

Of course, indifference can be tempting – more than that, seductive. It is so much easier to look away from victims. It is so much easier to avoid such rude interruptions to our work, our dreams, our hopes. It is, after all, awkward, troublesome, to be involved in another person's pain and despair. Yet, for the person who is indifferent, his or her neighbours are of no consequence. And, therefore, their lives are meaningless. Their hidden or even visible anguish is of no interest. Indifference reduces the other to an abstraction.

Over there, behind the black gates of Auschwitz, the most tragic of all prisoners were the *Muselmänner*, as they were called. Wrapped in their torn blankets, they would sit or lie on the ground, staring vacantly into space, unaware of who or where they were – strangers to their surroundings. They no longer felt pain, hunger, thirst. They feared nothing. They felt nothing. They were dead and did not know it.

‘When adults wage war, children perish.’

Rooted in our tradition, some of us felt that to be abandoned by humanity then was not the ultimate. We felt that to be abandoned by God was worse than to be punished by Him. Better an unjust God than an indifferent one. For us to be ignored by God was a harsher punishment than to be a victim of His anger. Man can live far from God – not outside God. God is wherever we are. Even in suffering? Even in suffering.

In a way, to be indifferent to that suffering is what makes the human being inhuman. Indifference, after all, is more dangerous than anger and hatred. Anger can at times be creative. One writes a great poem, a great symphony. One does something special for the sake of humanity because one is angry at the injustice that one witnesses. But indifference is never creative. Even hatred at times may elicit a response. You fight it. You denounce it. You disarm it.

Indifference elicits no response. Indifference is not a response. Indifference is not a beginning; it is an end. And, therefore, indifference is always the friend of the enemy, for it benefits the aggressor – never his victim, whose pain is magnified when he or she feels forgotten. The political prisoner in his cell, the hungry children, the homeless refugees – not to respond to their plight, not to relieve their solitude by offering them a spark of hope is to exile them from human memory. And in denying their humanity, we betray our own.

Indifference, then, is not only a sin, it is a punishment.

And this is one of the most important lessons of this outgoing century's wide-ranging experiments in good and evil.

In the place that I come from, society was composed of three simple categories: the killers, the victims, and the bystanders. During the darkest of times, inside the ghettoes and death camps – and I'm glad that Mrs Clinton mentioned that we are now commemorating that event, that period, that we are now in the Days of Remembrance – but then, we felt abandoned, forgotten. All of us did.

And our only miserable consolation was that we believed that Auschwitz and Treblinka were closely guarded secrets; that the leaders of the free world did not know what was going on behind those black gates and barbed wire; that they had no knowledge of the war against the Jews that Hitler's armies and their accomplices waged as part of the war against the Allies. If they knew, we thought, surely those leaders would have moved heaven and earth to intervene. They would have spoken out with great outrage and conviction. They would have bombed the railways leading to Birkenau, just the railways, just once.

And now we knew, we learned, we discovered that the Pentagon knew, the State Department knew. ...

... The depressing tale of the 'St Louis' is a case in point. Sixty years ago, its human cargo – nearly 1,000 Jews – was turned back to Nazi Germany. And that happened after the *Kristallnacht*, after the first state sponsored pogrom, with hundreds of Jewish shops destroyed, synagogues burned, thousands of people put in concentration camps. And that ship, which was already in the shores of the United States, was sent back. I don't understand. Roosevelt was a good man, with a heart. He understood those who needed help. Why didn't he allow these refugees to disembark? A thousand people – in America, the great country, the greatest democracy, the most generous of all new nations in modern history. What happened? I don't understand. Why the indifference, on the highest level, to the suffering of the victims?

But then, there were human beings who were sensitive to our tragedy. Those non-Jews, those Christians, that we call the 'Righteous Gentiles', whose selfless acts of heroism saved the honour of their faith. Why were they so few? Why was there a greater effort to save SS murderers after the war than to save their victims during the war? Why did some of America's largest corporations continue to do business with Hitler's Germany until 1942? It has been suggested, and it was documented, that the Wehrmacht could not have conducted its invasion of France without oil obtained from American sources. How is one to explain their indifference?

And yet, my friends, good things have also happened in this traumatic century: the defeat of Nazism, the collapse of Communism, the rebirth of Israel on its ancestral soil, the demise of apartheid, Israel's peace treaty with Egypt, the peace accord in Ireland. And let us remember the meeting, filled with drama and emotion, between Rabin and Arafat that you, Mr President, convened in this very place. I was here and I will never forget it.

And then, of course, the joint decision of the United States and NATO to intervene in Kosovo and save those victims, those refugees, those who were uprooted by a man, whom I believe that because of his crimes, should be charged with crimes against humanity.

'Together we walk towards the new millennium, carried by profound fear and extraordinary hope.'

But this time, the world was not silent. This time, we do respond. This time, we intervene.

Does it mean that we have learned from the past? Does it mean that society has changed? Has the human being become less indifferent and more human? Have we really learned from our experiences? Are we less insensitive to the plight of victims of ethnic cleansing and other forms of injustices in places near and far? Is today's justified intervention in Kosovo, led by you, Mr President, a lasting warning that never again will the deportation, the terrorization of children and their parents, be allowed anywhere in the world? Will it discourage other dictators in other lands to do the same?

What about the children? Oh, we see them on television, we read about them in the papers, and we do so with a broken heart. Their fate is always the most tragic, inevitably. When adults wage war, children perish. We see their faces, their eyes. Do we hear their pleas? Do we feel their pain, their agony? Every minute one of them dies of disease, violence, famine.

Some of them – so many of them – could be saved.

And so, once again, I think of the young Jewish boy from the Carpathian Mountains. He has accompanied the old man I have become throughout these years of quest and struggle. And together we walk towards the new millennium, carried by profound fear and extraordinary hope.

‘A great people has been moved to defend a great nation.’

George W. Bush

Address to the nation, 11 September 2001

George Walker Bush (known as George W. Bush to distinguish him from his father, former President George Bush) studied at the Philips Andover Academy in Massachusetts and then at Yale University, graduating with a bachelor's degree in 1968. He joined the Texas Air National Guard where he learned to fly fighter jets and reached the rank of Lieutenant. From 1972 to 1975 he attended Harvard Business School, then went into the oil business, forming an oil and gas exploration company, 'Arbusto' (a pun, using the Spanish word for bush). In 1977 he married Laura Welch: their twin daughters, Barbara and Jenna, were born in 1981.

In July 1986 Bush moved to Washington DC to support George Bush Senior's successful presidential campaign. After the election he moved to Dallas, Texas, where he became joint owner of Texas Rangers baseball team, making a profit of almost $15 million when he sold the team in 1998.

In 1994 he was elected Governor of Texas, showing considerable diplomatic skills and pushing through business friendly law reforms. In 1998 he won re-election by a big majority, the first Texas Governor to be elected to consecutive four-year terms.

Born 6 July 1946 in New Haven, Connecticut. Speechwriter Michael Gerson received a simple brief for the 11 September **address to the nation**: 'Our mission is reassurance'. However, the President insisted on including the phrase that became known as the Bush Doctrine, 'We will make no distinction between the terrorists who committed these acts and those who harbour them'. He considered the attacks an act of war and wrote in his diary that night: 'The Pearl Harbor of the 21st century took place today'.

In June 1999 George W. Bush won the nomination as the Republican candidate for President. His folksy style proved popular in the campaign but the result was an extraordinarily close and disputed contest. Bush was finally declared victor following five weeks of legal wrangling involving recounts in the key state of Florida.

George W. Bush became the 43rd President of the United States on 20 January 2001. On 11 September that year, Islamic terrorists flew hijacked passenger jets into the twin towers of the World Trade Center in New York and the Pentagon in Washington. In the wake of this event Bush made his famous speech, initiating the 'war on terror' that has characterized US foreign policy ever since.

In November 2004, Bush won a second term as President.

Good evening.

Today, our fellow citizens, our way of life, our very freedom came under attack in a series of deliberate and deadly terrorist acts. The victims were in airplanes or in their offices: secretaries, business men and women, military and federal workers, moms and dads, friends and neighbours. Thousands of lives were suddenly ended by evil, despicable acts of terror. The pictures of airplanes flying into buildings, fires burning, huge structures collapsing have filled us with disbelief, terrible sadness and a quiet, unyielding anger. These acts of mass murder were intended to frighten our nation into chaos and retreat. But they have failed. Our country is strong.

> ‘We're the brightest beacon for freedom and opportunity in the world.’

A great people has been moved to defend a great nation. Terrorist attacks can shake the foundations of our biggest buildings, but they cannot touch the foundation of America. These acts shatter steel, but they cannot dent the steel of American resolve. America was targetted for attack because we're the brightest beacon for freedom and opportunity in the world. And no one will keep that light from shining. Today, our nation saw evil – the very worst of human nature – and we responded with the best of America. With the daring of our rescue workers, with the caring for strangers and neighbours who came to give blood and help in any way they could.

Immediately following the first attack, I implemented our government's emergency response plans. Our military is powerful, and it's prepared. Our emergency teams are working in New York City and Washington DC to help with local rescue efforts. Our first priority is to get help to those who have been injured, and to take every precaution to protect our citizens at home and around the world from further attacks. The functions of our government continue without interruption. Federal agencies in Washington which had to be evacuated today are reopening for essential personnel tonight and will be open for business tomorrow. Our financial institutions remain strong, and the American economy will be open for business as well.

The search is underway for those who were behind these evil acts. I have directed the full resources of our intelligence and law enforcement communities to find those responsible and to bring them to justice. We will make no distinction between the terrorists who committed these acts and those who harbour them.

I appreciate so very much the members of Congress who have joined me in strongly condemning these attacks. And on behalf of the American people, I thank the many world leaders who have called to offer their condolences and assistance. America and our friends and allies join with all those who want peace and security in the world, and we stand together to win the war against terrorism.

‘None of us will ever forget this day.’

Tonight, I ask for your prayers for all those who grieve, for the children whose worlds have been shattered, for all whose sense of safety and security has been threatened. And I pray they will be comforted by a Power greater than any of us, spoken through the ages in Psalm 23: ‘Even though I walk through the valley of the shadow of death, I fear no evil for you are with me.’

This is a day when all Americans from every walk of life unite in our resolve for justice and peace. America has stood down enemies before, and we will do so this time. None of us will ever forget this day, yet we go forward to defend freedom and all that is good and just in our world.

Thank you. Good night. And God bless America.

Index of Speakers and Key Lines

Folk Tales of
JAPAN

Retold by Sheila Hatherley
Illustrated by Linda Forss

Titles in this Evans Folk Tales series are:

China
North America
Japan
South America

Illustrations by Linda Forss
Designed by Raul Diche

First published in the U.K. in 1993 by
Evans Brothers Limited,
2a Portman Mansions,
Chiltern Street,
London WIM ILE

ISBN 0 237 51307 2

First published in Australia in 1991 by
The Macmillan Company of Australia Pty Ltd
107 Moray Street, South Melbourne 3205
6 Clarke Street, Crows Nest 2065

Set in Bookman by
Superskill Graphics, Singapore
Printed in Hong Kong

Contents

The Strange Teakettle

A long time ago there was an old man who worked as a scrap dealer. He carried a large wicker basket on his back and as he walked from village to village people would give him things they no longer needed. Sometimes they would buy things already in his basket for a few coins.

One day, as he was walking, he found a badger caught in a trap.

'Poor animal!' he said. 'Why should anyone want to harm you? I'll set you free.' He loosened the trap and the animal scampered away.

Now this badger happened to possess magical powers. It felt very grateful to the scrap dealer for being rescued and wanted to reward him. It waited until the man took the basket from his back and sat down under a tree to rest, then the badger crept into the basket and, by its magic powers turned itself into a teakettle.

When the scrap dealer returned home he was very surprised to find among all the bits and pieces in his basket a very beautiful teakettle. Where had it come from? He couldn't remember anybody giving it to him. As he polished it carefully he decided to take it to a temple priest who had been kind to him in the past. He knew the priest would want to buy such a fine teakettle.

The next day he took it to the temple, and as he had expected, the priest thought it was a very fine piece of work and bought it. In fact he gave the scrap dealer far more money for it than he had dared to hope. The scrap dealer returned home happy and amazed at his good fortune.

The priest filled the beautiful kettle with water and put it on the fire to boil. That was when strange things began to happen.

The teakettle shouted, ‘It’s too hot! Much too hot! I’m burning!’ The badger’s grey head popped out from where the spout had been, then four paws and finally a tail sprang from the sides of the kettle. It hopped off the hearth and ran round and round the room.

By the time the frightened priest caught up with the badger-kettle the head, paws and tail had disappeared again. It was once more just a very beautiful but mysterious teakettle. Even so, the priest decided that he could not have such a thing in his temple. He sent for the scrap dealer.

‘Take back this kettle!’ he cried. ‘I cannot possibly keep it in the temple. It is bewitched! It speaks and runs round the room!’

Sadly the scrap dealer took back the teakettle and returned the money the priest had paid him. Poor man! He was very disappointed. He carried the kettle home and wondered what he could do with it. If it behaved in such a strange fashion nobody would want to buy it. He placed the teakettle on a shelf in the corner of the room and went to bed. He lay awake for a long time wondering what it all meant.

In the middle of the night he was awakened by a strange voice. Somebody was calling to him.

'Old man, old man, wake up!'

'Who is it?' he cried. 'What do you want at this time of night?'

The voice seemed to be coming from the corner of the room. It was the teakettle!

'Don't be upset,' it said. 'I may look like a teakettle, but I am really the badger you saved from the trap yesterday. You saved my life and I wanted to do something to help you. I wanted to use my magic power to help you earn more money and have an easier life. I'm sorry things turned out so badly at the temple.'

The scrap dealer didn't know what to think or say. How did one address a magical creature such as this?

'Thank you for trying to help me, Most Honourable Badger,' he stammered.

'I'll always be a teakettle now, I fear,' it said. 'Old man, I've been thinking things over as I sat here on the shelf. I believe you and I would make a good team. Why don't you take me with you on your journeys? I can perform all manner of tricks. I can sing and dance. People will pay well to see such a show.'

So that was what they did. People soon gathered in crowds to see the strange pair. They laughed and clapped as the teakettle danced on its little legs. They listened entranced as it sang all their favourite songs. The highlight of each performance was when the kettle walked along a tightrope before jumping back into the scrap dealer's basket.

In a short time the scrap dealer was no longer a poor man. Soon he and the teakettle became so wealthy they decided to retire and enjoy a more leisurely life. The scrap dealer often wondered, though, what would become of the teakettle after he was dead. There must be somebody who would value it and care for it.

Once more he went to the temple to see the old priest. This time he told him the whole story of how the badger he had saved turned into a kettle to try to repay him. The priest was astonished at the story.

'What a faithful creature! And what a fine teakettle! We will be delighted to accept it as a temple treasure.'

Some people say the teakettle is still among the temple treasures today.

Susanowo and the Eight-headed Serpent

Susanowo, the son of the great god Izanagi, was the god of storms. He was like a storm, too; dark, raging, and often quarreling with the other gods. They called him the Impetuous Male because he so often did rash and violent things without thinking about them first.

His bad behaviour so angered Izanagi that he banished his son from heaven. When he heard this Susanowo decided to visit his sister, Amaterasu, the sun-goddess. If he was to be banished, at least he would say goodbye to her first. Amaterasu distrusted the reason for her brother's visit. She felt that he most likely had plans to take away her power in the sky. She even prepared an army to fight him if necessary. When Susanowo saw her standing in front of her palace armed like a warrior, he burst out laughing.

'I have not come to make war,' he assured her. 'Izanagi, our father, has banished me from the heavens, and I merely wish to say goodbye to you before I leave.'

Since he came in peace, Amaterasu invited him to stay with her for a while. The visit was not a success, though. Susanowo's behaviour soon became worse than ever. He ruined his sister's rice fields, filled in the irrigation ditches and even trampled filth into her palace. At first Amaterasu made excuses for her brother's actions, but when his rough behaviour resulted in several of her maidservants being injured, Amaterasu could bear no more. She shut herself up in a cave and refused to come out until Susanowo had left her part of the sky.

Of course, without the sun in the sky, day and night ceased to exist. The world was plunged into darkness. All the other gods and spirits were greatly troubled about this, and tried every means they knew to coax Amaterasu out of the cave. When they finally succeeded, Susanowo was given a stern order, 'Leave the kingdoms of the sky and go down to earth.' This was an order he realised he must obey.

When he arrived on earth he found himself in the land of Izumo, near the mouth of the great River Hi. As he sat on the riverbank, wondering what to do next, he saw a pair of carved chopsticks in the water, being carried along by the current.

'If there are chopsticks, then there must be people living somewhere nearby,' he thought. He was curious to find out about the inhabitants of this strange, new place, and so he started to follow the river upstream. He walked for a long time without seeing a single person. The land seemed quite deserted.

Susanowo walked for most of the day, then suddenly he heard the sound of somebody weeping. He hurried round the next bend of the river and saw three people: an old man, his wife and a beautiful, young woman. They were all crying as if their hearts would break.

'What is the matter?' Susanowo asked. 'Are you in some sort of trouble? Maybe I can help you.'

The old man bowed and said, through his tears, 'Sir, tomorrow my daughter must die. You must be a stranger to our country, or you would have heard of the terrible serpent with eight heads. For eight years we have lived in fear and horror. Once I had nine beautiful daughters. Now I have only one. Already eight of my daughters have been sacrificed to this terrible beast, and now my last daughter will certainly be eaten when it appears again at dawn tomorrow.'

'Why do you stay in this place, then?' Susanowo asked. 'You have plenty of time to escape before tomorrow morning. Surely it would be best to move away, and live where this monster cannot find you.'

'We are earth spirits, my lord,' the old man told him. 'This place is where we belong. We may not move away.'

'Then why do you not kill the serpent?'

'If we could do so, we would, but it is not possible,' the old woman explained. 'The creature has eight heads. Even if some brave person could chop off one head, the remaining seven would tear them to pieces.'

Susanowo looked at the earth spirit's daughter and saw that she was very beautiful.

'If I rid the land of this eight-headed serpent, will you give me the hand of your daughter in marriage?' he demanded.

The girl's parents gladly agreed. 'But how will you be able to kill the creature?' they asked.

For once Susanowo, the Impetuous Male, thought carefully before he made his plans.

'Cut bundles of tall bamboo and build a high fence,' he told them.

The earth spirits did as he ordered. Then Susanowo took his sword and cut eight round holes in the fence.

'Place a table behind each hole,' he ordered. 'On each table set a large bowl and fill all the bowls with sake.'

Sake is a strong drink made from fermented rice.

'Now go to your home, for it is nearly night,' he told the earth spirits. 'Sleep well, and at dawn I will slay this bloodthirsty serpent for you.'

'But, where will you stay? The serpent will tear you to pieces,' the earth spirit's daughter said.

Susanowo drew his sword, 'I shall wait here behind the fence.'

Then he lay down to sleep with his sword beside him. Just before dawn he awoke and waited quietly. He did not have to wait long. As the first light crept over the mountains a gigantic serpent writhed into view. It was even more terrible than the old man had described. It did indeed have eight heads, with eyes that glowed like living coals. It had eight tails also, which lashed from side to side. Along its great, slimy back grew foul-smelling moss and fungus.

As it twisted and turned Susanowo saw flames leaping from its bloodstained belly.

The hideous creature stopped in front of the fence. The eight heads moved slowly to and fro, showing razor-sharp teeth. The beast seemed to be sniffing the air. Slowly, one after the other, the eight ugly heads found the round roles in the fence. They sniffed at the bowls of sake, then started to lap and guzzle until every drop was finished and the bowls were dry. Soon the strong drink took effect, and the serpent's eight heads fell forward in a drunken sleep.

Susanowo strode out from his hiding place, raised his sword and cut off each snoring head. Not content with that, he cut the entire serpent into pieces, until the River Hi ran red with blood. As he slashed at the last of the eight tails, his sword struck something hard. He cut down even deeper into the animal's flesh and discovered a great sword wrapped in a fine white cloth. This new sword had a very strange name. It was called 'Which Conquers Grass'.

The three earth spirits were amazed and delighted that the terrible serpent had at last been slain. The old man was pleased to give his daughter to Susanowo as he had promised. The young girl, too, was happy to give her hand to the stranger who had saved her life.

Susanowo built a grand palace at a place called Suga and married the earth spirit's daughter. They were very happy together. They had a large family, but the most famous of their children was their eldest son, Okuninushi. He became a great hero, and it was to him that Susanowo finally gave the great sword 'Which Conquers Grass' to go with him on his adventures.

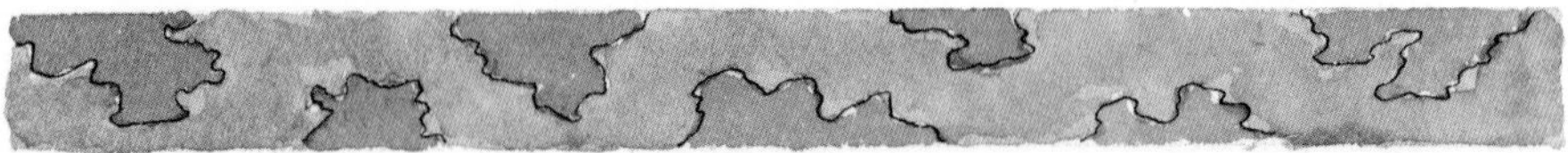

The White Hare

A beautiful white hare sat on the shore of the island of Oki and wondered how he could cross safely to the mainland. Only a narrow channel of water separated Oki from Inaba, and it would have been an easy journey for somebody with a boat. The hare, however, had no boat and it was too far for such a small animal to swim.

There were crocodiles in the water, too, and the hare feared they might fancy him as a meal. He wondered if there was a chance that he could trick them into helping him cross the water safely. One very large crocodile lay in the mud quite near to him, so he struck up a conversation with it. Very soon they were arguing about how many crocodiles and hares lived on the island.

'There are more of us than there are of you,' the crocodile rumbled.

'I beg to disagree,' the hare replied politely. 'But to make sure, why don't we each count how many there are? You first! Line up all the crocodiles nose to tail, and see if they reach as far as the coast of Inaba. I will count each one, then I will call all the hares together, and you may count us. Right, Sir Crocodile?'

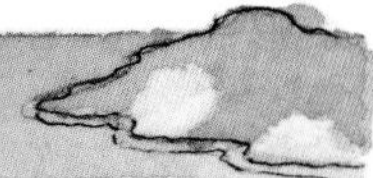

The crocodile agreed to this idea and called all his friends and relations together. Soon a long line of crocodiles stretched away over the water towards the mainland. The hare scampered over their rough, leathery backs, counting as he went, 'one, two, three, four'.

He was still counting when he reached dry land on the other side of the channel. 'Forty-nine, fifty,' he sang out as he hopped ashore. 'Thank you, crocodiles, for bringing me home safely. That was all I really wanted from you. It doesn't matter how many crocodiles and hares there are on the island of Oki. Here I am, safely home in Inaba. Thank you!' And he rolled on the sand laughing at the trick he had played.

The crocodiles realised they had been made to look foolish and were furious. They rushed out of the water and ripped the hare's beautiful white fur until his skin was raw and bare.

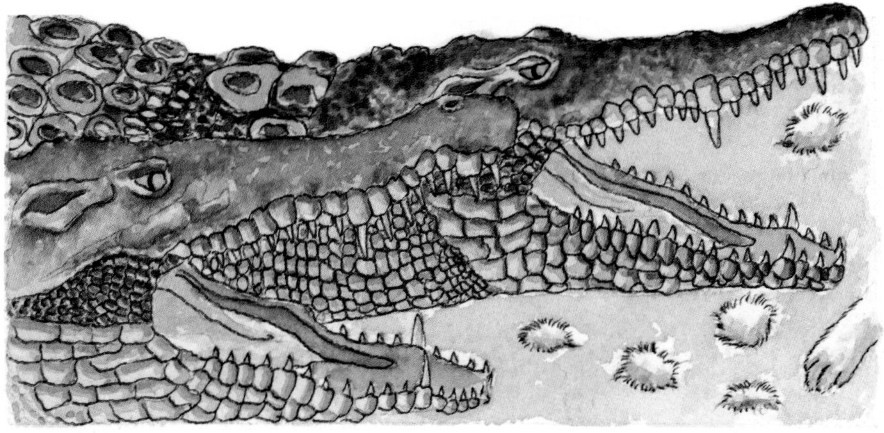

The poor hare was still shivering with pain when three young men came hurrying along the beach. When they saw the injured animal they stopped.

'Whatever happened to you?' one of them asked. 'What happened to your fur?'

The hare told them the crocodiles had attacked him.

'You should bathe in the sea. Salt is good for raw skin like yours. Then sit in the wind until you are dry.'

The hare took their advice, but of course the salt made his raw skin hurt more than ever. The young men laughed, as if it was a good joke to see an animal in pain, and went on their way.

The hare lay there helpless, wondering what he could do to ease the soreness, when another young man came past. He, too, stopped and put down the heavy pack he was carrying.

'You poor animal! Who has done this to you?' he asked, his voice full of pity.

The hare told him what had happened, 'Three young men told me that bathing in the sea would help me. It made my pain much worse.'

'Of course it would,' the young man cried. 'What a stupid, heartless thing to do! Now we must wash off the salt and treat your sore skin. Let me help you.'

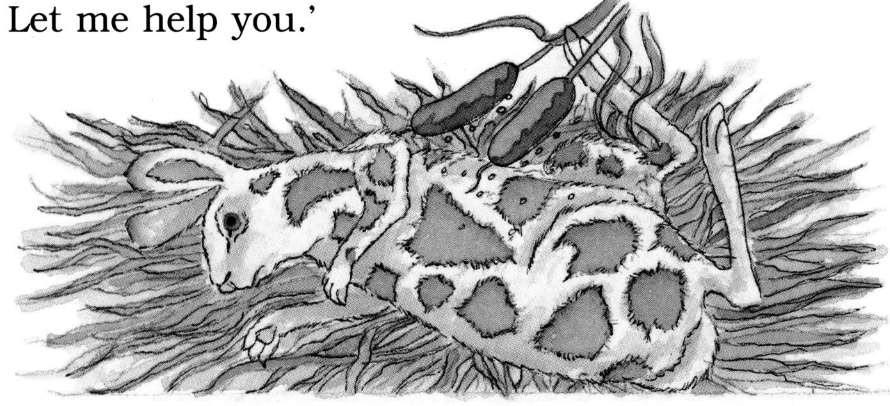

The young man picked up the shivering hare and carried him to a river not far away. There he washed off the salt and gently dried him. Next he cut a number of spikes of bull-rush flowers which were growing in the river and shook them over the animal's raw skin.

'The pollen from bull-rushes is very soothing,' he assured the hare. 'You will soon feel more comfortable.'

Immediately the animal's skin healed and his fur grew back, soft and white as before.

'What is your name, young sir?' the hare asked. 'I see you are a person with great powers.'

'They call me Okuni, the Lord of the Plain of Reeds and eldest grandson of the great Lord of the Sky, Izanagi. I am ashamed to say that the men who treated you so badly are my young half-brothers.'

The hare bowed respectfully, then asked, 'Is it right for Your Highness to be travelling alone and carrying a heavy pack, like a servant? You say that the three young men who treated this humble animal with less than kindness are your half-brothers. Surely it would be more fitting if Your Highness walked in front and your half-brothers followed carrying the pack?'

Okuni smiled. 'They are young and thoughtless. We are all on our way to see the Princess Yakami to ask for her hand in marriage. It is said that she is both beautiful and wise, and is looking for a suitable husband. My young brothers were so anxious to meet the Princess that they forgot one very important rule of politeness. When seeking favours from such an important person as a princess it is good manners to take gifts. I'm afraid they rushed away leaving their gifts for the Princess behind.'

'So Your Highness is carrying their gifts for the Princess Yakami as well as your own,' the hare said thoughtfully. Then he went on, 'Not only are you a Prince with great powers, you are also a kind and gentle man, full of pity. Your brothers are cold-hearted and cruel. You are wise and thoughtful, while they are foolish and careless. I know who the Princess will choose to marry. She will certainly give her hand to Your Highness.'

After this the hare thanked Okuni for his help, and for having restored him to health. Okuni continued his journey to meet the Princess.

Outside her palace he met up with his brothers. He gave them the gifts they had left behind, but they hardly bothered to thank him. They were much too concerned about what they would say to Princess Yakami, and which of them she would choose to marry.

The Princess received them all with great courtesy. She smiled politely as Okuni's three half-brothers boasted of their bravery and talents and tried to win her with grand speeches. Her glances, however, were all for Okuni, who was waiting patiently for his turn to speak with her.

Then it was shown that the white hare had been a wise little animal when he said that the Princess would choose Okuni.

Having listened to the three half-brothers for some time she rose and held out her hands to Okuni.

'It is you, Noble Prince, that I choose to marry.'

Years later their children never tired of hearing the story of the beautiful white hare their father had met as he journeyed to meet their mother for the first time. A clever animal who foretold that Yakami would choose Okuni as her husband.

Urashima and the Island of Jewels

For three long days and nights Urashima, the fisherman, had been at sea in his little boat and had caught nothing. Time after time he had cast his net into the water and hauled it in empty.

The small amount of food and water he had brought with him had all been used up, and Urashima knew that he must soon return to his village. He felt ashamed of having to go back empty-handed. His father would think he was a failure, a fisherman who could catch nothing, and if he had no fish to sell there would be no money for his parents. They relied on him to help them, for they were growing old.

He decided to cast his net one last time before returning home. He threw the net high and wide and waited. At first it seemed as if he was going to be unlucky this time, too. Then suddenly there was a sharp tug. A catch at last! It must be a huge fish, too, Urashima thought excitedly, as the creature struggled and fought to get free. As he hauled the net in he was surprised to see not a fish, but a large tortoise. With some difficulty he heaved it into the boat, where it lay helplessly on its back. Then to Urashima's amazement it spoke to him.

'Please spare me! Do not kill me, and I will reward you.'

He was even more amazed when the tortoise turned into a beautiful, young woman.

'Who are you? What are you?' Urashima cried. He was very afraid, for this was certainly the strangest and most mysterious thing he had ever known.

'I am the Princess Mizunoe,' the girl replied. 'If you take me back to my father's island he will reward you.'

'But where is that? How shall I find the way?'

'Close your eyes and I will take you there,' she told him.

Urashima thought this was an odd way to navigate a boat, but he did as he was told. When next he opened his eyes they were near the shore of an island such as he had never seen before.

As they beached the boat he saw that the shoreline was scattered with pearls, which seemed to grow out of the ground. There were trees with leaves made of emeralds and agates, and the flowers growing by the wayside were jewels, too. Rubies, sapphires and diamonds nodded on slender stalks as they passed.

High on a hill above the beach Urashima saw a great palace gleaming in the sun.

'That is my home,' the Princess told him. 'Come with me!' She led the bewildered fisherman past the jewelled trees and flowers and up the path to the palace.

The Princess's father was delighted at her safe return and welcomed Urashima joyfully.

'You have brought back my daughter, Mizunoe, and you have my heartfelt gratitude. Let us feast and celebrate this happy day!'

The feast, which lasted all day and all night long, was the most splendid ever seen. There was rich and wonderful food served on golden plates. Musicians played while the guests, all dressed in costly silken robes, celebrated the return of Princess Mizunoe.

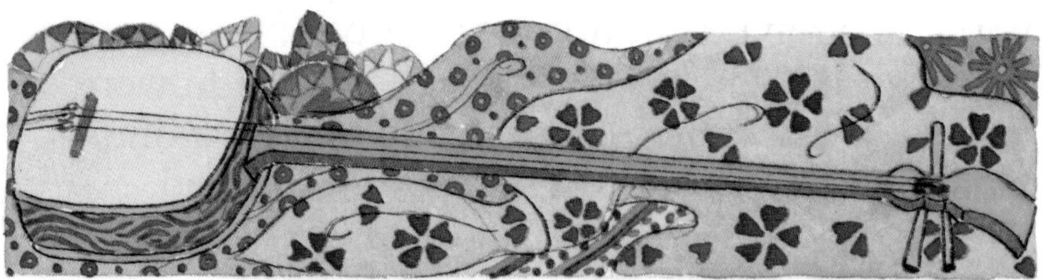

Of course Urashima fell hopelessly in love with the Princess. They were married, and for a while Urashima completely forgot his former life as a poor fisherman. He forgot his parents and the village in which he had grown up. He was so happy with Mizunoe.

Then, after about two years of great happiness, he began to remember things from the past. He thought longingly about his home in the village by the sea. He wondered, too, about his parents and his friends and became very sad.

The Princess asked him, 'Why are you so unhappy? What has happened to spoil our wonderful life together?'

'I do so long to see my native land again,' Urashima admitted. 'I have a father and mother, too, and I often wish I could see them.'

The Princess loved Urashima dearly, but she could not bear to see him so unhappy.

'You shall go back to your village,' she promised. 'But before you leave I have a gift for you.' She gave him a beautiful comb-case with a jewel-encrusted lid. 'Never open it,' she warned him, 'or we may be separated for ever. Now, close your eyes!'

Urashima did as he was told, and when he opened them again he was standing on the shore near his native village.

But was it really his village, he wondered unhappily. How it had all changed! The houses looked different from his memories of them, and there were many new buildings, too. He looked out for his friends, but did not see a single familiar face. The village was full of strangers.

He raced down the street towards his father's house, then stopped short in amazement. It had vanished, and in its place stood a much larger, grander house. He stopped a man who was passing by.

'I am trying to find my father and mother,' he said. 'They used to live in a little house where this one now stands. I have been away for a few years, and did not know they had moved.'

The man gave him a strange look and said, 'This house has stood here for many years. I know of no other. What is your name?'

Urashima gave his family's name. 'I am their son, Urashima,' he said.

'I know of nobody with that name,' the man replied, 'but there is one man who may be able to help you.' He took Urashima to see a very old man who had lived all his life in the village. The old man listened to his story, then shook his head.

'I cannot remember your family,' he said, 'but your name reminds me of a story my grandfather told me when I was a boy. There was once, a long time ago, a fisherman called Urashima who went to sea in his boat and was never heard of again. The sea just swallowed him up, boat and all, but all that happened nearly two hundred years ago. So you can't possibly be that Urashima, can you, young sir?' the old man chuckled.

Urashima felt as if his heart had turned to ice. Two hundred years? He looked at his altered village, full of strangers, and realised the terrible truth. He had indeed been away for two hundred years, not two, as he had believed.

He left the village in despair and went down to the sea. In his hands he carried the box Mizunoe had given him. He lifted the lid, and from the box a white mist rose and floated out over the sea. Urashima realised now that he would never see his Princess again, and he cried aloud in sorrow. From the white mist a voice floated back. It was Mizunoe's voice.

'Never forget me, Urashima! Never forget me!'

As he listened, grief-stricken, a change came over Urashima. His face became old and wrinkled. His strong back became bent and his hands trembled with age. His glossy black hair turned as white as snow. Urashima had become an old, old man, the oldest man in the village.